SCIENCE AND INTERNATIONAL AFFAIRS SERIES
Melvyn B. Nathanson, Editor

CRIME AND MODERNIZATION
THE IMPACT OF INDUSTRIALIZATION AND URBANIZATION ON CRIME

Louise I. Shelley

SOUTHERN ILLINOIS UNIVERSITY PRESS
Carbondale and Edwardsville

Copyright © 1981 by Southern Illinois University Press
All rights reserved
Second printing, March 1982
Printed in the United States of America
Designed by Quentin Fiore

Library of Congress Cataloging in Publication Data

Shelley, Louise I
    Crime and modernization.

    (Science and international affairs series)
    Bibliography: p.
    Includes index.
    1. Crime and criminals.   2. Underdeveloped areas—
Crime and criminals.   3. Technology—Social aspects.
I. Title.   II. Series.
HV6025.S458   364.2'5   80-24044
ISBN 0-8093-0983-1

To my mother and in loving memory of my father

CONTENTS

FOREWORD

Until recently, the study of crime has been extraordinarily insular with respect to time and place, and in relation to the basic disciplines upon which it must depend. Historians have begun to redress their part of this imbalance, as have a few anthropologists, sociological criminologists, and legal scholars. Louise Shelley is one of these, having firmly established herself as a knowledgeable student of crime in the Soviet Union and its sphere of influence. The comparative study of crime remains in its infancy, however, despite the vigorous efforts of these few, as well as the good offices of the United Nations and several international professional associations.

Organizational efforts of the latter, it should be noted, are concerned largely with the most primitive matters necessary to international cooperation in control and development of a knowledge base—e.g., legal definitions, communication and reporting systems, descriptive research—rather than analytic and integrative study.

Despite this state of affairs, important beginnings have been made, and stock-taking is very much in order. Louise Shelley here makes a signal contribution to this enterprise. *Crime and Modernization* is a pioneer attempt to draw together the large research literature on crime in many countries insofar as it bears on the relationship between crime and the modernization processes of industrialization and urbanization. Importantly, the study is historically based, and it compares socialist and capitalist nations.

Shelley's thesis can be quickly summarized, though doing so eliminates richness of detail and necessary qualifications. Crime patterns over the past 200 years in many countries throughout the world exhibit a consistent response to the developments subsumed under the term *modernization*. Societies characterized by a predominance of violent crimes come to be dominated by crimes against property. The critical period of industrialization and mass migration to urban

ix

centers is the most disruptive of traditional family and other institutional patterns. Violence rises, but then declines as new institutional controls are formed. The rising standard of living accompanying modernization is then followed by increasing property crime. The latter results from relative, rather than absolute deprivation, in greatly oversimplified terms. The ascendance of secular over traditional values and the pecuniary nexus of modern societies combine to make economic crimes a hallmark of modern societies, socialist and capitalist alike.

Differences among and between socialist and capitalist countries reflect and inform the role of historical and cultural factors related to crime. Success in preserving traditional values, for example, have enabled Japan and Switzerland to avoid—to date—the major disruptive forces of modernization. By controlling internal migration, socialist countries, too, have avoided some of these impacts.

Comparisons such as these join the issue of the balance between freedom and control, as Shelley makes clear. They do little to resolve questions of the consequences of socialism v. capitalism. Nor do the data available solve all questions of crime causation, as Shelley readily acknowledges. The role of technology, independent of an economic system, in speeding up social change—and thereby accelerating problems of adaptation—has not yet been fully assessed. The implications of alternative systems of social control have hardly been conceptualized as a problem.

Clearly much remains to be done. Until recently, scholarly work in this area has been desultory and esoteric, rather than systematic and rigorous. Louise Shelley has advanced both an understanding of the study of crime and a challenge to future scholars. Theories purporting to account for crime may no longer claim ignorance of the historical and comparative analyses she examines, nor of her own synthesis of these analyses. Hopefully, her assessment will also inspire more systematic inquiry in this important area.

JAMES F. SHORT, JR.

ACKNOWLEDGMENTS

This book grew out of an interest in comparative criminology maintained since my first days in graduate school. It focuses on one particular aspect of the subject—the impact of the process of development on crime internationally. Although this study is based on the belief that crime should be studied comparatively in terms of many different variables, I have chosen to focus on two primary ones, industrialization and urbanization.

The publication of this book gives me the opportunity to acknowledge publicly the efforts of many individuals who have made this work possible. As the origin of this work lies in my years as a graduate student, I would like to recognize the three professors who helped guide me in the present direction: Marvin Wolfgang who suggested that I pursue my interests in international studies, Sir Leon Radzinowicz who urged me to continue my work on comparative criminology, and John Hazard who gave me the moral support and intellectual guidance necessary to complete my dissertation and whose encouragement has helped me pursue my academic career. I would also like to thank the dean, Richard Myren, and my colleagues at the School of Justice, American University for their suggestion that I teach a course in comparative criminology that helped prepare me to write this book.

I would also like to thank the Fulbright-Hays Fellowship Program and the International Research and Exchanges Board (IREX) for supporting my studies in the Soviet Union and in Eastern and Western Europe.

I also appreciate the assistance of friends and colleagues who read parts of the manuscript and provided me with suggestions. For this help I want to thank Walter Connor, Stephen Crawford, George Gibian, and Tina Johns. I am deeply in the debt of my mother, Ricca Shelley, who read through the entire manuscript and provided serious substantive and editorial assistance.

I am also grateful for the assistance of many individuals who helped me obtain the diverse information needed for this study. I, therefore, want to thank Patricia Kelley and the rest of the staff of the American University Library; the staff of the National Criminal Justice Reference Service; and Tadeusz Sadowski, Dr. Ivan Sipkov, and Dr. Miklos Radvanyi of the European Law Division of the Library of Congress.

I also would like to thank two of my teaching assistants, Janet Paull and Hope Fried, for their help in obtaining and compiling materials. I want to acknowledge the help of Chris Cormier, Ann Critzer, Joanne Flynn, and Grace Lewis for their excellent secretarial assistance.

Last, but not least, I would like to acknowledge the support of my husband, Donald E. Graves, who has patiently waited for the completion of this manuscript.

Washington, D. C.   LOUISE I. SHELLEY
June 1980

INTRODUCTION

Modernization has affected rates and forms of criminality in the past two hundred years in both capitalist and socialist societies. This book documents the historical transition in international crime patterns that is a consequence of socioeconomic development. With this transformation in historical perspective, it is possible to evaluate the extent to which development, rather than unique cultural and social characteristics, is responsible for observed changes in criminality.

Crime was studied in terms of larger social forces in the late nineteenth and early twentieth centuries by such scholars as Durkheim, Tarde, and Bonger.[1] This tradition has been sustained more recently by such scholars as Shaw and McKay, Gurr, and the collaborative efforts of French and Eastern European scholars.[2] Little effort has been made by these scholars to examine the relationship of crime and development in a more global context; instead they have focused primarily on the relationship between crime and development in one society or in a region. A notable exception has been the relatively recent work of Clinard and Abbott that examines crime in the geographically dispersed developing nations.[3] But even this work does not bring the entire problem of the relationship between socioeconomic development and criminality into perspective.

Substantial evidence demonstrates that the process of modernization has a distinct and generally consistent effect upon both rates and forms of criminal behavior. Despite this fact, scholars have generally failed to examine comparatively the impact of development on crime "since most students of modernization per se have only marginal interest in nonpolitical forms of deviance, and most students of deviance have relatively little concern with the broader aspects of modernization."[4] This too frequently neglected topic is, however, of crucial importance to an understanding of the phenomenon of criminality.

Introduction

Only by studying crime in a comparative context, examining both historically and cross-culturally its evolution as a consequence of modernization, can we understand the alarming contemporary crime rates and the general threat they make to the social order.

This examination of the effect of modernization on crime in developing, developed capitalist, and socialist countries is an attempt to synthesize a broad body of information and to extract from it some tentative conclusions on the impact of diverse social and economic forces on crime and the criminal offender. The level, form, and geographical distribution of diverse criminal offenses as well as the nature of the offender population of societies with various levels and forms of socioeconomic development will be examined. While the focus of the study is modernization, the impact of social and political controls exercised over individuals and their influence on national crime patterns will not be ignored.

The book focuses on no particular group of crimes, criminals, or region of the world. The crimes analyzed include the full range of crimes against property and the person as well as the crimes unique to a particular form of socioeconomic structure. The only category of criminality not fully incorporated into the analysis is political crime; definitions of these offenses are too subjective for comparison because the political system of each country determines whether such a category of criminality exists and the extent to which violators of these articles of the criminal code are prosecuted. While the majority of crimes in most societies are committed by adult males, in order that a representative picture of total criminality be presented, other groups of offenders, such as juveniles and women, are included in this analysis.

The study integrates data from all regions of the world, from societies with different forms and levels of economic development, and from diverse cultures and political systems. Primary crime statistics, as well as analyses conducted by reputable scholars of criminality of one or more societies, are included. The only societies excluded from this analysis are those such as China, Cuba, and several African societies for which crime data are not available, a result either of the intentional desire of officials to mask the true extent of their country's crime or of the lack of statistical sophistication of their criminal justice systems. Because crime data and analyses are available from so many other societies, despite these national omissions, the study of the relationship between crime and development in a truly international context is still feasible.

Introduction

The level, form, and distribution of criminality as well as the nature of the offender population are examined in terms of several distinct sociological measures of development: the extent and speed of the urbanization process, the degree of industrialization, changes in the social structure of society, and the impact of the criminal justice system. To a lesser extent, the study incorporates social variables that affect the psychological state of the individual. Such factors, which affect the individual and his potential for crime commission, are the destruction of the traditional way of life, internal migration and the concomitant separation of families, and the isolation of peer groups. The impact of social forces on contemporary crime is the focal point of the analysis. But the study does not discount the fact that psychological and even biological factors are needed to explain the etiology of crime on the individual level. A comparative discussion of the influence of these factors is, however, outside the scope of this book.

The sociological variables incorporated in the analysis address a variety of questions concerning the effect of the developmental process on patterns of criminal behavior. Crime statistics from a diverse group of nations are analyzed to establish the impact of modernization, but secondary sources, as well as historical and descriptive analyses, are used to examine historical periods and societies for which few hard data are available.

These different sources are used to ascertain fundamental relationships between the process of socioeconomic development and the quantity and quality of criminality. The following questions that probe the fundamental effects of modernization on crime will be examined in the book in both the historical and contemporary context: What is the effect of modernization on rates of crime both in the initial stages of the developmental process and after the transition to development has been made? Does the process of modernization affect the relative rates of the two fundamental forms of crime—crimes against the person and crimes against property? Does the process of development affect the relationship between crimes against property and crimes of violence against the person? Does the rate at which the transition to development occurs affect the observed patterns of criminal behavior? Does the modernization process affect the nature of the criminal population? In attempting to answer these questions, the book will show that there is a profound and complex relationship between society and crime and that the crime phenomenon, though no less tragic in its ramifications, is not as senseless as it at first appears.

The book does not oversimplify the relationship between crime and development. The relationship between industrialization and urbanization and changes in levels and forms of criminality is shown never to be a simple linear one. Every effort is made to show that it is the complex social changes accompanying these two major manifestations of development that contribute to the observed patterns of criminal behavior. This analysis shows that a complex relationship exists among different variables associated with the process of development and the phenomenon of crime. Among these variables are the geographical mobility of the population, changes in social and familial structure, and the economic organization of society. The book, using historical and international comparisons, shows that there is nothing haphazard about the observed crime patterns; instead, they are a comprehensible response to changing social conditions. Stated more simply, society gets the type and the level of criminality that its conditions produce.

Definitions of the terms employed are a necessary prerequisite to the evaluation of the impact of the developmental process on the crime phenomenon. Unfortunately, there are no absolute definitions of modernization, development, and crime as these concepts can be defined from many ideological and disciplinary perspectives. It is not an easy task to find definitions broad enough to allow for historical and cross-cultural comparisons of social, political, cultural, and economic forces but not so narrow as to constrict the scope of the research. One of the most suitable definitions of development for the purposes of this book is one provided by the United Nations Educational, Scientific, and Cultural Organization (UNESCO): "Development, in short, is an integral and interacting process, both requiring and precipitating far-reaching social, political, cultural and economic changes. It is by no means a unilinear process that moves steadily and smoothly toward some predetermined set of models and values . . . it is typically turbulent, often a downright disorderly and painful process."[5]

This quotation suggests the societies that are currently undergoing the process of development or have already made the transition to modern societies may differ significantly in their social, political, cultural, and economic characteristics. The speed at which these societies underwent the transition towards modernization and the response of the inhabitants to the processes of social change result in very great differences among societies that bear the appellation "developing" or "developed." Despite the heterogeneity of countries grouped under these umbrella terms, these nations share common characteristics because they have reached similar levels of socioeconomic development as a result of the process of modernization. They, therefore, can be grouped together for the purposes of criminological analysis.

An equally complex problem in analyzing the phenomenon of crime in these disparate countries is that definitions of criminality differ so significantly among individual developed and developing nations. Such variations exist because a country's criminal code is a reflection of its political and economic system as well as of its national culture. National diversity accounts for the fact that no two societies choose to define any criminal act in the same way. Even homicide, which has the most concrete and measurable consequences of any crime, is defined differently in such culturally similar Scandinavian countries as Sweden and Norway.[6] These definitional problems preclude precise comparisons of crime rates for individual offenses, but the general agreement among societies on the nature of criminality makes broad comparisons of criminal behavior feasible. Most of the book is devoted to discussion of internationally recognized crimes against the person such as homicide, rape, and assault and such crimes against property as theft and robbery.

No attempt is made by the author to establish internationally valid definitions of criminal behavior because such an effort deserves its own book. Instead, a nation's crime patterns will be defined solely in terms of its legal definitions of criminality. Its total crime rate will be based on the crimes it chooses to report, and its conviction rate will be a reflection of the number of offenders that its criminal justice system chooses to prosecute. Every attempt will be made to avoid imposing the legal values of one society upon another.

Several other means are used in this book to circumvent the problems created by distinct national definitions of criminality. Much of the discussion in the book will focus either on the total crime rates of individual countries or on the aggregate rates recorded for crimes against the person and property, thus avoiding the problem of lack of comparability of definitions for specific offenses. When definitional problems are unavoidable and affect the generalizability of criminological findings, mention will be made of the limitations of the analysis.

Major methodological problems also confront the researcher who examines the relationship between modernization and criminal behavior. The impact of socioeconomic development could, of course, be studied using the crime statistics of different countries. Using multiple regression analysis, the internationally available crime data could be analyzed in terms of certain tangible measures of modernization. Such extensive quantitative research seems premature until such time as the available data merit such methodologically complex analysis. The author of the study has, therefore, chosen to eschew such an approach. It is unlikely that such a lengthy and inherently problematical analysis could shed more light on the impact of modernization upon crime than can an analysis and synthesis of research that has already been conducted.

A comparative, cross-cultural, and historical study of the impact of development on crime is feasible at this time because enough descriptive and small-scale statistical studies have appeared on the evolution of crime in the modern age. This research has not been conducted by a particular school of scholars; therefore, it has been necessary to draw on a wide body of literature that is international and truly interdisciplinary. A conscious effort has been made to draw on a significant body of literature from many countries to broaden the perspective of the book.

As previously mentioned, the analysis of the impact of modernization on crime has generally been ignored by both students of modernization and contemporary criminality although each group has written on these topics. The subject of this book makes it necessary to draw on both of these distinct bodies of literature as well as on historical analyses of criminality and civil disorder. The primary research source has been the international body of criminological literature. Research on the crime problems of individual nations has been used although cross-cultural comparative studies have been emphasized as they generally provide greater insight into the relationship between social forces and criminality.

The diverse readings have provided both historical and contemporary perspectives on the impact of the developmental process on levels and forms of criminality. The insights provided by the modernization process are distinctive as the limited analysis previously done on the relationship between crime and socioeconomic development has generally made little allusion to historical precedent. Conversely, the historical analyses have failed to do more than speculate on the similarities between present trends and those observed in the past century. The book has required the synthesis of a large body of literature in order to ascertain the extent to which the process of socioeconomic development produces similar changes over time in culturally distinct and geographically separated nations.

The book coordinates theoretical writings on the impact of modernization on crime with research on the state and transformation of criminality in the past two hundred years. This analysis, conducted within the context of social structure and control, examines the fundamental changes in criminality that result from rapid social changes and increasing societal affluence. The first chapter of the book lays out the primary theoretical problems addressed in the following chapters, examining recent writings on the impact of modernization and current explanations of the causes of both adult and juvenile crime. It evaluates the extent to which the research examined in the following chapters can shed light on these theoretical explanations of the etiology of criminal behavior and the relationship between socioeconomic development and crime. The criminological theories presented in the initial theoretical chapter are woven into the more substantive chapters that follow, but no effort has been made in these later chapters to present evidence that will either directly support or refute these theories. Instead, the implications of the evidence presented in chapters 2 through 5 on the relationship between development and crime for contemporary criminological theory will be synthesized in the book's conclusion.

The second chapter—on crime and development in historical perspective—provides the background for the discussions in the following chapters on the nature of contemporary criminality. The chapter shows that previous historical periods also experienced serious crime problems and that the relationship between urbanization and crime was already established before the advent of modernization. Apart from providing a historical perspective on contemporary crime patterns, it synthesizes both theoretical writings of the nineteenth and twentieth centuries on the impact of the developmental process on crime as well as tangible evidence that either supports or refutes these suppositions. The chapter's conclusion delineates the crime patterns associated with the advent of modernization and, thereby, provides a basis for the examination in the following chapters of the relationship between development and crime in the contemporary period.

Chapters 3 through 5 focus exclusively on present-day international crime patterns. For analytical purposes, the world's countries have been divided into three groups—developing, developed, and socialist countries. The three groups are not mutually exclusive as socialist countries can be divided into those that are developing and those that are already developed. The division of countries according to their level of social and economic development is a necessary prerequisite to an analysis of the effect of modernization on patterns of criminal behavior. By differentiating between capitalist and socialist societies, it becomes possible to determine which crime patterns are influenced by the overall process of economic development and which result from the form of socioeconomic development that a country has chosen to pursue and the degree of social and political control that a government has chosen to exercise over its population. Division of the world's nations in this way permits a test of the socialist claim that only the capitalist form of economic modernization is conducive to increased criminality whereas the socialist form of development is exempt from disruptive social consequences. These three chapters lead to tentative conclusions concerning the impact of social structure and control in the modern period on the qualitative and quantitative nature of contemporary criminality.

All three chapters focus on the patterns of criminality, the geographical distribution of criminality, the offender population, and the efforts made to control the problem of crime. These aspects of criminality are discussed in the three chapters in reference to either a few representative countries or in terms of overall regional patterns of crime commission.

The third chapter on crime in developing countries examines the extent to which developing countries are presently replicating the changes in rate and form of crime commission (noted in the previous chapter) that occurred in nineteenth-century Europe during the initial stages of the modernization period. Although great similarities are found between the crime patterns of both sets of nations, the impact of the increased population mobility and greater technological sophistication of the modern age is shown to differentiate contemporary crime trends of developing nations from those observed in Europe during the past century. Similarities and differences between both periods are established by focusing on changes in rates and patterns of criminal behavior, regional variations in criminality, the nature of the offender population, and national attempts to control the burgeoning problems of criminality. The great increase in property crime and the reduction in violence that accompanies the developmental process is examined as a consequence of the large-scale population migration from rural to urban areas. The skyrocketing crime rates of certain developing nations and the relatively stable ones of others are analyzed in terms of differences in social structure and means of social control. Predictions are made for future patterns of criminality based on the current experience of developed countries.

The fourth chapter—on crime in developed countries—shows that the crime patterns of these societies have continued to evolve in the direction initiated during the first phases of nineteenth-century modernization. Contemporary developed societies maintain the relationship between property crimes and violent crimes against the person established at the onset of modernization. The similarities in the quality of criminality in developed society are not matched by similarities in quantity of criminality. Although the developed countries, as a group, have higher overall crime rates than developing nations, a great range exists in the crime rates recorded in developed countries. Chapter 4 explains these differences in rates of criminality in terms of variations in societal structure and social control. The increase in female criminality and juvenile delinquency that accompanies development is analyzed as well as the impact of large-scale international population movements on the level and distribution of criminality in developed countries. Tentative predictions concerning the future state of criminality in presently developed nations are based on analyses of the offender population, recent crime trends, the impact of the criminal justice system, and the predominant values of the society.

The fifth chapter focuses on the criminality of socialist societies, primarily of the Soviet Union and those countries of Eastern Europe for which criminological data are available. These countries are grouped together because they have followed a different form of economic development which ideologues claim exempts these societies from many of the pernicious consequences of modernization. The socialist economic system has produced many definitions of criminality that are inherently different from those in other nations of the world. The primary question addressed in this chapter is whether the socialist authorities, through their system of economic and population controls, have produced more fundamental changes in their crime patterns than the definitional ones previously named. The geographical distribution of criminality, the level and types of crime observed in socialist societies, and the nature of the offender population in these countries are all discussed in an attempt to answer this question. The analysis reveals that the general forces of socioeconomic development have a more significant effect on observed patterns of criminality than the form of economic development followed. Although the forms of criminality and the geographical distribution of crime have been affected both by the definitions of crime and the population controls unique to socialist countries, socialist societies have not prevented the transformation and unfortunate rise in criminality that accompanies the developmental process.

The conclusion of the work synthesizes the substantive discussions of the impact of socioeconomic development on crime with contemporary theories of criminal behavior. It determines the extent to which contemporary theories of criminal behavior are sufficient to explain the impact of modernization on criminal behavior and the degree to which the phenomenon of development suggests new explanations of criminality.

PART ONE

CRIME IN PERSPECTIVE

I

Crime in Theoretical Perspective

Anthropologists, political scientists, geographers, and other social scientists have studied the impact of modernization on contemporary society. Criminologists refer to the concept loosely without attaching any particular definition to modernization. In diverse studies scholars of crime refer to the "modernization theory" of criminality, but this theoretical approach has never been fully expounded in the literature.

Two decades ago criminologists first focused their attention on the impact of modernization on the development of patterns of criminal behavior. These initial studies were never fully developed and, therefore, the analysis of the effect of development on criminal behavior has remained in the embryo stage. Research on crime produced in the past 20 years and especially in the last decade by scholars in many disciplines has made it possible to reexamine and expand our understanding of the impact of this form of social change on crime and the criminal offender.

The expansion and the application of a theory of modernization to criminal behavior have not been possible for most American scholars because they lack the linguistic skills prerequisite to this necessarily historical and comparative research. But European scholars who possess the language skills fail to focus on modernization theory because their research concentrates primarily on studies of characteristics of individual offenders or criminological problems of national concern.

The development of a full-blown theory of modernization applied to criminality had not previously been possible because of the absence

3

of sufficient research or a body of researchers capable of filling the intellectual gap. This book attempts to describe the impact of modernization on crime during the past two centuries. The relationship between modernization and crime is studied in terms of the level and form of economic development. Two economic modes of modernization will be examined, capitalist and socialist. The book analyzes whether the achievement of economic development through private enterprise or its achievement through the socialization of the means of production have different impacts on crime. Modernization is analyzed primarily in terms of two of its most important effects, urbanization and industrialization, and to a lesser extent, in terms of such other variables as changes in family life, educational level, and the growth of the working class. These latter effects will generally be considered to be subsidiary because it is urbanization and industrialization that contribute to the breakdown of the family, an increased demand for education, and the development of an urban working class engaged in industrial production.

A theory of modernization and crime provides a comprehensive explanation of criminality. Any new theory must be examined in terms of the general theoretical perspective of the discipline. This is especially true of a modernization theory that has sweeping implications for our understanding of the relationship between social change and crime and the role of crime in contemporary society. As the following analysis will demonstrate, the process of societal development produces change in the nature and level of criminality and the character of the criminal population. These conclusions make it necessary to rethink some of the emphasis placed previously on other explanations of criminality.

Criminological theory emerged with the works of Quetelet and Lombroso. Lombroso chose to focus on the characteristics of the individual offender.[1] For Quetelet, the central task of criminology was to explain the existence and distribution of crime in society, and his natural tendency was to see social factors as of overwhelming importance.[2] Quetelet was followed by the French scholar Guerry who likewise chose to study crime in terms of a variety of social factors. Both these scholars analyzed the effects of age, sex, race, education, profession, and economic and meteorological conditions on crime. Guerry and Quetelet, both writing in the first half of the nineteenth century, noticed a striking similarity and regularity in the crime patterns of the nations they studied and subsequently concluded that scientific methods could be applied to the study of criminal behavior.[3]

The observed consistency in national crime patterns did not last long for, as Engels noted in his *The Position of the Working Class in England* and as Marx wrote in *Model Government Belgium,* crime rates rose rapidly with the industrialization of society.[4] This fact did not go unnoticed by other nineteenth-century scholars who were concerned with the relationship between social forces and criminal behavior. The analysis of the relationship between rising crime rates and societal change was pursued by Tarde and Durkheim who, in contrast to Marx and Engels, asserted that it was the changes in social relations of society rather than in the economic system that were responsible for this sudden transformation in what previously were relatively constant crime rates.

Tarde asserted that change in society has a profound effect on the nature of crime, the types of crime committed, and the nature of the offender population. He believed that a variety of social factors contributed to the existing crime patterns, and though he did not focus on any particular ones he did see certain recent social forces as especially conducive to criminal behavior. Among the factors he cited were the growth of urban areas which served as breeding grounds for criminal activity, the greater material advantages of industrialized society, and the chance of evading horrific penalties that were no longer dispensed by the more humane justice systems.[5]

Durkheim, like Tarde, also focused on the impact of larger social developments on criminal behavior. He perceived the rapid evolution of criminality in the mid-nineteenth century in terms of the larger social changes accompanying the urbanization and industrialization of society. Durkheim was concerned by the high crime rates of industrialized society and suggested that these rates might exceed "the normal" and indeed be pathological. The findings discussed in the following chapter on the disproportionately high crime rates of the initial stages of the industrial process support his claim. Durkheim's most significant theoretical contribution to the field of criminology is his formulation of the concept of anomie. According to this theory, society has the need and the moral right to regulate the behavior of its citizens. When society is in a state of rapid transition, the rules of society break down and people no longer can appraise their situation, "ambition was perpetually stimulated but never satisfied. This condition Durkheim called acute anomie."[6] Chronic anomie occurs when overwhelming importance is attached to economic progress as the supreme goal in and of itself and secondary consideration is given to the regulation of human conduct and the control of individual ambition. These conditions which prevailed in the nineteenth century contributed significantly to the variety of social problems observed in that society.[7]

The line of nineteenth-century criminological reasoning initiated by Quetelet and culminating in the writings of Durkheim focuses on the vital importance of larger social forces and societal evolution on the rates and forms of criminality. Unfortunately, these scholars never fully developed their thoughts on the impact of industrialization and urbanization on criminality. They left to their successors the full exploration of the impact of social modernization on criminal behavior.

The pioneering work in criminological theory passed in the twentieth century from Western European to American hands. Sir Leon Radzinowicz, the eminent English criminologist, gives the following explanation for this phenomenon. The United States has achieved the highest degree of affluence and at the same time the most threatening crime rates. The break with Lombrosian thought had been complete and serious empirical research replaced this semiscientific research as a range of new criminological hypotheses were tested empirically.[8] For these reasons American criminologists for most of this century have taken the theoretical lead from their European colleagues, but American research has focused on the development of smaller-scale explanations of criminal behavior than those attempted by the nineteenth-century Europeans.

Seven American criminological theories dominated international criminology in this century until recently when the radical and conflict schools of criminology increased in importance. These theories are anomie, opportunity theory, differential association, culture conflict, social disorganization, relative deprivation, and delinquent subcultures. None of these theories attempts to explain the impact of contemporary conditions on criminal behavior.

Robert K. Merton's theory of anomie is possibly the most widely acknowledged explanation of deviant behavior. According to this theory, deviance is most likely in societies in which success is a major societal objective but where many of the inhabitants are unable to acquire the material possessions or social status that denote success. His theoretical argument is formulated in terms of the societally recognized goals that individuals strive for and the institutionalized means used to regulate access to these desired objectives. Merton recognizes that these goals and means are not equally available to all individuals because of the differentiated class and ethnic structure of American society. Striving for success within a society that is achievement oriented, some individuals for whom traditional paths to achievement are closed follow illegitimate or deviant means to attain success within that society.[9] Although this theory was originally developed in terms of American society, it has been applied to many of the world's other industrialized societies as an explanation of the persistence of criminal behavior.

Culture conflict, proposed by Thorsten Sellin in the same year as Merton's theory of anomie, is another widely applied explanation of criminal behavior. Culture conflict has remained as autonomous theory: Although Sellin's ideas about crime causation were incorporated into criminological theories of the 1940s and 1950s,[10] his overall view that norm conflict contributes to criminality has remained untouched by successive criminologists. Conflicts between the norms of different cultural codes may cause clashes on the borders of contiguous cultural areas, when the laws of one cultural group are extended over the territory of another and when members of one cultural group migrate to an area with a different culture.[11] This theory is applicable to movement between geographically separated areas as well as between contiguous regions within the urban environment. Today's ready mobility makes this theory of particular contemporary relevance.

Edwin H. Sutherland, a contemporary of Merton and Sellin, is viewed by many as the father of American criminology. He is the author of a number of the most significant theories and studies of criminality, including such topics as white-collar crime, the professional thief, and differential association. It is this last explanation of the etiology of criminal behavior that has attained the most universal recognition and acceptance.

Sutherland's formulation of differential association "began to congeal around the view that cultural conflict or complex social organization resulting from social and economic changes involved in the industrialization of the Western world had generated a pervasive individualism and other conditions conducive to criminality."[12] In diverse contemporary societies, people encounter a wide range of individuals, some of whom have a positive effect on their lives while others may promote the commission of societally condemned acts.

The possibility of varied acquaintances in modern, complex society led to the formulation of the theory of differential association, which holds that criminal behavior is learned through interaction with others. The extent to which criminal norms and habits are acquired is determined by the intensity and duration of the association. The mechanisms for learning criminal behavior are no different from any other kinds of learning. Sutherland asserts that "while criminal behavior is an expression of general needs and values, it is not explained by these general needs and values since non-criminal behavior is an expression of the same needs and values."[13] Briefly, stealing is no more motivated by the desire for material goods than is honest employment. In the latter case, however, the individual is sufficiently committed to the society's norms and values to channel his desires through legitimate means while in the former case, the individual will pursue his goals by illegitimate methods.

Sutherland's theory of differential association has met with broad acceptance in the United States and abroad. The theory has gained extensive support because it is not culture bound and, therefore, appears to have a universality not present in other theories of criminal behavior. Differential association is not based on probabilities that an actual phenomenon will occur but makes a better claim than most other theories to a universal and consistent explanation of criminal behavior in contemporary society.

Social disorganization, a theory advanced by Clifford R. Shaw and Henry D. McKay in the 1930s, has not attained the degree of international recognition accorded differential association, but its validity has been shown outside American society, particularly in regions that are only now undergoing the process of economic development.

According to the theory of social disorganization, delinquency has its roots in the dynamics of a community. In areas with low rates of delinquency, uniform and consistent attitudes towards child care, law, and general societal values exist. In urban areas characterized by high rates of crime, there are competing and conflicting moral values. In these neighborhoods, crime is a viable means of obtaining a livelihood and is seen by community residents as a means of acquiring social and economic status.[14]

Children in areas without common values turn to delinquent behavior because the youthful members of the community are alienated from their parents and the social institutions around them. Unrestrained by the traditional forms of social control, they turn to deviant forms of personal expression. The theory, however, lacks validity at later stages of community transformation when social and personal mobility decrease and the community is not as disorganized as it was earlier. The theory of social disorganization is incapable of explaining the perpetuation of high levels of urban criminality in these later developmental stages.

A major set of American criminological theories is concerned with delinquent subcultures. These theories developed primarily in the 1950s by such scholars as Albert Cohen, R. A. Cloward and L. E. Ohlin, and Walter Miller, focused attention on the structure and causes of gang delinquency,[15] a topic ignored in the two decades since the Chicago School's initial formulations on the subject. These different scholars, addressing the impact of delinquent subcultures on working-class neighborhoods, examined the psychological problems of the members of delinquent groups, the relationship of the delinquents to the world around them, and the absence of legitimate opportunities for advancement. The broader applicability of the latter concept of opportunity theory will be discussed more fully.

Delinquent subculture theories maintain that boys in such a subculture have adopted their own values that are frequently variants of traditional middle-class values. Their values are a collective solution to their inability to succeed within the established structure of society. They strive to achieve on their own terms, and their activities are directed towards the attainment of short-term objectives rather than long-term status. The predominance of these values among lower-class youths explains their widespread delinquency and the relative severity of their acts of criminality. Critics of delinquent subculture theory accuse the authors of these theories of explaining more delinquency than actually exists and of isolating criminal behavior too completely in the lower class. Critics such as David Matza suggest that significant amounts of criminality exist among middle-class youths and stress the similarities between delinquents and other youths of the same age group.[16] The rejection of middle-class values by members of the delinquent subgroup is not as extensive as the subculture theorists suggest.

The opportunity theory of Cloward and Ohlin developed from Merton's anomie theory. Unlike Merton's theory, which was applied to no particular group in the population, opportunity theory was formulated strictly in terms of lower-class American boys. According to opportunity theory, lower-class boys seek to acquire a higher class position in terms of the criteria of their present social group rather than of those of the middle class. The lower-class youths want to achieve success in life, but they perceive correctly that their opportunities to acquire material success and social status are limited; therefore, they look for other means to attain their objectives. The discrepancy between what they desire from life and what they can realistically expect to attain causes them to seek their desired goals by other than legal means. The absence of legitimate opportunities causes youth gangs to participate in criminal subcultures that engage in acts of property crime and often lead to adult criminal careers. Drugs provide a retreat for those boys who cannot participate successfully in either the legitimate or the illegitimate world that surrounds them.[17]

Opportunity theory has often been applied in a larger context than Cloward and Ohlin originally intended. It is no longer applied just to juveniles but also to all urban residents who seek the fruits of societal prosperity but lack the legitimate opportunities needed to acquire these tangible signs of success. Opportunity theory thus becomes a broader explanation of the reasons for extensive deviant activity in the urban environment.

Relative deprivation is another explanation of criminal behavior in the urban environment. Unlike the previously discussed American theories it is not primarily a theory of criminal or deviant behavior but has been used to explain a wide variety of human conduct in modern industrialized society. When applied to criminal behavior, the state of relative economic deprivation becomes a primary explanation for the preeminence of property crime in modern society. Relative deprivation is more conducive to criminal behavior than absolute deprivation because the visibility and accessibility of material goods proves more of an incentive for committing crimes than the absence of goods or the opportunity to secure them.[18]

Relative deprivation is not an explanation of all forms of crime but only those offenses related to property. Relative deprivation exists not only in industrialized societies whose less affluent members feel economically disenfranchised but also in developing societies where new urban residents are exposed to a quantity and diversity of material possession they have never previously known.

All these American theories of criminal behavior represent partial explanations of the problem of contemporary criminality. They are predicated on the conditions of modern urban, industrializing societies in which the traditional way of life has broken down and in which contemporary city life has raised community and personal anxiety. The affluence of industrialized society in which many live beyond the subsistence level merely heightens the adjustment problems of masses of individuals accustomed to living at the edge of survival.

Each of the seven theories previously described addresses different consequences of the phenomenon of modernization. These consequences affect the individual, the community in which he lives, and the general nature of urban life and modern contemporary society. Anomie theory addresses the impact of urban life on modern man suggesting that conflicts often arise in contemporary society because what man strives to attain is not accessible to him. This situation is characteristic solely of modern society because limited social mobility existed before the advent of industrialization. Individuals in agrarian society could expect to maintain a life-style very similar to that maintained by their parents or grandparents. They had no reason to expect more in the future and consequently in premodern societies an individual had little opportunity to feel any conflict between his level of achievement and that which was accessible. Therefore, anomie is a new phenomenon unique to the conditions of modern society.

Culture conflict theory is not as inextricably linked to the conditions of modern society as the theory of anomie, but the mobility of the contemporary world produces more situations conducive to culture conflict. Culture conflict can arise in any historical period, but, as it is predicated on the confrontation of individuals of different cultures, the enhanced mobility of the modern age makes it a more plausible explanation of contemporary criminal behavior than it would have been in the past. Increased mobility of all social and economic strata leads to more crime. The employment of migrant workers, skilled technicians, and businessmen abroad; tourism; and the gravitation of different rural cultural groups to urban areas make culture conflict more likely. With modernization, large numbers of individuals are exposed regularly to unfamiliar cultures making culture conflict a particularly salient explanation of criminal behavior during the past century.

Differential association, social disorganization, delinquent subculture, opportunity, and relative deprivation theory all explain the etiology of criminal behavior in terms of the urban community. Tarde originated the concept of proximity in his criminological theory of imitation, the forerunner of Sutherland's differential association. Tarde's theory of criminality was a natural outgrowth of the conditions created by an increasingly urban society. Differential association could not be a primary explanation of criminality in a rural society because the preconditions for this behavior do not exist. When most individuals are in close contact only with members of their families, criminality cannot be learned as readily as in the intensely congested conditions of the urban environment.

Social disorganization theory applies to urban neighborhoods affected by intense internal immigration where common values are not held by members of the particular community. Urban neighborhoods with unusually high crime rates have existed traditionally because many area residents do not share the law-abiding norms of their fellow urban dwellers. By supporting similar populations for centuries these so-called disorganized neighborhoods had considerable stability until the advent of modernization. With increasingly rapid urbanization, traditionally stable neighborhoods were besieged by an influx of migrants unaccustomed to the conditions of urban life, resulting in particularly high rates of criminality. Only as society makes the transition from a primarily rural to an urban society does the theory of social disorganization become a primary explanation of criminal behavior. Delinquent subculture theory, like the theories of social disorganization and differential association, is predicated on the conditions of a highly urbanized society. For without the concentration of humanity in urban areas and the relaxed adult supervision that accompanies city life, little opportunity would exist for the formation of delinquent subcultures. As is pointed out repeatedly in this book, juvenile delinquency was itself a rare phenomenon prior to the advent of industrialization because youths had little independence and were closely supervised by their parents. The urban environment and parental employment outside of the home have contributed to the development of youth crime that is frequently peer oriented and, therefore, conducive to delinquent subcultures.

The theory of relative deprivation, more than many other theories, is linked to the conditions of modern society. Prior to the industrial revolution, most Europeans resided in rural areas close to the subsistence level except for the rare member of the rural gentry or nobility who resided on his estate. The peasants did not feel deprived in relationship to the nobles because the hiatus between their position and that of the manor lords was rigidly established. The class structure of society make it hopeless to aspire to the status or possessions of the nobility. The growing preindustrial bourgeoisie were satisfied with their social and economic gains and therefore were not subject to relative deprivation. After the industrial revolution and with increased urbanization, the social situation was transformed as urban residents were exposed to more material possessions, and social mobility increased. No longer were individuals compelled to live their lives at the same economic level as that of their parents, and cities provided ample personal models to emulate. The urban environment of industrialized societies made large numbers of individuals feel deprived in comparison to the standard of living of their fellow city residents. The city provided increased exposure to material possessions and greater financial expectations for those who resided there. Therefore, one of the unfortunate consequences of the increasingly urbanized society was a growth of property crime as individuals attempted to compensate illegally for their perceived deprivation.

The previous analysis demonstrates that the most prominent American criminological theories, widely accepted both in the United States and abroad, during the last four decades, are not universal explanations of criminal behavior. They apply only to the changes that have accompanied the process of modernization. None of these seven theories explain the changes that have occurred in crime commission in the last two centuries but merely explain the dynamics of crime in the present urban environment. They focus on the dynamics of individual crime commission, the impact of urban decay, and the increased opportunities of city life for the attainment of success. They do not examine the transformation of crime in the rural environment or the dislocation of crime from rural to urban areas, nor do they provide an overall theoretical framework to explain the emergence of new categories of criminal offenders, like juveniles and females, in the period since the advent of the industrial revolution.

Modernization provides the theoretical framework necessary to analyze the evolution of criminality in the last two hundred years. All the major American theories of crime commission can be subsumed under the theory of modernization. They all explain the dynamics of crime commission in terms of the conditions of increasingly urbanized modern life. All analyze the impact of modernization on crime in terms of the individual, the community in which he lives and the general effects of urban life. Not one of them individually nor all of them combined, however, are sufficient to explain the etiology and nature of complex contemporary criminality. Only a theory of modernization that looks at crime in terms of the total dynamics of society, as did the theories of many late nineteenth-century thinkers on crime, can hope to explain the proliferation and transformation of crime in the contemporary period.

Conflict and radical theories of criminal behavior, developed in recent decades, compensate for certain omissions from contemporary theories, but they fail to provide a theoretical framework necessary to explain the transformation in criminal behavior that has occurred in the last two centuries. Radical theorists contend that earlier American criminological theories have ignored the role of social conflict in the formulation of criminal law and of the development of lawbreakers. The pluralism of rapidly changing societies, the conflict theorists assert, leads to heightened tensions and increased dependence on law to control the conflicting aspirations of different economic and political interest groups. Conflict theorists assert that the disproportionate criminality of the poor is not a result of the social disorganization of their residential communities or their delinquent subcultures but is a consequence of the differential enforcement of laws in urban areas. Political changes in the social system are deemed necessary for a restructuring of the crime problem. Some radical theorists support Marx's contention that the crime problem will be eliminated once the means of production are socialized.[19]

Certain radical theorists contend that the economic precariousness of individuals in capitalist society contributes to the high level of property crime in contemporary western societies.[20] The fear of economic insecurity as well as the unequal distribution of property lead many individuals to criminal careers. The surplus population created by the growth of technology in modern capitalist societies has produced a body from which criminals and other forms of deviants are drawn.[21] The mass educational system created to enlighten the general population has instead produced alienation and antagonism among those who are not part of the status quo. Still another radical perspective on crime in capitalist society attempts to explain the extensive participation of juveniles in serious criminality in modern industrialized capitalist society. The theory of delinquency and the age structure of society suggests that juvenile theft is motivated by the desire to participate in social activities, when the funds needed to finance this activity by legitimate means are absent. More importantly, juvenile delinquency is a direct result of labor market conditions of advanced capitalist societies because little employment is available to teenagers despite their training.[22]

The problem inherent in all these radical and conflict theories is that they are ethnocentric, based on uniquely American or Western European experience. Their formulations of the crime problems of capitalist societies are based almost solely on analyses of one capitalist society, and no attempt is made to compare the crime problems of capitalist nations with those that have followed the socialist form of economic development. Although radical theorists argue that socialist societies are not truly socialist and therefore not deserving of such a comparison, they cannot disagree with the fact that these societies have eliminated the problems of economic insecurity, teenage unemployment, and surplus populations—conditions that these theorists contend are conducive to the emergence and proliferation of crime in capitalist societies. Despite the elimination of these criminogenic conditions, the crime patterns of socialist societies are not very different from those observed in capitalist societies undergoing the process of development. This conclusion again suggests that it is the process of modernization rather than the economic context in which it occurs that determines the patterns of criminality observed in contemporary society.

This brief survey of the significant criminological theories of the past century shows that the theorists of this century have strayed far from the more global theories of criminal behavior formulated in the nineteenth century. The process of modernization posited in this book, as a significant explanation of contemporary criminality is reminiscent of the attempts of earlier theorists to explain crime in terms of larger social forces. Yet, this theory of modernization and crime advances beyond those initial formulations because it subsumes the individual twentieth-century criminological theories that explain the impact of contemporary society on the criminality of individuals and communities. By analyzing modernization in the context of both developing and developed capitalist and socialist societies, this book overcomes the weaknesses of criminological theories based solely on the capitalist form of economic development. As the following analysis demonstrates, the process of modernization has a significant and consistent impact on crime in all societies.

2

Industrial Development
and Crime

All too frequently, contemporary criminologists with little knowledge of historical precedent make statements based upon unfounded generalizations about the uniqueness of present-day crime problems and overstate the irreversibility of contemporary crime trends. A historical discussion of past patterns of criminality since the advent of industrialization in England at the end of the eighteenth century places the current phenomenon of developing and developed countries in perspective. It shows that fluctuations in criminality were observed in earlier centuries and that the transformation in criminality presently observed in developing countries is not unique to contemporary societies. Only by examining the antecedents of contemporary crime trends is it possible to make assertions concerning the criminological consequences of the developmental process or to comprehend current crime patterns of both developed and developing capitalist and socialist countries.

The following historical discussion will focus on both the crime patterns prior to development as well as the changes that occurred as a result of the developmental process. Contemporary scholarship as well as that of nineteenth-century scholars will be used to determine whether the process of modernization or particular national, cultural, and political differences are more useful in explaining observed patterns of criminality. Several national case studies will be employed to examine the transition in forms and levels of criminality that accompany the phenomenon of industrialization. This historical analysis leads to some fundamental conclusions concerning the use of criminality as a barometer of social change that will be corroborated in later chapters. Sociological theories will be used to explain criminal behavior, but crime data will not be used to prove these theories.

CRIME PRIOR TO DEVELOPMENT

While this study does not attempt to provide a historical survey of world crime patterns, some knowledge of crime patterns prior to industrialization is a necessary prerequisite to the appraisal of the impact on crime of the transition to modern economic development. Because crime statistics are a relatively recent development, it is not possible to provide a highly quantitative analysis of crime patterns in Europe several centuries ago, but sufficient descriptive materials are available to give some broad indication of the level and forms of crime predominant at that time. Despite the absence of statistics, analysts of the period have found it possible through the use of legal archives to comment on trends in different categories of criminal behavior.[1] Other scholars have relied heavily on literary texts,[2] and still others have used journals and annals of the period in question.[3]

These different sources reveal that crime was not an isolated phenomenon in the centuries before the advent of the industrial revolution; in cities, along highways, and in villages, individuals were threatened by both violent and property crimes. Observers indicate that France, Germany, and England had significant crime rates and diversified forms of criminality. Reports of crime in Germany in the seventeenth century reveal that "the number of experts among thieves in general seems to have been almost as large in the sixteenth and seventeenth centuries as it is today."[4] In medieval England "there is a host of violent crimes"[5] and "Elizabethan London was . . . probably more dangerous . . . than the city we know today."[6]

The urban environment, as these quotations suggest, has been a bastion of criminality for centuries, and it is not just the recent process of urbanization that has contributed to crime. Urban authorities have traditionally had to contend with the problem of crime and their varied attempts at law enforcement within their jurisdictions have produced changes in patterns rather than reductions in levels of total criminality. For example, in France in the period before the Revolution, criminals had become skilled and crafty because the authorities of the period had become more sophisticated in handling the less professional criminals who had previously dominated city life.[7] These changes in crime patterns as a result of administrative behavior only produced changes in the professionalism of the offender. Actual changes in the social conditions of the urban environment were required to produce variations in the rate and form of urban criminality. When such changes occurred, a significant transformation in the crime patterns was observed. The stabilization of the urban environment that occurred in the seventeenth century produced a noticeable modification in urban criminality: "From the end of the seventeenth century, in fact, one observes a considerable diminution in murders and, generally speaking, in physical acts of aggression, offenses against property seem to take over from crimes of violence; theft and swindling, from murder and assault."[8]

Criminality remained rampant despite any transformations in patterns of criminality. Partly as a result of extensive criminal misconduct the city's reputation for iniquity was already firmly entrenched before the industrial revolution. The extent of urban crime may, however, have been slightly exaggerated because urban law enforcement was superior to that of rural areas where the groups of roaming vagrants were poorly controlled by the limited criminal justice resources.[9] The urban monopoly on crime, while not as complete as many observers of preeighteenth-century crime suggest, did provide a significant threat to the internal order of cities of this period.

Property crime was the predominant form of urban criminality, occurring at greater rates in cities and towns than in the countryside. The reasons for the prominence of such crimes were that access to goods was greater in cities and that poor urban residents were forced to daily contrast their standard of living with that of wealthier urban inhabitants. Picking pockets was a common offense,[10] and many other types of thievery were common[11] despite the severity of the punishments meted out to those found guilty. Property crimes were not necessarily free of violence, and many victims were hurt as a result of the offenses perpetrated. Urban residents therefore had to contend both with straight acts of violence as well as those associated with other forms of criminality.

Those who committed these crimes were primarily members of the lower class, and in many different countries the criminals belonged to families of offenders where professional skills were passed on to successive generations. These groups of offenders seem to have been descendants of the organized criminal bands of the later Middle Ages.[12] The highly organized criminal groups with an established division of labor and systems of training recruits[13] continued into the nineteenth century when one of their ranks was immortalized in the character of Fagin in Dickens' *Oliver Twist*. John Gay's *The Beggar's Opera* (1728) provided a vivid account of the organization and pervasiveness of the criminal underworld.

Apart from the organized crime figures of the urban scene, highwaymen operated both within and outside of the city limits. Accurate reports of their activities are not available, but the literary descriptions of many of their exploits, though often exaggerated, provide some understanding of the extent and form of their illegal activities. In England their heyday was in the first half of the eighteenth century when Dick Turpin brought fame to the ranks of those who had transcended their earlier careers as petty thieves.[14] German literature had its highwayman dramatized in a play by Schiller in the eighteenth century, and Stenka Razin, the courageous freebooter, served much the same role in Russian literature.

These bandits were championed by the poor[15] and cast in the image of rebels, a role they were incapable of fulfilling.[16] The bandits stole exclusively from the rich and distributed some of their ill-gotten gains to the poor. Their choice of victims and their attitude towards their spoils were calculating rather than philanthropic because the poor, who had nothing worth taking, protected the bandits from the nobles and law enforcement officials. Bandits were the only criminal group to confine their activities to the countryside.

Most information on prenineteenth-century criminal behavior concerns offenses committed in urban areas because this was the locale most visible and accessible to the chroniclers of the period. An analysis of crime in rural areas prior to nineteenth-century industrialization demonstrates that, unlike cities, rural areas had generally stable rates and forms of criminal behavior. While political upheavals and changes in the system of judicial administration (apprehension and punishment of offenders) had pronounced effects on the state of urban order, rural crime patterns were not as susceptible to these forces that produced noticeable fluctuations in rates and forms of crime commission.[17]

Rural areas had traditionally low rates of criminality. While urban areas, even before the advent of industralization, contended with offenders who were "harassed" and "ill-fed,"[18] the rural environment provided at least a subsistence income for most of its inhabitants. Its crimes were, therefore, not those of desperation and need but rather ones that resulted from interpersonal tensions exacerbated over time. Rural areas were characterized by a high level of violence and a low level of property crime and an overall crime rate lower than that in towns and cities.

Crimes of violence, the most frequent of rural offenses, were characterized by their seasonality. Crimes of assault and murder were frequently associated with alcohol consumption or the maintenance of family honor. Increased alcohol use at feast times combined with the increased proximity of individuals on these occasions produced an upsurge in violence as long-submerged hostilities surfaced. Not only have chroniclers recorded these sometimes gory feasts, but Bruegel in his realistic representations of village life often depicted the bloody consequences of this holiday merrymaking.

Rural festivals were not the only occasions for violence in rural life. Because families resided in the same community for centuries, hostilities among different families were sometimes perpetuated through successive generations. The close proximity of these families and their continued antagonisms often led to the resolution of familial differences through blood feuds or violent assaults against the members of an opposing clan or family. These pronounced conflicts, though not present in all societies or communities, contributed to rural violence in many areas.

Certain forms of criminal activity were associated exclusively with rural preindustrial society. Social banditry is a primitive form of illegal social protest that expresses "vengeance on the rich and the oppressors."[19] These activities are an expression of innate political feelings, are not associated with any political movements, and exist only before the rural population has developed a general political consciousness. Another form of criminality associated with rural pre-industrial society is vagabondage.[20] With the advent of industrialized society both social banditry and vagabondage were transformed by the new social conditions.

Opportunity theory helps explain the characteristic forms of rural criminality. The presence of rural violence and the general absence of property crime can be understood in terms of the characteristics of the agricultural community. Property offenses were rare because most individuals residing in rural areas had little worth stealing and the wealthy landowners and nobles who resided in the countryside were generally guarded by their staff of household servants. Only the servants had access to the property of their masters and their petty thievery was taken for granted.[21] The only possessions of the landowners accessible to the masses of the population were the nobles' woods and game which were carefully guarded against potential poachers.

The social structure of the rural community also served as a deterrent to property crime. The interrelationship of the lives of rural residents increased the probability of detection and ensured that the perpetrator could not escape further contact with the victim of his offense or his family. The conditions of rural life also ensured that property offenders had little to gain and much to lose as a result of their criminal behavior.

These generalizations about rural life, its deterrent effect on criminal behavior, and its greater propensity for violence remained true only as long as individuals born in rural areas were assured of spending the rest of their lives in the same or adjoining community. When mobility was absent from the lives of rural residents, the traditional rural life "dominated by spontaneous, informal social organizations founded upon tradition and kinship and characterized by collective responsibility"[22] deterred criminality. Rural crime rates were further suppressed as individuals deprived of a means of financial support in the countryside gravitated towards the city, further swelling the ranks of the urban criminal population.

A definite geography of criminality characterized preindustrial society. This distribution of criminal offenses was a direct result of the complex interaction of social, political, and economic forces. The process of urbanization, although not as accelerated as during the nineteenth and twentieth centuries, had already begun in England and to a lesser extent in other European countries. The transition from the agrarian way of life to the anonymous city with insufficient employment for its masses of "expendable" residents[23] was conducive to increased rates of urban criminality.

While the economic and social forces were promoting new levels and forms of criminal behavior, other forces were serving to suppress traditional or existing criminality. The impersonality of the city helped reduce the common internecine feuds that marked rural life; as the lives of individuals were no longer interwoven with that of their extended family, a major source of interpersonal violence was eliminated.

Two other conditions contributed to decreased urban criminality—the improved quality of urban life for all but the lower classes and the emergence of criminal justice systems in many European states more capable of coping with the problem of crime and urban violence.

As Lenski points out, from the sixteenth century on the lives of criminals were usually cut short at an early age because the urban police force and the rest of the criminal justice system were becoming increasingly sophisticated and capable of controlling urban disorder.[24] In addition to the interference of the criminal justice system, disease, malnutrition, and infanticide served further to deplete the ranks of the lowest urban classes[25] whose numbers were only replenished by the arrival from the countryside of other displaced peasants and artisans.[26]

This brief analysis of crime prior to the industrial revolution indicates that, though certain pivotal factors help explain the observed crime patterns, no direct correlation exists between crime and a single social, economic, or political condition. Crime was and continues to be a complex response to intricately connected societal forces.

THE INDUSTRIAL REVOLUTION AND CRIME

The advent of the industrial revolution was seen as a watershed in the evolution of criminality both by contemporary observers of the phenomenon and by present-day historians of crime. Prior to the industrial revolution crime rates were already high, a distinct geography of crime existed, and significant changes had been observed in the relationships among different categories of crime. How can one then contend that the nineteenth century brought significant changes in criminality? The previous historical discussion deflates some of the arguments for the distinctiveness of the crime patterns of the industrial revolution, but there are still strong reasons to view the nineteenth century as a turning point in crime patterns of the western world. The speed of the general societal transformation and the irreversibility of nineteenth-century urbanization[27] in Western Europe and parts of the United States heralded a permanent transformation in the crime patterns of rural areas and, in particular, towns and cities. The criminal groups associated with preindustrial society, primitive rebels and vagabonds, disappeared almost entirely from modern urban communities.

The following theoretical discussion of the effect of social change on criminal behavior in the nineteenth century is based on writings of the period as well as on contemporary scholarship. These theoretical speculations are followed by case studies of changes in criminality in several European countries during the nineteenth century.

Nineteenth-century social thinkers were concerned with the impact of large-scale urbanization and industrialization on the traditional way of life. The problems of deviant behavior and social order, while not central to these scholarly discussions, were considered among the most revealing symptoms of the societal transition. Marx and Engels were among the pioneers in the examination of the effect of urban life on patterns of criminality. Their analysis focused on the impact of the economic structure of society on patterns of criminality while other scholars formulated their views of industrialization without giving as much priority to the economic forces behind development. The writings of Weber, Durkheim, and Simmel advanced a view of urbanization in which secular values, the decline of collective sentiments and restraints, and an increase in stress and anxiety were emphasized.[28] Their theories assumed that more people would become criminals because the absence of social cohesiveness in the urban environment would create greater impersonality, thereby facilitating the commission of crimes.

In retrospect, it appears that the intense societal transition was more conducive to crime commission than the urban milieu itself, but the commentators of the nineteenth century, led by Marx and Engels, stressed the pernicious influence of the urban environment. In *The Position of the Working Class in England,* Engels gave eloquent testimony to the increased criminality and general depravity of urban life during the initial phases of industrialization. In one of his descriptive analyses, he commented that the horrible residential conditions of the workers were responsible for an unprecedented rise in crime.[29] In a statistical analysis of the crime trends of the period, he comments:

> Hence with the extension of the proletariat, crime has increased in England, and the British nation has become one of the most criminal in the world. From the annual criminal tables of the Home Secretary, it is evident that the increase of crime in England has proceeded with incomprehensible rapidity . . . [from 1805 to 1842 criminal offenses] increased seven fold in thirty seven years. . . . In Scotland, crime has increased yet more rapidly, there were but 89 arrests for criminal offenses in 1819, as early as 1837 the number had risen to 3,176 and in 1842 to 4,189.[30]

The sudden increase in criminality that coincided with industrialization and the concomitant urbanization were not confined to British society but affected other societies as they followed England's lead in the industrial revolution. To demonstrate the generalizability of his findings, Engels also commented on the crime trends of Belgium in the middle of the nineteenth century. He concluded that their crime problem was also alarming, particularly among juvenile offenders whose commission rates doubled every year from 1845 on. From these analyses of criminality, Marx and Engels concluded that the economic system accompanying industrialization resulted in human degradation and ultimately crime.[31]

Durkheim believed that the degeneration of urban life, of which crime was one of the most visible symptoms, should be attributed to the transition from the *Gemeinschaft* to the *Gesellschaft*.[32] This change occurs when individuals move from a traditional, family-oriented life to the impersonal and transient life of the city. Crime and other manifestations of social and personal disorder were consequences of this significant societal transition.

Thus, while Marx's thought forced him to conclude that the position of man would decay further under capitalism and that crime rates would continue to rise, Durkheim's analyses of the social situation did not provide such ominous predictions for future crime trends. According to his analysis, urban life would suffer most during the initial stages of rural to urban migration because the new urban residents would be unaccustomed to life without the usual controls that result from intimate personal associations. After the initial transition, Durkheim believed that human adjustment would result in a stabilization of social patterns.[33]

Marx and Durkheim never reexamined the relationship between crime and development at later stages of industrialization. A retrospective view of the impact of nineteenth-century development on crime has been left to other scholars. Unlike their predecessors, more recent scholars have generally chosen to focus almost entirely on the question of crime;[34] they have not examined the impact of the industrial revolution in terms of the larger question of societal structure and evolution.[35] Recent studies by Hobsbawn, Tilly, and Gurr, for example, make the development of social and political conflict the central problem rather than a subsidiary topic of their analyses.[36]

Recent studies of nineteenth-century criminality lead to several fundamentally different interpretations of the effect of modern economic and social development on illegal behavior. Perhaps the most widely held belief on the subject is a synthesis of the writings of Marx, Durkheim, and the criminologist Tarde.[37] According to this interpretation of the impact of development on crime, the noticeable rise in crime recorded during the first half of the nineteenth century is attributable to the unfortunate and immediate consequences of the rapid urbanization accompanying industrialization. (That is, the problems created by the tangible conditions of insufficient employment for the masses of job seekers, poor educational and medical facilities, and overcrowded housing were compounded by the generally depraved moral atmosphere of the urban milieu.) These larger social conditions had a direct impact on the life of the worker's family and resulted in the breakdown of familial relations, individual disorientation, and anomie,[38] all of which contributed to increased rates of criminality. A restoration of social order occurred only with the deceleration of the urbanization process that allowed the established urban residents to acclimate themselves to their new conditions, without the impediment of the masses of new urban migrants. This change in the urban environment that occurred later in the century convinced observers of the period that it was not the city that was itself "criminogenic" but it was "the youthful urban environment, prior to its integration, that was conducive to criminal activity."[39]

Another interpretation of the crime patterns of the nineteenth century adds a biological dimension to the previous social-economic interpretation of development. Such theorists assert that biological factors need also to be considered because of their preeminence in influencing the "physical characteristics of populations."[40] Crime is seen as the direct result of the pathological state of the city racked by disease, death, and the generally enfeebled health of the population.[41] Overwork resulting in exhaustion, absence of sleep and recreation, and general ill-health increased the tension in the lives of urban residents. It is these biological factors which one scholar maintains were responsible for the "brutalities of the street, the workshop and the barricade"[42] or in other words for crime and general social disorder. In the nineteenth century, biological factors overlaid with economic, social, and moral factors contributed, as in the past, to the development of existing social conditions and urban problems.[43]

The demographic explanation of the observed criminality in many ways complements the biological view because according to both theories the physical state of the working population explains much of the observed crime. According to the demographic view, industrialization depresses birthrates and increases longevity but it also creates the teenage stage of life.[44] With industrialization and its concomitant passage of child labor laws and the expansion of formal education, teenagers—presently the most crime-prone age group—emerged as a distinct entity.[45] Industrialization not only caused this demographic change but also caused a large-scale emigration to the cities, which resulted in a disproportionately old population in the rural areas and a youthful one in the cities.

The biological and demographic explanations help elucidate the proportional contribution of particular groups to the crime rate, but they do not explain the root causes of large-scale criminal behavior. The following theoretical views see crime as a rational response to existing social conditions.

The Marxist interpretation of these developments that has been adopted by many conflict theorists emphasizes the rational and calculating aspects of the growing crime phenomenon. Crime is seen to be too closely associated with the "values and norms it violates to be considered as simply anomic in respect to them"; crime the converse of legal activity is too similar to be seen as truly deviant.[46] Crime, therefore, fulfilled the expressed need to protest against the social conditions of society and in this respect it was not pathological but utilitarian.

Howard Zehr has advanced one of the most distinctive and convincing explanations of the impact of the nineteenth-century developmental process on crime; he maintains that the change in rural and urban crime patterns was a manifestation of modernization. The transition from the preeminence of rural patterns of crime based on violence to those of the urbanized society where crimes against property predominate, occurred, because of changing values and social systems and not because of normlessness or social disorganization. He contends that to explain crime as a "symptom of social and moral disorganization" would not even be partially convincing as an explanation of criminality except at the initial stages of the industrial revolution because crime is a rational response to a situation.[47] Zehr expresses the following opinions:

> Rising theft rates indicate rising expectations, the spread of 'modern' economic values and, with some qualification, are characteristics of modern, urban society ... Violence, on the other hand, represents a traditional form of criminal behavior, and its rise in a situation of change reflects the retention rather than the breakdown of traditional behavior. Thus ... drops in violence indicate reductions in tension and, in the long run, the abandonment of traditional forms of behavior.[48]

Other social thinkers go even beyond this view of property crime to suggest that theft is a form of class conflict and an expression of social discontent.[49]

This theory of crime and development at first seems to be very

26

much at variance with the previously presented explanations of criminality. The first three theories of crime addressed man and his moral and physical state while the latter two theories approach the rationality of his behavior in response to social circumstances. While social disorganization is emphasized in the first theories, the latter theories abandon this concept and substitute the formulation of transitional values.

While these theoretical differences may at first appear to be fundamental, a closer examination of these approaches to crime during the nineteenth-century industrial revolution reveals certain striking similarities. These theories, unlike explanations of criminal behavior for the preindustrial period, attest that a very significant and irrevocable change had occurred in the structure of society.[50] The advent of the industrial revolution, therefore, represents a break with the old order of society and the substitution of new ways of living, and consequently different patterns of criminal behavior. To these social theorists, crime is indicative of larger changes in the social order and assumes a significance greater than previously attributed to it. The booming crime rates of the first part of the past century are tangible evidence of the massive transition heralded by the advent of the industrial revolution.

CONTEMPORARY CASE STUDIES OF CRIME AND DEVELOPMENT

These explanations of the relationship between development and crime, while provocative, need to be substantiated by historical evidence. Recent research by social scientists and historians evaluates the impact of the industrial revolution and the concomitant urbanization on both crimes of violence and property. Their studies demonstrate that these societal changes had a very similar effect on many of the Western European societies examined.

National crime patterns ceased to be dominated by the offenses of the countryside as the large-scale movement of the population to cities and towns made urban crime patterns the preeminent form of national criminality. Urbanization produced an irreversible increase in overall crime rates since the recorded rates of criminality for the mid-twentieth century are appreciably higher than those recorded prior to the onset of the industrial revolution. The motivations for urban criminality were also transformed following the initial traumatic transition to industrialization. By the advent of the twentieth century, acute need had ceased to be a primary cause of property crimes,[51] but the desire for and exposure to luxury assumed an increasingly important role in the perpetration of nonviolent crimes. Significant changes were observed in regards to offenders as well as offenses. The phenomenon of crime, once confined primarily to adult offenders and their families, suddenly became an activity of many young town dwellers [52] and unattached children who formed gangs to perpetrate thefts.[53]

Recent studies of crime in the past century suggest that the larger forces of social change overcame existing cultural and historical differences to produce common crime patterns in these societies. Despite the similarities between countries in research findings, contemporary scholars provide strikingly different interpretations of available data. These differing analyses of the data result from diverse social and ideological views rather than disagreements on the validity of available data.

Most contemporary historians of crime are in general agreement that available nineteenth-century criminal statistics lack reliability. Crime statistics are generally among the most questionable of social or moral statistics available because all crimes are not reported and reporting rates depend on the offense involved. Rape has one of the lowest reporting rates and homicide one of the highest with most property crimes lying between these two extremes. Not only do the reporting rates contribute to the lack of reliability of crime statistics, but the criminal justice system, seeking to prove its effectiveness, frequently removed unsolved crimes from the public record. However, the development of crime should not be ignored because of the potential problem posed by the distortions in crime statistics.[54] Historians agree that, despite these limitations "comparisons among periods, places and groups" are feasible.[55] As Zehr comments,

> The biases and distortions in crime records must not be glossed over, however, a close study of various crime indices from both the nineteenth and twentieth centuries indicated that nineteenth-century crime statistics are more plentiful and provide better indices of actual criminal activity than is commonly assumed. Crime indices are not random variables; records from the nineteenth century yield recurrent and comprehensible patterns of crime which can not be attributed simply to biases in the records or to the activities of agencies which compiled them.[56]

Researchers should be aware of certain important distortions in the crime rates of the past century. First, rural communities because of their greater degree of social order were probably more tolerant of small collective "outbreaks" of minor violence. Urban dwellers, residing in communities where the state of order was more precarious and informal relationships between law enforcement official and offender did not prevail were more concerned by violence. Therefore, rural violence may have gone unreported more frequently than that in urban areas in the nineteenth century. Property crimes that were already rarer in rural than in urban areas may have been disproportionately documented by rural authorities because of their perceived seriousness. Conversely, urban residents, already cynical about the ability of law enforcement authorities to restore stolen property, may have been more reluctant to report the loss of goods to law enforcement authorities.[57] As a result of these factors there appears to be a consistent distortion operating in both rural and urban areas. If these biases are taken into account in conducting analyses of crime patterns, then the comprehensible patterns can be used to probe some important questions.

If it is possible to make as much sense out of the crime statistics as Zehr and the work of the scholars to be discussed suggests, then the following case studies of crime and development should contribute to our understanding of the impact of different social processes on crime.

Major studies of the development of crime in England, France, Germany, and Sweden in the nineteenth century and in Russia in the twentieth century have been conducted by reputable scholars. These studies all analyze crime in the context of urbanization, economic transition, and the social conditions of these populations. The authors of the studies isolate fluctuations in criminal behavior attributable to changes in law and judicial practice from those resulting from social forces.

Zehr's comparative study of French and German criminality from 1830 on establishes quite remarkable similarities for the crime patterns of the two countries at parallel stages in their development. This study corroborates and quantifies some of the relationships[58] established in Louis Chevalier's similar but more descriptive study of Parisian crime and social disorder during the first half of the nineteenth century.[59] The Parisian study suggested that crime and collective violence were a response to urban tensions. While a more recent study negates some of the findings of this analysis of Parisian criminality,[60] its research conclusions may be faulty because they are based on an unrepresentative data sample.

The study of French and German crime analyzed the data in a

different way, focusing solely on the crimes of homicide, assault, and theft because the former two offenses were deemed the best measures of violent misconduct while theft was considered to be the most representative of property crimes. Using an analysis of the commission rates of the two violent crimes as compared to the rate of theft, Zehr established clear results concerning the impact of urbanization and modernization on German and French patterns of crime.[61]

During the urbanization of France and Germany, crimes of violence, after an initial increase, became less frequent and ceded their preeminent place to property offenses. Proportionately more violence was committed in rural than in urban areas, and, as urbanization progressed, this relationship became ever more pronounced. What these data suggest is that the trend toward urbanization resulted in a lower rate of violence not only in the short term but in the long term as well, indicating that the phenomenon of urbanization had more than a transient effect on observed patterns of crime. Urbanization was a social process that brought more of the population under the direct surveillance of the criminal justice system, resulting in fundamental changes in national patterns of crime commission.

A closer examination of this study reveals that these data were valid in the aggregate and in the individual case as well. The highest levels of violence in relationship to property crimes were found "without exception" in the most rural French administrative districts while all the highly urbanized regions had the converse relationship.[62] The crime patterns of urbanization, or low rate of violence in relationship to theft, was most pronounced in the largest and oldest urban centers.

While the relationship between types of offense differed according to the age of urban centers, no difference could be discerned in the crime rates of cities of differing degrees of industrial maturity. All French cities, regardless of age, experienced remarkable growth in their theft rate as evidenced by a rise in prosecutions for this offense of 230 percent between 1831–39 and 1900–1909,[63] an assertion incorrectly disputed by another recent study of nineteenth-century French criminality.[64] Comparable figures are not available for Germany, but figures on rates of conviction by community size indicate that the number of offenders rose with the level of urbanization.[65] However, the two studies of French criminality, as well as the German conviction rates, suggest that violence, unlike theft, does not appear to be associated with the degree of urbanization. Though violence grew in urban areas, its growth in France and Germany appears to have been greatest during the initial period of industrialization. Evidence for this is that "assault and battery rose in Germany for several decades after 1880, when the industrialization process was in full swing, then turned downward by the end of the period."[66] The observable trends in France were similar and growth was greater in violent crime before 1870 than afterwards, a relationship not as apparent if all crimes against the person were examined in aggregate.[67]

The observable trends for France and Germany can then be summarized in the following way: with urbanization, both theft and violence rose but the rate of increase for theft was much higher than that for assault and homicide.[68] Violence rose primarily during the initial stages of urbanization, but theft increased not only with the process of urbanization but remained after urbanization had already transpired. Modern patterns of criminal behavior appear after agrarian society characterized by violent criminality is replaced by urban society where the theft of material goods becomes the pervasive form of crime. Crime is no longer counted in isolated incidents but becomes a major threat to the very order of the urban community.

These conclusions based on Zehr's major study of French and German crime rates call into question some of our commonly held ideas of the recently urbanized environment as a place where both property crime and violence reign. It is therefore important to examine some other crime data of other countries to see if the process of modernization and development induced similar effects on their crime rates.

London, unlike Paris and those German cities that have been studied in terms of this tradition, had a considerable tradition of urban disorder dating from the Middle Ages. Its reputation was such that it was alluded to as a "monstrous city, the city of poverty and crime." This heritage means that scholars of London's criminality must examine the crime patterns of the nineteenth century in terms of this historical precedent.[69]

A marked decline in crime occurred in eighteenth-century England immediately before the advent of the industrial revolution. This reduction in criminality was noticeable both for those offenses committed to trial and for the number of convictions. One explanation for this decline in criminality was that the criminal justice system, designed by the wealthy, was repressing ever more rigorously the criminality of the masses.[70] The death penalty was extended to an increasing number of crimes and was used almost exclusively to punish property offenders. The brutality of this punishment, however, resulted in its lessened application.[71]

The social conditions of the urban environment, the laws, and the operation of the criminal justice system account for the crime trends observed at the beginning of the 1880s. In the early 1800s property crimes again rose but the number of violent offenders diminished, continuing the decline initiated in the previous century. Murder remained a fairly infrequent crime and decreased in frequency despite temporary upswings in the mid-1840s and mid-1860s.[72] Examination of the statistics for the other major crimes against the person, assault, reveal very similar trends.[73] The assault rate fell almost consistently from 1830 onward, except for a major upswing during the late 1840s, a period of both economic and political instability.

London crime patterns are quite similar to those previously discussed for German and French cities. The intense period of industrialization of the 1820s and 1830s was marked by an unprecedented increase in the urban population, primarily a result of the mass movement of the rural population into cities. Between 1821 and 1831, "Manchester's population increased by almost 45 percent,"[74] paralleling a similar national trend towards urbanization. "In 1750 less than one-fifth of the population lived in towns of this [Manchester's] size."[75] The rural emigrants brought their traditional patterns of criminal behavior to their new environment, and, as a result of this importation of criminality, the rates of violent criminality for metropolitan London were highest during this stage of population transition.

As the new residents of London accustomed themselves to the conditions of urban life, crimes against the person stabilized, only to rise momentarily in the late 1840s and 1860s. This rise in criminality coincided with the new, unfamiliar economic and political conditions in the urban environment. Chartism, the first great movement of the British working class, was primarily an urban phenomenon of the 1830s and 1840s.[76] It affected most significantly the members of the population who contributed disproportionately to their nation's criminality. This destabilization of the urban environment may account for the upswings in criminality.

The decline in violent offenses and their early peak appear to result directly from the early onslaught of industrialization in England prior to its emergence in other European countries. The patterns observed for property crimes are somewhat different from those observed in crimes against the person. Property crime did not peak during the first stages of industrialization, but during the 1830s. From that point until 1873, the recorded statistics note a fourfold decline in the most common property crime of theft with a gradual increase in the most serious forms of acquisitive crime such as robbery, burglary, fraud, and embezzlement. No decline is evident in these more serious and sophisticated forms of property offenses until after the 1870s.

The relationship between property and violent offenses observed in Germany and France during their later period of modernization after 1850 was foretold by events in London during the 1820s and 1830s. After the onset of industrialization in England, violent offenses ceded permanently their once preeminent position to the increasingly common property crimes. In all three countries, the mature years of industrialization were characterized by fewer violent offenses and more frequent though less threatening crimes against property.

A study of criminality in Sweden during its period of development reveals differences from the three European countries previously discussed because a very small percentage of the Swedish population was urbanized at the advent of the industrial revolution. Even after the onset of industrialization, the nation as a whole, with the exception of Stockholm, proceeded to urbanize at a relatively slow rate, a result of health and economic problems as well as of large-scale emigration to the United States. As most of the Swedish population continued their residence in rural areas, Stockholm proved exceptional in Sweden's modernization because its population doubled between 1840 and 1850.[77] Although Stockholm followed the developmental patterns of other major European cities at the time, the rest of the country did not.

The availability of consistent crime statistics for Stockholm for a large number of offenses enabled analysts to make accurate comparisons over time for many categories of criminality. The patterns observed in this city are reminiscent of the countries previously discussed. Crime rates for assault and breach of the peace were high in the 1840s and declined gradually between 1850 and 1880 and sharply from 1880 onwards.[78] This pattern further confirms the observation that crimes of violence rise at the beginning of a period of urbanization and decline with its maturation.

Whereas the patterns of violence observed for Stockholm during this period resembled those of other European cities, its patterns of theft were sharply different from those observed in England, France, and Germany during the period of industrialization. With some slight fluctuations, theft rates for the city of Stockholm declined from 1840 onward. Among property offenses only fraud and embezzlement showed a consistent and long-term increase.[79] This overall decline in most forms of property crime is atypical of the patterns observed in other countries undergoing simultaneously the process of development.

The Swedish statistics support the contention that the initial period of industrialization and mass migration to urban centers is most disruptive of the social order of the urban community. This is shown by the commission rates for violent and property crimes, which were highest during the early stages of the industrial revolution. Property crimes are not, however, the indices of modernization in Sweden that they appear to be in other industrializing European nations. The Swedish case may be exceptional because large-scale emigration to America reduced certain economic tensions that may have otherwise resolved themselves in criminality. In this significant respect, the recorded decline in Stockholm's urban theft parallels that observed in London during the eighteenth-century when problems of urban criminality were relieved by the mass deportation of property offenders to the American colonies and Australia.[80] This parallel drawn between eighteenth-century London and nineteenth-century Stockholm suggests that some of the consequences of urbanization can be averted by alleviating some of the social factors leading to nonpolitical urban disorder and by promoting an effective criminal justice system respected by the citizenry.

The last country to be examined in this historical discussion of the impact of industrialization on crime is Russia / the Soviet Union. Though a study of the entire developmental process is not possible because of the cessation of criminological research at the end of the 1920s, it is possible to document the dramatic changes that occurred in the initial years of industrial development at the turn of the twentieth century.

The analyses of crime during this period were conducted by Soviet researchers acquainted with the criminological research of other societies. Because the process of industrialization occurred in Russia several decades later than in the Western European countries, it was possible for Soviet scholars to place some of the changes they observed in comparative perspective.

Soviet crime data for the period available duplicate some of the trends observed in the other countries that were studied. Rural criminality prior to the onset of the industrial revolution was limited but highly violent. This high degree of violence was closely associated with alcohol use among offenders which helped provoke spontaneous outbursts of aggression.[81] Whereas crimes against the person were a frequent occurrence in the countryside, the poverty of rural life and the close associations of members of the rural community provided little opportunity for the commission of property offenses.

With the advent of industrialization at the beginning of the twentieth century, millions flocked into the cities of Moscow and Leningrad resulting in intense overcrowding in already inadequate housing facilities. Criminologists closely monitored the impact of this urban migration on crime patterns of the largest city, Moscow.[82] Of particular concern to the researchers were the high rates of urban violence and particularly the rates recorded for homicide. Theft was by far the most frequent property offense and far exceeded the commission rates for armed robbery, swindling, and other categories of property crime. Property crime represented 30 percent of all crimes,[83] a significant change for a society that had previously experienced very few crimes in this category.

The process of urbanization in the Soviet Union cannot be studied in its entirety because after Stalin's ascent to power the impact of modernization cannot be differentiated from the influence of his dictatorship. The initial stages of modernization of Russia and the Soviet state are, however, reminiscent of the countries of Western Europe where large increases in the rate of commission of violent and property crimes accompanied the birth of the industrial revolution.

Is it possible from these five brief case studies to discern a relationship between the process of development and patterns of crime commission? Are the social, economic, and cultural changes that accompany the transition from a rural to an urban society so significant that they produce very similar crime patterns in countries with very different cultural, economic, and political histories? The answer appears to be a resounding yes, at least at the initial stages of the industrial revolution. The crime patterns of societies at more advanced stages of modernization are, however, more individualized, reflecting the influence of national historical differences in social structure and the effectiveness of the criminal justice system in dealing with increased threats to urban order.

The analysis of crime and modernization in five countries suggests that rural and urban areas are characterized by different types of crime, and as development proceeds these environmental differences become even more pronounced. While theft was a rare phenomenon in rural life and crimes against the person were very much more frequent, the advent of industrialization and the subsequent movement of the population to urban areas produced a very different form of criminal behavior. During the first stages of large-scale urbanization, cities experienced an increase in commission rates for both violent and property offenses while rural areas continued to suffer primarily from the consequences of personal violence.

Urban areas in the transitional stage to modernization suffered their worst crime problems as urban and rural patterns of criminal behavior converged. Their tradition of violence accompanied rural migrants to the cities, and their adjustment problems aggravated their usual response to social tensions. Thus, unprecedented rates of urban violence accompanied new levels of property crime as recent urban arrivals expressed their unfulfilled desire for the fruits of industrialization. Only as urbanization progressed and the recently arrived urban inhabitants adjusted to city life, did crimes of violence cede their once preeminent place to crimes against property.

The transition from a society dominated by crimes of violence to one characterized by property offenses is the hallmark of mdernization. Though many believe that another characteristic of this societal transformation is a steady increase in total rates of crime commission, all available evidence does not substantiate such a trend. Urban crime per capita did consistently exceed those of agricultural communities, but increasing urbanization did not necessarily result in unilateral increases in reported commission rates. The fact that property crime, the dominant form of criminal behavior after the onset of the industrial revolution, did not increase in all societies with increasing development substantiates this observation. In Sweden, for example, where emigration abroad provided an outlet for unfulfilled material aspirations, spiraling crime rates for all categories of theft were arrested.

Of the four countries for which data are available, the maturation of the developmental process brought a stabilization in the reported crime rates. In evaluating the significance of this change, it is necessary to determine whether this leveling off of the crime rate is an indication of social adjustment to new conditions or represents a transference of dissatisfaction to another arena. This slip in the crime rates was prolonged but, in the long term, temporary because crime rates again ascended in the middle decades of the twentieth century. It is, therefore, necessary to conclude that the decline in criminality represented both an adjustment to the conditions of modern life as well as an abatement of those political, social, and economic conditions conducive to criminal behavior. As high crime rates coincided with increases in civil disorder, it suggests that in some countries crime may be another form of political expression of the hostilities created by modernization. The stabilization of crime rates between 1870 and 1930 in societies that underwent industrialization in the first half of the nineteenth century, is an indication of the political, social, and economic accommodation of the urban population to the forces of modernization.

Thus, crime rates at all stages of the developmental process appear to be a barometer of the problems associated with this major societal transition. Property and violent crime are therefore important measures of social order and societal transition and assume a significance greater than that previously attributed to these forms of societal misconduct. Violent criminality is both a symptom of rural life as well as an indication of the problems associated with the adjustment to urban life. Property crime is a natural consequence of modern urban settlement with its emphasis on material goods unequally distributed to all inhabitants.[84] The crime rate and the relationship between property and violent crime provide indices of a society's transition towards modernization.

PART TWO

CRIME IN CAPITALIST NATIONS

3

CRIME AND DEVELOPING COUNTRIES

The process of development knows no geographical limits, and countries on all major continents are presently undergoing the transition from rural agricultural to industrialized urbanized societies. Despite the significant social, cultural, political, and economic characteristics that differentiate these developing countries, few of these nations have avoided one of the most visible consequences of this developmental process, the growth of criminality. With the onset of modernization, these diverse societies, which had previously enjoyed low crime rates, are plagued suddenly by an alarming increase in criminality that proves a threat to the urban order and the very process of societal development.

The criminological consequences of twentieth-century development in many ways parallel the experiences in the nineteenth century of currently developed nations. This repetition of historical patterns provides further support for the thesis that the process of development and its accompanying social changes produce common patterns of criminality in what were once and remain culturally diverse societies.

The following discussion of crime rates, patterns of criminality, criminal offenders, and crime causation shows the repetition today of nineteenth-century patterns of crime and development. Overall trends in crime commission confirm that the process of modernization produces criminal behavior that not only reflects social change but provides a major threat to the continuity of this societal transformation.

Forms of Criminality

Prior to the initiation of the modernization process, currently developing societies had generally low rates of crime commission. Like the developed societies prior to industrialization, the criminality of developing countries was confined primarily to rural acts of violence and property offenses were generally an urban phenomenon in a society dominated by rural life.[1] These traditional patterns of criminal behavior, as in nineteenth-century Europe, are disappearing as these nations enter a new type of social order.

Developing countries are currently affected by an increase in both crimes of violence and property offenses. Property crime presently provides the most serious threat to the social order,[2] recalling the trends observed in nineteenth-century Western Europe. A recent United Nations study of world crime patterns has concluded that the growth in theft and robbery in developing countries is "substantial and serious." Both these categories of crime grew by over 40 percent in the six-year period from 1970 to 1975. During this same period, crimes against the person and property were almost equally responsible for 90 percent of the crimes committed.[3]

Drug offenses compose most of the remaining 10 percent of crime commission not associated with crimes against the person or property.[4] This category of criminality, dependent on the mobility of the modern age and, therefore, practically unknown in the past, has assumed an increasingly important role in the overall crime patterns of developing countries.

As commission rates for crimes against property are now rising at a faster rate than those for all categories of crime except drug offenses,[5] property crimes will soon be more frequent than crimes against the person. Violent crimes, as they cede their formerly preeminent position in developing countries to crimes against property, will repeat the transformation in criminal behavior associated with development in nineteenth-century Europe. This anticipated transformation in crime patterns would be further confirmation that violence is associated with rural life and the disruptive transition to urbanization and rising theft is the offense that epitomizes the advent of modernization.

The overall crime rate of the developing countries in the first half of the 1970s has been calculated at approximately 800 offenses per

100,000 population or approximately 40 percent of the rate recorded in developed countries. This amount is not static but has risen at the rate of 2.5 percent per year with rates for female offenders increasing during this period at the more accelerated rate of 30 percent a year.[6] The rates of increase for total criminality and for female offenders are considerably higher than that reported in developed countries.

Crime rates for offenses against the person in the transitional period from a rural society to a modern developed nation have traditionally been high. It is, therefore, not surprising that violent crimes against the person comprise a disproportionately larger percentage of the total crime picture in developing countries than in developed countries. The commission patterns are not, however, dissimilar. The most serious forms of violent criminality occur less frequently than the less serious violent offenses. Kidnapping and intentional homicide are relatively rare offenses while assault and armed robbery, a combination of both the major offense categories, are important threats to the social order of developing societies.[7] The unreliability of rape statistics and the variability of definitions of this offense make cross-cultural comparisons of this category of criminal behavior infeasible. The relative frequency of these different offenses is explained by the conditions of life in developing countries. Kidnapping, an offense requiring offender mobility and some sophistication in communications, is less feasible in this environment than armed robbery, which requires little more than force and the personal ingenuity of the criminal. The low rate of intentional homicide is explained by the context in which murders are committed. As explained in the previous chapter, violence is common in rural areas because animosities or grudges often manifest themselves in assaults when traditional social controls are relaxed by alcohol consumption on holidays. The spontaneity of these assaults results in low rates of intentional homicide and a high probability that the victim and the assailant are acquainted.[8] Therefore, though crime rates for premeditated murder are low, the rate for other categories of homicide is much higher.[9] Of the 25 countries with the highest rates of homicide in the 1960s, 21 of them were developing countries.[10]

High rates of assault are recorded simultaneously with high rates of other forms of violent crime because assaults are frequently unsuccessful homicides in which the victim survives the attack of the assailant. The principal reasons given for the high incidence of this violent crime in rural areas before and during modernization are as follows: Apart from the sporadic violence that accompanies feast times, aggression provides an important outlet for members of rural communities. Violence is legitimated as a means of dispute settlement[11] because traditional bureaucratized forms of settling antagonisms are not available and private mediation is not always feasible or successful. Violence for young males, especially in Latin American societies, is a means of demonstrating their manliness and is part of the whole cultural concept of "machismo."[12] The probability of violence is further compounded by the rapid rate of social change and concomitant culture conflict[13] that frequently results in crimes of violence against the person.

For these reasons rates of violence have traditionally been high in rural areas. With the process of development, rural residents flock in large numbers into cities bringing their traditional patterns of rural violence with them. Thus, prior to the acclimation of these new urban residents to city life, both urban and rural areas record high rates of crimes against the person.

The availability of goods and the proximity and impersonality of city life make increasing rates of property crime a natural outgrowth of the process of urbanization. The paucity of material possessions among many city dwellers is both a cause and a constraint on this form of criminality. Material need plays a very significant role in the motivation of property offenses in many urban areas.[14] While need affects the lives of many recent settlers, others desire the manufactured goods inaccessible to individuals of their financial means.[15] The desire for otherwise unattainable goods has resulted in increasing violence in the commission of property crimes. The process of development has also produced the violent property offender and the gang, which commits acts of aggression against personal and social property. The growth of *kondoism,* or armed robbery, in Uganda[16] is characteristic of many developed countries where collective behavior has become increasingly frequent.[17]

The limited mobility of many of the recent urban migrants causes many of them to commit crimes close to their place of residence, thereby often victimizing individuals of not very different financial status. Therefore, most of the property crime committed in developing countries, apart from armed robbery, does not involve large-scale loss of property.[18] Instead, research from several geographically dispersed societies suggests that the goods or money stolen are used by the offenders, who infrequently engage in wanton acts of destruction.[19]

The only property crime in developing countries that causes

large-scale losses is financial corruption, which encompasses a wide range of criminal offenses such as corruption of governmental officials through bribery, payoffs, and kickbacks. These crimes are not confined to just one part of the developing world but have been observed extensively in Latin America, Africa, Asia, and the Middle East. The universality of this phenomenon has led certain analysts to suggest that it is the very process of modernization that is conducive to this form of criminality.[20]

Though certain developing countries have taken action against corruption in recent years, in many countries officials feel powerless to control it.[21] The problem is now endemic, not only among officials who believe that such financial incentives are part of their remuneration but also among ordinary citizens who believe that services cannot be obtained without providing a bribe or payoff.[22] Payments to political officials are considered one of the costs of doing business in developing countries.

While this form of economic behavior is being discussed here as a crime, only in some of the developing countries are these types of activities defined as criminal. Even in those societies that outlaw this conduct, payments and gifts to officials are considered natural and necessary and certainly not the equivalent of assaulting an individual or stealing livestock or a personal possession. Therefore prosecutions for corruption in developing countries are as rare as the prosecution of white-collar offenders in developed nations.

Though the traditional property and violent crimes predominate in developing countries, these societies are not immune to the problem of victimless crime. Drug offenses and prostitution are problems of increasing magnitude in these societies presently undergoing rapid transition. The perpetration of drug crimes, facilitated by modern communications, makes these crimes among the most unfortunate consequences of modernization. Drug-related crimes are presently the fastest growing crime category and comprise 8 percent of all known offenses in developing countries.[23] The majority of crimes in this category involve traffic in drugs not only to developed countries but to other developing countries as well. Research on cannabis revealed that "a large proportion of the traffic is based on indigenous production and consumption in the Far East, Central and South Africa"[24] which augments the traditional commerce of the Middle East. The increase in drug traffic is both a consequence of modernization and a threat to the continuation of the process of development.

The principal reason that this category of criminality is so prevalent in developing countries is that these societies are the prime producers of opium and other drugs.[25] Drugs are raised by farmers in areas that are threatened presently by mass rural emigration because of the absence of another lucrative crop in a cash-dependent economy. Increased cultivation of drugs is, therefore, a consequence of the processes of urbanization and industrialization. The unfortunate consequences of this distinctly modern crime are experienced both at home and abroad as more individuals are drawn into the highly profitable but criminal international drug trade. Drug crimes have increased so significantly[26] as a result of contemporary circumstances that many experts forsee further growth in this category of illegal behavior.

Prostitution is another type of illegal behavior in developing countries that is widespread and of increasing frequency. Whereas prostitution is relatively rare in most traditional societies because of the strong tribal and village customs surrounding marriage and the prohibition against premarital sex,[27] its rapid growth in developing societies is a direct result of the process of modernization. As urbanization proceeds, the mass migration of youthful males to cities promotes the breakdown of the traditional way of life. The youthful male migrants, alone in cities and removed from familial controls, many of them with money available to them for the first time, seek out prostitutes. With such a lucrative market for prostitutes, many women choose or are forced into careers of prostitution.

The status and careers of prostitutes differ significantly among developing nations. In Africa prostitution is more informal than it is in the Far East, and women often choose to become prostitutes as a lucrative means of establishing their personal independence and providing a nest egg for future business ventures. Though different classes of prostitutes exist, none of their activities appear to be linked with other categories of criminal behavior.[28] The absence of commitment to the criminal way of life and the voluntary nature of their participation in prostitution makes it possible for these women to acquire money and consequently status, thereby enabling them to leave prostitution and enter marriages.

In Southeast Asia, prostitution is much more organized; and the women, unlike their counterparts in Africa, do not have control over their own activities as many of them are sold to brothels by their families to pay off debts or are seduced into this activity through deception. In this area where prostitution is more formally structured, connections to the larger criminal underworld are firmly established.[29]

The majority of the crimes previously discussed have been transformed rather than created by development. Though these offenses now occur with increased frequency, they were not unknown in previous centuries. The modern age has created new forms of crime that differentiate the twentieth-century developmental process from that of the nineteenth century. Among the recently created crimes are those associated with modern mobility and the complexities of contemporary commerce. Crimes that fall into this category are vehicular offenses involving automobiles, motorcycles, and airplanes as well as bank robberies.

The automobile, a recent arrival in most developing countries, has produced two significant forms of criminality—traffic accidents and automobile thefts. The former is a particularly acute problem because the poor condition of the roads and the inexperience of the drivers lead to a large number of auto fatalities. In Africa and many parts of the Middle East little attention is paid to road signs or speed limits, and this reckless driving, illegal of itself, results in high rates of negligent homicide as well as some of the world's highest auto fatality rates.[30]

The automobile is a symbol of even greater prestige in developing than in developed countries because people are unaccustomed to the car and fewer individuals possess them. Because of the mobility and glamor it provides its owner, the car is an attraction to youthful offenders, and it makes the car a desirable piece of property to the more sophisticated professional thief. Auto theft is common both for the purpose of joyriding and of resale.[31] Joyriding, primarily an offense of juveniles, is one of the few forms of destructive property crime found in developing countries.

New forms of theft as well as the vehicular crimes have been created as a result of the automobile. The pervasive problem of short supply of imported goods in developing countries is conducive to the theft of automobile parts from other vehicles. In the Soviet Union, as in other developing countries, professional thieves steal car parts to fulfill the requests of their customers.

Other offenses related to mobility are crimes associated with airplanes. Airplanes have been hijacked and subjected to other forms of terrorism.[32] In some cases hijacking represents a modern form of piracy, but the act is motivated more often by political ideologies than by financial objectives. This form of political terrorism causes a more dramatic transition in developing countries than in developed ones because not only are the automobile, the airplane, and communication systems new to their people but criminal acts connected with this modern technology were previously unknown to them.

Another new form of crime in developing countries is the bank robbery. Since individuals in rural societies had little of value and cash was of minimal significance in the economy, this offense was unknown. But as the developing nations have become more industrialized and barter and exchange have yielded their place to cash exchanges, the bank has become a necessary institution. The emergence of this financial institution surprisingly did not lead immediately to bank robberies but their occurrence can be traced to the importation of techniques from abroad. Scholars of crime in Yugoslavia maintain that bank robberies began in their country only after migrant workers returned from France and Germany where they became acquainted with this offense.[33] The introduction of the bank robbery, usually an armed offense, has led to an even higher level of violence in the already violence-prone developing countries.

Though a detailed discussion of political criminality is outside the scope of this book, some mention needs to be made of this category of criminal behavior. Political crime is not more frequent in developing countries than in developed countries, but the definition of the offense varies considerably among the developing countries. The concept of political criminality though almost universally understood is not as often defined as criminal behavior as the illegal acts previously discussed. In some societies the criminal code makes no special provisions for politically motivated offenses and they are treated under the criminal code as ordinary crimes. This is true in most developing countries with socialist economies while in other countries special provisions are made for acts not motivated by personal or material motives. Political acts of criminality include such behavior as sabotage, seizure of buildings and aircraft, bombings, and acts of violence committed by terrorists.

A political act of criminality, though confined to one country, may transcend national boundaries and affect the citizens of other nations as well. This is particularly true of acts of terrorism which are carried out on international airliners or against buildings and officials outside their native countries. Examples of this are the Moluccans in the Netherlands, Arab terrorists who operate in Europe, and Croatian terrorists in the United States. These political offenders go abroad to perpetrate their crimes in more economically advanced societies where they will gain more visibility for their cause.[34]

Historical, cultural, and political differences explain the significant variations observed in patterns of political criminality. The process of development, therefore, explains less about the form and extent of this criminality than the other categories of illegal behavior that are more influenced by social and economic transition.

The developing countries have invented no new forms of crime. They have either acquired crimes facilitated by their increased technological capabilities or have modified their traditional forms of criminality to their new social and environmental circumstances. These countries have not yet relinquished the influence of the traditional way of life, and rural life still influences not only the types of crime that are committed but the means by which they are perpetrated.

The tradition of rural violence prevails and many of the crimes against the person and property involve the use of arms and force.[35] Though not much of the violence appears to be wanton, unrelated to or excessive to the demands of the crime, the level of violence does provide a threat to the way of life in developing countries.

Property crimes, the offenses that characterize the developmental process, have grown rapidly but still do not involve large losses of property because of the highly restricted mobility of the generally poor offenders. Increasingly, property crimes are accompanied by acts of violence though a large professional criminal class has not yet developed.[36]

Developing countries have not only changed their traditional forms of criminality but have acquired new crimes associated with the advent of modern mobility and commerce. These crimes, only recently introduced in developed countries, have proved more disruptive to the social order of societies only now making the transition to modernization.

Rates of Criminality

The level of crime in developing countries is considerably below that of developed countries but as these nations move towards modernization their crime rates are approaching those of the more impersonal, industrialized societies. The rate of increase in criminality for the period 1965–1976 is, however, generally less than the rate of population growth for developing nations.[37] Crime rates are increasing rapidly for all offenses and in particular for drug offenses and for crimes against property, especially those involving violence. In this way, patterns of crime in the developing countries are moving towards the model of the more developed societies where property offenses represent a large share of all criminal offenses and crimes against the person assume a merely secondary role. Though national and regional differences will remain, a convergence of criminal patterns may result as the economic, social, and cultural characteristics that distinguish developed countries disappear.

The apparent similarities observed in the crime patterns of developing countries should not obscure the fact that significant regional and national differences still characterize the nations that are presently undergoing industrial development. Differences exist both in the frequency of crime commission and the types of crimes that are committed. For example, the crime rates of the Caribbean nations are quite high and those of the countries of the Middle East are low, while the developing nations of Latin America, Africa, and the rest of Asia lie between the two extremes.[38] The explanations given for the wide variance in levels of criminality are based on social structure, religious institutions, geographical location, and foreign influences.

Many of the Middle Eastern and North African countries are characterized by low and stable crime rates. This fortunate circumstance appears to be a consequence of the preservation of cohesive family structure and the strong religious foundation of the societies. Even in those societies experiencing rapidly increasing affluence like Iraq, Qatar, and Saudi Arabia, this dramatic change in the societies has not resulted in the criminological problems that often accompany rapid economic development.[39] The contrast between the financial position of the migrant workers imported by many of these Middle Eastern societies and that of the wealthy native population has not, except in Kuwait, been conducive to increased criminality. Only in Kuwait, where the immigrant labor force outnumbers the nation's citizens, has a noticeable increase in reported rates of criminality been observed.[40] The maintenance of a traditional way of life appears to have been successful in averting some of the most unfortunate consequences of societal development.

Israel, another Middle Eastern country, generally shares the crime patterns of its neighbors and also the explanations for its preservation of a low and stable crime rate despite a tense and unstable domestic situation. Although the national crime rate has risen recently, the strong religious and familial foundation of the society appears to have overcome the influence of such normally criminogenic factors as a high level of internal violence (war raids and terrorist attacks), the presence of large numbers of children of migrants, and an extremely heterogeneous urbanizing population.[41] Research conducted there, however, corroborates the observations of criminologists in other societies concerning the relationship between migration and crime. The highest rates of delinquency are associated with the children of immigrants or the first generation to be born in the new country. The greater the differences between the immigrants and the predominant resident population, the greater the recorded rates of criminality.[42]

The Caribbean nations, in contrast, have not avoided the negative effects on their crime rates of the contrast between affluence and poverty. The Caribbean situation is the reverse of the Middle Eastern one because domestic poverty is confronted by the affluence of tourists who provide a ready target for offenders while simultaneously promoting expectations of an improved material existence. Thus, high rates of theft coexist with the traditionally high rates of rural violence in these small Caribbean countries.[43] The proclivity of this region for criminal behavior is compounded by its geographical location between the drug-producing countries of South and Central America and the readily accessible drug markets of the United States. The financial temptation provided by this lucrative illegal traffic results in particularly high rates of drug-related crimes in this region.

The crime rates recorded in Asia, Latin America, and non-Moslem Africa lie between the rates of the Caribbean and the Middle East, but the extent of difference is hard to calculate because of the inaccuracy of recorded crime rates. In all of these societies similar factors—unbalanced economic growth, economic stratification, breakdown of traditional society and migration to the city—are seen as particularly conducive to the generally observed rise in criminal behavior.[44]

Regional differences exist not only in total rates of crime commission but also in the frequency of individual offenses. These regional differences in relative frequency of offenses are explained by cultural, historical, and geographical factors. For example the geographical location of the Caribbean nations accounts for their leading the developing countries in the frequency of drug-related and property crimes. However, no one region of the world manifests distinctively high crime rates for all categories of violent criminality. "Latin

America displays the highest rates of intentional homicide closely followed by the Caribbean."[45] nations which also led the rest of the world in their recorded rates for assault. Asia, Latin America, and the Caribbean shared equally high rates of robbery. Generalizations about the distinct characteristics of African criminality were difficult to make because of the absence of statistics from many countries but this region, according the general reports of authorities, suffers particularly from such forms of financial corruption as embezzlement, fraud, smuggling, and illegal currency transactions.[46]

Though it is possible to examine the crime patterns of developing countries collectively, the regional differences previously noted suggest that the process of development does not have the homogenizing effect on international crime patterns that a cursory examination might suggest. The combined impact of urbanization, societal transformation, and great economic contrasts between poor and rich city dwellers all appear to be conducive in most societies to increased crime rates. However, the extent of growth and the crimes most affected by this societal transition vary among countries and geographical regions. The factors that account for these variations are historical and cultural traditions, the extent to which the government is controlling the process of development, and the location of the country relative to other high crime regions.

THE CRIMINAL POPULATION

Although the majority of offenders in nearly all countries are adult males,[47] this characterization is particularly true in developing countries, where juveniles and women have only recently assumed a more important role in crime commission. As adults and the dominant members of society, men have had the greatest opportunity to perpetrate offenses. Now that women and juveniles share a greater opportunity for the commission of crime, opportunity alone does not account for the rapid increase in the criminality of these two groups of offenders.

The following discussion of juvenile delinquents shows that the phenomenon has regional similarities and some universal characteristics, but historical and cultural differences still result in different patterns and motivations for criminal behavior.

Juvenile delinquency has become a problem in developing countries only since the advent of urbanization and industrialization. Internationally, these traditional societies previously had very few cases of male delinquency[48] and an even lesser problem among teenage girls. Females in most developing countries are now responsible for less than 10 percent of the delinquent acts. The youth contribution to total national criminality is steadily increasing, and juveniles commit as much as one-third of the total crime in some developing countries.[49] Juvenile crime is almost exclusively a problem of urban areas. Modernization has merely accentuated the problem of crime in cities, but it has not precipitated a rise in crime in rural areas.[50]

The criminality of juveniles is generally within a narrow range of activities and frequently not of a serious nature. Juvenile criminality is confined primarily to theft although in some nations delinquents are committing robbery, rape, and other violent offenses with increased frequency.[51] Juveniles are also represented significantly in acts of public disorder.

The motivation for thefts by many of the poorest delinquents is acute need.[52] As many of the developing countries do not have or do not enforce child labor laws, the conditions of youths, especially in urban areas, is often one of acute deprivation and need. Children living under these conditions are denied the leisure that characterizes childhood in other societies, and their exploitation pushes them to commit acts that help alleviate their difficult situation.[53] Increasingly, however, delinquents in many developing countries are perpetrating property crimes that do not appear to be motivated by need but are inspired instead by the desire for luxury goods.[54] Like recent adult migrants to urban areas, juveniles are impressed by the quantity and variety of goods that surround them and seek to acquire tangible goods that denote status within the community.

Gangs of youthful offenders are not as widespread in developing nations as in the developed countries. Although researchers in Mexico have commented on the development of gang subcultures in the principal cities, studies in other societies indicate that the majority of delinquents act alone or with a limited number of individuals. Drug usage among juvenile offenders appears to be concentrated primarily in those countries where delinquent behavior is committed collectively.[55]

The reason that urban crime has increased so precipitously is that the social processes accompanying industrial development have resulted in conditions conducive to increased criminality. Family stability, close parent-child relationships, and extensive supervision of youthful members of a family are conditions usually associated with low rates of criminality. After the onset of economic development, these conditions cease to exist for large numbers of young people. With the initiation of the process of modernization, large numbers of rural inhabitants migrate to urban areas where a stable life-style, comparable to that existing in the rural environment, is not available. Research on the social background of delinquents in diverse developing nations reveals that among delinquents and their families the negative effects of recent urbanization are felt acutely. Delinquents generally have a low educational level, and in many societies they are dropouts from primary school.[56] Delinquents are disproportionately the offspring of recent urban migrants, and their home lives reflect the instability of their parents' existence. Broken homes and alcoholic and unemployed parents of low social and educational status characterize the biographies of numerous delinquents. Juvenile delinquency is only one of the problems associated with these families.[57]

Juvenile delinquency is not a homogeneous entity in most developing countries as youthful offenders are drawn in many societies from both middle-class and lower-class homes. The crime patterns and motivations of these two groups differ significantly. Lower-class delinquency is generally of much longer standing and may have an established place in the community. An example of this is the behavior pattern of delinquents in Taiwan.[58] A brief examination of research from three different continents will highlight some of the significant variations in delinquent behavior.

In Taiwan, two forms of delinquency exist simultaneously. The *Liu-mang* is the long-established term for lawbreaker, and members of this group are not distinguishable from the poor urban Chinese population. The boys, acting without female accessories, are ready to engage in professional criminality. Though closely associated with temple life, they are active in prostitution, gambling, and other categories of victimless crime and are a source of financial support to their families. The structure and the function of the group is very similar to those of groups which operated in prewar Japan and existed until recently in Thailand. At the same time that the *Liu-mang* are engaged in crime as a full-time profession, *tai-paus*, delinquents drawn from the middle and upper-middle classes, are often still enrolled in school. Participation is not limited to members of·one sex, and members attract attention through their dress and manner. Their criminal activities do not serve an established need in the community, and their illegal behavior resembles that of their counterparts in more affluent societies.[59]

Though many developing countries do not have such strictly delineated boundaries between their different classes of delinquents, social differences do exist among groups of delinquents. The principal difference that exists between the lower-class delinquency of the Far Eastern countries and that of many other developing countries is that delinquents in many other developing societies do not perform a function desired by the community in which they reside.

Criminological theories based solely on the experiences of more industrialized societies should not be applied automatically to developing countries. Lois B. DeFleur discovered all too quickly in her study of delinquency in Cordoba, Argentina, that the American theories of juvenile misconduct were not applicable in this new environment. Contrary to expectations, the offenders she observed did not commit their crimes close to their place of residence but ventured far from homes to the city center to steal where wealth was most concentrated. Their criminality was characterized by little violence as the motivation for their illegal behavior was primarily need.[60] The delinquents, themselves migrants or the children of recent immigrants from the countryside, though influenced by the new abundance of material possessions available to them in the city, are concerned primarily with satisfying their immediate and real physical needs. Consequently, the juveniles of Cordoba and their counterparts in many other developing countries steal only what they need and will go to great efforts to secure it.

In most African countries, juvenile delinquency is primarily a recent phenomenon that coincides with the process of urbanization. Though a recent rural background is common to most of the juvenile offenders, it is their life in cities that propels them into criminality. Many African delinquents are not the originators of their offense but commit their crimes under the guidance of older criminals. The influence of peers is as important as that of adults and, consequently, delinquents in Asia, Africa, and Latin America participate in crime with other youthful offenders.[61]

The influence of peers has been identified as a significant factor in the delinquency of many youths in developing nations. The types of recreational outlets, the selection of friends, and the influence of adults were found in many studies to be significant in determining whether a youth would turn to criminal behavior.[62] The influence of adults on the criminal careers of juveniles is more significant in many developing countries than it is in more industrialized societies where juvenile gangs and adult offenders associate little with each other. Adult influence over juvenile offenders was observed in nineteenth-century England, and the same patterns of behavior may exist in developing countries for similar reasons. The traditional structure of rural life characterized by close intergenerational relationships and the criminal apprenticeship of the city result in a closer coordination of youth and adult criminal activities.

The previous analysis of juvenile delinquency does not explain the high rate of joyriding among youthful offenders. The juveniles who commit such offenses are not motivated by material need but by the presence of material goods that carry status as a result of their high cost and limited availability. This crime is more reminiscent of that of the more affluent youths of developed societies where the feeling of relative deprivation rather than actual need provides an important incentive for juvenile criminality.

Although the structure, pervasiveness, traditions of, and severity of juvenile delinquency differ among developing countries, there seem to be certain characteristics that distinguish this group of offenders. Delinquent behavior appears to be collective and highly influenced by need and by adults. Offenders are generally poor and recent migrants to urban areas.[63] Traditional forms of youthful criminality prevail in certain parts of the Far East whereas in many other societies in Africa and the Middle East, the phenomenon of large-scale juvenile delinquency is tied exclusively to the urbanization process accompanying industrialization. Though material need is more important than the desire for luxury, the latter motivation has become increasingly important among more affluent groups of youthful offenders.

The increase in juvenile delinquency accompanying the modernization process has been startling to many of the nations affected, but even more surprising has been the increase in crimes perpetrated by female offenders. In traditional societies women rarely committed crimes as their lives were restricted almost entirely to home and family. Even for such frequently domestic crimes as homicide, women had very low commission rates as shown by a detailed study of suicide and homicide among many African tribes 20 years ago. Women were more frequently victims of the crime than perpetrators but in most cases of homicide women were neither assailants nor victims.[64]

Even though there has been an unprecedented rise in rates of female criminality in developing countries, women do not as yet commit a significant share of all offenses. Because women previously committed crimes so rarely, this growth in female criminality is more significant for the behavioral change it heralds than for the social danger it provides to the community. In developing countries, adult males are 12 times more frequently perpetrators of crime than women while the comparable difference for juveniles is a factor of 8.[65] In some particularly traditional countries like the Middle Eastern nations, women commit an even smaller percentage of the crime, but in some countries where women are more integrated into society, their level of participation is much higher. Though the gap is narrowing between the commission rates of the sexes especially among youthful offenders, it will be a long time before scholars can even suggest a convergence between male and female patterns of criminal behavior.

At present female rates in developing countries are growing on an average 30 percent faster than the comparable figure for men but this increase is not evenly distributed internationally. Brazil and India reported especially dramatic increases, but these countries were far from unique in reporting this transition. The noted increase appears to be concentrated primarily in traditional female offenses such as prostitution, abortion, and petty theft rather than in the more traditionally male crimes of violence.[66]

Female criminality is almost unknown in the countryside and women confine their illegal activities almost exclusively to the urban environment.[67] The location of female criminality is explained by the social and economic position of women. In rural areas, women have a very circumscribed role in society and are restricted almost exclusively to the family sphere. In more urbanized communities women have a more active societal role, thus providing them with more opportunities to commit crime and frequently a greater need to support themselves.

Recidivists are not a firmly established part of the criminal community in developing countries. Because of the problems of record keeping in developing countries, little is known about the extent of recidivism in these nations. Studies have examined the extent of repeated criminality in limited regions and have discovered significant fluctuations among geographical regions.[68] Little, however, is known about the community or correctional factors associated with recidivism.

The relative rarity of the criminal underworld and of professional criminality accounts for a lesser proportion of recidivists in developing countries than in developed countries. Most of criminality is not confined to a select group of professional criminals who derive their livelihood almost exclusively from crime but appears to be a much more broadly based phenomenon with more individuals involved in less serious forms of criminal behavior.[69] The reasons for this difference is that crime is not so deeply rooted in these societies and there has not been a large older generation of criminals to train youthful offenders in professional techniques.

GEOGRAPHY OF CRIME

Urban and rural areas in developing nations have both different patterns and levels of criminality. While little change has occurred in the types of crime found in rural areas, a dramatic transformation has occurred in the urban environment. Rural areas adhere to their traditionally low rates of crime commission and contribute only a small share of each nation's total crime rate. The process of development has caused the crime-prone age groups to exit en masse from the countryside, reducing the potential for criminality in an area already highly immune to criminality and magnifying the problem in the recipient urban areas already highly susceptible to the problems of criminal behavior.

The transformation of the urban environment can be attributed to the massive migration of the rural population to cities. This migration is so extensive that "in some African cities more than 80% of the population are under the age of 40."[70] The figures are equally dramatic for some Latin American countries[71] and less so but still significant for developing countries in other parts of the world. The largest cities appear to suffer disproportionately from the criminological consequences of modernization as the already colossal problems of urbanization are compounded by the sheer mass of humanity assembled.

Uncontrolled urban growth has been a direct consequence of the conditions of rural life and the process of urbanization. Agricultural areas are incapable of supporting the ever increasing number of rural inhabitants, and the transition from labor intensive to highly mechanized agriculture has made much of the rural population superfluous. Migration from rural areas has become increasingly necessary as developing societies convert to cash economies making it obligatory that some family members obtain paying jobs in urban area.

Urban areas that have grown rapidly as a result of the industrial revolution serve as magnets for the underemployed rural population. Most of the developing countries do not control population mobility, and few coordinated efforts are made to decelerate the process of urbanization or to divert individuals to areas that might benefit from an increase in manpower.[72] Therefore unprepared cities are receiving masses of youthful immigrants without preparing adequately for the employment, medical, and residential needs of the new urban work force. This seemingly unstoppable movement of masses of individuals to ill-prepared urban areas has disrupted all aspects of urban existence.

The migration presently observed in developing countries has consequences similar to European migrations of the past century. However, it differs in certain fundamental aspects. First, urbanization developed more slowly in the nineteenth century in Europe than it is developing now in Africa, Latin Ameria, and certain other developing areas.[73] Second, in the nineteenth century the move to the city was made by individuals from communities adjoining the city or from towns not far removed from urban centers. Only as the process of urbanization accelerated did migrants arrive from more far-reaching towns and communities. In Africa, particularly, and to a lesser extent in other developing nations today, the transition from village to city has been sudden as the migrants have made the immediate jump from remote communities to far distant cities. In Columbia and Mexico, a medium-sized community is usually an intermediate step between the countryside and the city.[74] In both continents the transition from one environment to another is not easily made.

The city is attractive to the most crime-prone age group of youthful males who, because of their lack of responsibilities, possess increased personal mobility. The very factors that contribute to the ready mobility of the youthful male population are the same conditions that make them susceptible to the disorienting and criminological consequences of the developmental process. These young males, relieved of traditional family responsibilities and removed from the usual constraints of close family life, are more prone to misconduct than individuals more established in the community.

Many of the migrants, poorly educated and ill prepared for the demands of the more developed area, are incapable of finding employment, and must resort to illicit means to support themselves. Others who find employment for the first time in their lives are unaccustomed to the cash they earn and turn to such victimless crimes as gambling and prostitution to fill the void created by the absence of their traditional ways of life.[75] Thus, the uncertainties and novelty of the urban environment appear to have a potentially criminogenic effect on both the employed and the unemployed.

The conditions under which these recent urban migrants live are hardly amenable to the maintenance of community order. A sharp difference exists between the expectations of the migrants and the conditions that await them. Urban life is attractive to migrants because of the reputed access to the conveniences made possible by electricity, transporation, education, medical care, and the general excitement associated with the city.[76] Unfortunately, these advantages are not available to many of the recent arrivals. Migrants are crowded into the most substandard of housing sometimes far removed from the basic amenities. In South America these squatter communities are situated far from the city center, removed from public transport while the wealthy, unlike many of their counterparts in more developed societies, reside in the city center. These slum communities and shantytowns are not confined to Latin America but exist as well in many countries in Africa and the Far East.

The criminogenic influence of the slums, already a subject of study by nineteenth-century social scientists, has been further examined by contemporary researchers of developing countries. The majority of crimes are committed by slum dwellers, and though much of it is perpetrated against neighbors, very often offenders reach outside their immediate community and commit crimes against the more affluent members of the community.[77] For this reason there appears to be no solitary zone of criminality in urban areas.

The social disorganization of the poor urban community described by Shaw and McKay in the United States during the 1930s[78] also appears to be characteristic of the social and family life of slum dwellers in developing countries. The cohesive family structure and the association patterns based on kinship characteristic of rural society disappear in the urban slum as individuals are separated from their extended family and encounter the tribulations of city life. The extended family cedes its central position to the nuclear family. Marriage bonds are loosened, and individual coupling rather than family alliances becomes the principal objective of marriage.

Slum culture is similar in both developed and developing countries and its effects are comparable in both types of societies. A younger generation is raised in conditions in many ways physically worse than the communities they left because recreational opportunities are limited and care from extended families is no longer available. The recently urbanized youthful population spends much time on the streets, a carry-over from the rural society as well as a natural reaction to the limitations of their home environment. The youths, spending their lives together away from parental influence, often develop a subculture that fosters and legitimizes their illegal behavior. The youths who emigrate to the cities without their families are even more strongly influenced by the criminal subculture that exists in many slum communities.[79]

Some slum communities appear to be more successful in warding off criminality than others. A study a decade ago of crime in Kampala, Uganda, revealed that certain slum areas had rates of property crime eight times higher than others with similar physical conditions and economic status. The different social structure of the two communities explains the divergent crime rates. The lower crime rates are found in the community that has more visiting, less mobility, and greater participation in local community organizations, including religious groups. More members of the low crime community shared negative attitudes towards fighting, prostitution, and bootlegging, but both communities concurred in their condemnation of stealing. The high crime area had less stable family relations and more tribal diversity.[80]

It appears from this research that Durkheim's conclusion, based on observations of nineteenth-century Europe, that close familial ties prevent criminality is also applicable to developing countries presently undergoing a similar process of urbanization. Possession of common values, continuity of societal traditions, and strong familial relations can help alleviate some of the criminological consequences associated with the traumatic transition from rural to city life.

Regardless of the level of crime commission found in a particular slum community, the city is generally characterized by very different and more diversified forms of criminal behavior from those found in rural areas. The crimes that are most common in the urban environment are also those that are the most frequent in developing countries because the vast majority of crimes committed in these societies are perpetrated in the city. All forms of theft and property crime are common in cities since items often are not well guarded and individuals carry with them, rather than safeguard, objects of value. The severity of property crimes ranges from pilfering from vendors in market places to armed robbery. In between these two offenses lie picking pockets, stealing from stores and individuals, and vandalism. Swindling is common in developing countries because of the lack of sophistication of many urban inhabitants. Victims are cheated into believing the swindler capable of growing money through simulated acts of magic that resemble the charms of tribal figures.[81]

White-collar crime is almost unique to the urban environment because offices and business are centralized in cities. The low wages paid to members of the bureaucracy and the contrast between the financial position of owners and employees of businesses are seen as conducive to both large-scale and small-scale embezzlement. More elaborate forms of corruption such as bribery, graft, and kickbacks are also pervasive in urban areas in almost all developing countries.[82]

Violence has been an increasingly urban phenomenon as well as the predominant form of rural criminality. Violence is not confined to armed robbery; some scholars maintain that homicides and assaults occur with increasing frequency in cities. There are some who speculate that they have already observed a downturn in urban violence in developing countries[83] which would support the observation made of nineteenth-century criminaltity, that violent behavior declines with the stabilization of city life. This trend has, however, not yet been sustained.

The victimless crimes of prostitution, gambling, and abortion are known almost solely in cities. This is true because the first two types of criminal behavior rely heavily on ready supplies of cash which are available almost exclusively to city dwellers. The tight controls of village life make prostitution rare and abortions unnecessary as children conceived are desired and absorbed by the families into which they are born.

There are almost no forms of criminality unique to the rural environment; crime in rural areas is merely less diversified and less pervasive than in urban areas. Cattle theft is a problem in some developing countries, and illegal drugs are produced by farmers in Latin America and Asia. Apart from these crimes and petty theft, most rural offenses belong to the category of violent behavior.

The social and economic factors that account for differences between urban and rural criminality will ensure the continuity of this divergent behavior. As the cities are more affected by modernization than are rural communities, a significant difference will persist between the crime patterns of the two environments.

FUTURE PATTERNS OF CRIMINALITY

The previous discussion of crime in developing countries suggests certain crime trends for the future. Crime rates of developing countries, though rising rapidly, are still far behind the overall rates recorded in developed countries. It is natural to expect that this increase in criminality will be sustained and may even accelerate as the increasingly youthful population of developing countries reaches the most crime-prone age period. This predicted rise in juvenile delinquency will also be accompanied by a similar rise in female rates of crime commission. As women leave the domestic sphere and have more opportunities to commit crime undeterred by family restraints, it follows that their commission rate will increase.

Changes will be observed not only in rates of crime commission but in the proportional contribution of each offense to total criminality. As property offenses and drug-related crimes are rising at a faster rate than all other categories of illegal behavior, it is only natural that property crimes will shortly become the most frequent type of criminal behavior in these nations of the world. Crimes against the person, which presently occur with the same frequency as property offenses, will then assume second place because the rate of increase of these offenses has decelerated with increasing development. Drug-related crimes, presently increasing at an unprecedented rate, will assume an increasingly large share of total criminality in developing countries, though the frequency of these crimes will still be significantly less than that of the two major categories of criminal behavior.

Developing countries are thus duplicating the nineteenth-century trends in criminal behavior which saw, with increasing industrialization, violence cede its former preeminence to the less threatening but more pervasive crimes against property. The growth of international drug traffic and other drug-related crimes is a development unique to the twentieth century and was not foretold by events in the past century.

The present geographical distribution of criminality will continue and the differences may be even further intensified by the departure of young males from the countryside. Rural criminality will be even more closely identified with crimes of violence though the frequency of these crimes will decline because of the exodus of the most crime-prone age group. The urban environment will continue to be the source of most criminality recorded in developing countries, and the largest cities will be susceptible to the highest rates of criminality. The full range of property, violent, drug, and political offenses will be present in the urban environment as well as the corruption presently endemic in developing countries.

The recent trends in criminal behavior in developing countries have been alarming but the prognosis for the future is hardly more promising. Until these developing societies adjust to the major transition presently transpiring in their countries and establish means to equalize the distribution of wealth and power, crime will remain both a symptom of societal transition and of the inequalities of modern society.

CRIME PREVENTION AND CONTROL

A detailed discussion of the judicial and legislative response to the crime problem is outside the scope of this book, but at least a cursory acknowledgment must be made of the fact that many developing countries are not passively observing the dramatic increase in criminality. Many of them are trying to alleviate some of the environmental conditions conducive to criminality and to establish a justice system that reforms individuals who have embarked on criminal careers.

Few societies have, however, established sufficient controls over the population to prevent the disruptive immigration process or to channel the immigrants into communities that are more prepared to receive them. Though this approach, tried in many socialist societies and discussed later in this book, denies much personal freedom, it is successful in averting some of the worst consequences of the urbanization process. Because many of the developing countries are societies not known for their respect for personal freedom, their absence of controls in this area is even more surprising.

The measures used to control rising criminality appear to be the approaches established by European countries in the twentieth century. This is especially true of those societies that were only recently under colonial rule. They appear to be repeating many of the mistakes made in the past century and a half by those societies that have experienced the ever growing problem of criminality. Thus, the response of many of the developing nations to their increasing crime problem has been to expand the police, impose longer sentences, and establish juvenile and adult penal institutions.[84] These costly measures for the administration of justice have done little to avert the rise in criminality.

The ineffectiveness of the criminal justice system in controlling the problem of crime has been pointed out by Radzinowicz[85] and Gurr[86] in their lengthy studies of historical patterns of crime and criminal justice. Though their observations were made in reference to developed countries a century ago, their analyses appear to be valid today. As the primary causes of criminality appear to be rooted both on the societal and the person level in the social structure and the disruptions of societal transformation, there is little that can be done by governments or individuals to control the problem of crime. This unfortunate conclusion provides further confirmation for Durkheim's statement that crime is a normal, natural, and consequently an uncontrollable phenomenon in society.[87] At the same time it provides further evidence for Tarde's and Quetelet's statement that changes in criminal behavior occur only with changes in social structure[88] and the transformations in crime patterns reflect fundamental societal change.

CONCLUSION

The enduring validity of these French sociologists' analysis, based on their observations of the impact of nineteenth-century development on crime, suggests that the effects of contemporary development are not inherently different from those of the past century. Though regional differences in patterns of criminality exist today as did national variations in Europe in the past century, overall contemporary trends suggest a repetition of historical patterns.

The primary cause of the presently observed increase in criminality appears to be the same as that of a century ago: the transformation brought by economic development. As a result of rapid urbanization, thousands of migrants have moved from the countryside into the rapidly expanding urban centers. These cities are not physically equipped to deal with an ever increasing number of inhabitants and are incapable of assimilating this manpower into the urban work force. Consequently, slums have arisen at both periods of history, and these urban regions have been the primary source of criminal behavior. Youths, raised under these conditions, have increasingly turned to criminal behavior both as a means of support and as an outlet for personal tensions.

These similarities that have been observed between the impact of nineteenth- and twentieth-century development on crime do not present the entire picture. Modern mobility and improved communications have brought changes to countries presently undergoing development that make the experiences of these societies not entirely comparable. The advent of the automobile, the airplane, and modern commerce not only have resulted in new categories of criminality but also have made offenders more mobile. The relative ease with which criminals can travel has resulted in international drug crimes and political offenses. It facilitates crime commission outside the residential region of the offender. Financial and political corruption assume a much larger role in overall crime commission in contemporary societies than in those of the past. Certain countries, particularly in the Middle East, even though they are developing rapidly, have been able to avert some of the severe disruptions caused by development.

Though very strong similarities exist between the impact of development on crime in the twentieth and nineteenth centuries, the experiences are not entirely comparable. The primary reason for this difference has been increasing technological development that has affected both developing and developed countries simultaneously.

4
Crime in Developed Countries

The developed countries will be defined as the countries of Western Europe, Canada, the United States, Japan, Australia, and New Zealand. While certain countries of Eastern Europe might be grouped in this category as a result of their histories, their present social, political, and economic situation differentiate them from the developed countries. They will, therefore, be discussed in the next chapter, devoted to crime in socialist countries.

The developed countries are generally grouped together for the purposes of social, economic, and political analysis, but does it make sense to group them together for the purpose of criminological analysis? The following discussion will address this question. Despite their many historical, ethnic, religious, and cultural differences, the developed countries are generally grouped for criminological analysis, and findings indicate that their common transition to modernization causes them to have similar crime patterns, although different rates of criminality. In establishing points of comparison among developed countries, the effect of development on crime should not be exaggerated, and consideration should be given to the political, cultural, and social characteristics that explain, for example, the very different crime rates of Japan and the United States.

The countries that are presently characterized as developed have progressed through a very definite period of modernization, prior to which they were primarily rural with economies based on agriculture. Though significant differences existed among them before the industrial revolution, these countries were generally characterized by a hierarchical system of government in which individual citizens had little chance of participation. Social classes were sharply differentiated, and the rural and urban populations lived very different lives.[1]

Significant exceptions exist to these generalizations. The United States, for example, had developed a representative system of government even before the advent of the industrial revolution. Yet, despite such national peculiarities, it is possible to state that prior to this period of modernization, the characteristics of a primarily rural society predominated.

With the arrival of the industrial revolution, at different time periods, depending on the individual country discussed, significant changes were noted in the political, social, and economic structure of these countries. The changes that these societies underwent have been fully discussed in chapter 2 on crime and development in historical perspective, but it is worth noting again the main effects of this societal evolutionary process.

As a result of the process of modernization, these countries changed from highly rural to primarily urban societies whose economies were based on industrial rather than agricultural production. The lives of individuals no longer centered on the extended family but were based instead on the more impersonal ties developed in towns and cities.[2] Democratic or republican systems of government were established in most of the societies of this group. These significant changes in the social, economic, and political structure were, in turn, reflected in the crime patterns of the individual nations.

PATTERNS OF CRIMINAL BEHAVIOR

Many of the same problems encountered in comparing the crime patterns of developing countries apply to comparative criminal analysis of developed countries. And although international crime statistics did not exist before the establishment of the United Nations and the International Police Organization (Interpol), compilation of statistics during the last 25 years has made analysis and comparison of contemporary international crime feasible.[3] Of course, broad variational allowances for age and offense must be taken into account.

International crime statistics reveal that criminality has increased in the United States, Europe, and the British Commonwealth in the period since World War II. While these countries were relatively successful in controlling their crime problem in the latter part of the past century and the beginning years of this one, the institutions that helped control the rising tide of criminality in the past have not been as successful in the present period. Although the increasing affluence of modern society can explain the growth of property crime, it does not explain the increased frequency of violent criminality.[4] Homicide rates tend to increase in participatory nations during and after wars, and though this could explain some of the increase in this form of criminality in the postwar years,[5] it is not a sufficient explanation for a trend that has continued for a decade after the war when these nations should have ceased to experience the consequences of war. It has been suggested that the growth in both types of criminal behavior is explained by a loss of general morality and a sense of alienation and selfishness displayed by youths,[6] whose contribution to the increase in crime has been particularly significant.

But why consider changing mores as a possible cause for increases in criminality when social and economic forces can be shown to explain these increases? Demographic and labor market trends as well as the maturation of the urbanization process appear to be of significant influence in explaining presently observed fluctuations in criminal behavior. The postwar baby boom appears to account for much of the growth of juvenile crime internationally,[7] and economic growth and the stabilization of the process of urban expansion appear to work in opposition to the population trends.

By comparing the growth rates of criminality in developed and developing nations, the present state of crime in western countries appears less ominous. Developed countries are still experiencing growing crime rates, but the rate of increase has slowed down considerably since the initial stages of the developmental process. Developed countries are currently experiencing an annual growth rate in crime of 1 percent[8] which is two-fifths the present rate of increase of developing countries. This is a result of the higher initial rates of criminality, the stabilization of the process of urbanization, and the lower birthrates which result in fewer potential offenders in the crime-prone years.

The crime patterns of the developed countries at the present time are a natural outgrowth of the process of social and economic development that occurred in the nineteenth century. Both in the aggregate and by individual offense, crimes against property far exceed those committed against the person. Property crimes comprise 82 percent of all offenses in developed countries, followed in frequency by crimes against the person and drug-related crimes.[9] Political crimes, though disruptive of the social order, comprise a negligible percentage of total crime commission in these nations.[10]

Significant variations exist in the crime rates for individual property offenses and crimes against the person. Internationally, homicide and kidnapping occur more than assault, though the most serious category of homicide has been rising at a rate of 35 percent per year.[11] Theft has consistently been the most common form of property crime but it has increased by approximately 35 percent during the 1970s as compared to the dramatic 322 percent recorded simultaneously for the more violent crime of robbery.[12] Drug-related offenses which are increasing more rapidly among developed countries are a small but growing share of total crime.[13]

The chapter on the relationship between development and crime asserted that during the period of nineteenth-century industrialization, the ratio of violence to theft changed and the latter offense became predominant. The relationship appears to remain valid even after the transition to development has been made. A recent study of Interpol crime statistics reveals that the relationship between murder and larceny rates still appears to be one of the best indicators of development.[14] These international statistics show that almost all the societies with high rates of larceny and low rates of murder were developed countries. In Europe, the only exceptions were Ireland and Italy, where strong family ties, the age of the populations, and continuing emigration cause both countries to score low in murder and larceny.

These results lead to the conclusion that there is a close correlation between a number of conventional indicators of "industrialization and development such as nativity and mortality rates, number of telephones relative to population, number of persons employed in industry, degree of urbanization, literacy rate, newspaper circulation . . . and the size of per capita gross national product" and the recorded crime rate.[15] The relationship between violence and property crimes established 150 years ago appears valid today, suggesting more continuity in international crime patterns than is usually presumed.

The internationally known property and violent crimes are the predominant offenses in developed countries, but several other categories of criminal behavior are central to an understanding of the overall crime picture of these nations. These crimes are related to the advent of the modern age, the structure of contemporary society, business, and present-day social concerns. The crimes that fall into this category are computer crimes, automobile, and airline offenses, organized crime, white-collar crime, and environmental crimes.

The technology of the modern age has created possibilities for new offenses. These offenses that involve harm either to the person, property, or the community order have become widespread only in recent decades. Computer crime, for example, exists on a significant scale only in developed countries that have large numbers of sophisticated computers and highly trained personnel capable of perpetrating offenses on these complex machines.[16] The probability of vehicular offenses and crimes employing aircraft is greater in developed countries because of the widespread use of these forms of transportation.

Organized crime appears to be a phenomenon present almost exclusively in developed countries. Nearly half of the developed countries report having this type of criminal behavior, and almost a third of these economically advanced societies contend that they face a serious problem in this area.[17] Organized crime, in many respects, is simply a modernized form of the traditional justice system based on the family blood feud that prevailed prior to industrialization. Before the destruction of the extended family in the contemporary period (except in those European countries having a predominantly Anglo-Saxon heritage, where this phenomenon does not apply), the property and personal welfare of individuals were the responsibility of family members. Intentional violence, before the advent of development, was used almost solely as a form of protection, and only during its long evolution has this family-based activity turned into present-day organized crime based on economic interests. "Although the *mafiosa* began as a vendetta system over a century ago, it was transformed into a social form of political and economic control not dissimilar to organized crime in the United States."[18]

The development of organized crime has not only become feasible in the contemporary period but its growth appears to be a logical response to the contemporary conditions of modern societies. The spread of organized crime through much of the developed world has become possible only as a result of modern mass communications and personal mobility. Organized crime is a natural response to the absence of legitimate opportunities for advancement by societal members lacking required technical and educational skills demanded by a highly complex economy. For this reason, the network of organized crime is often run and staffed by individuals who are not native to the society in which they reside. In the United States, different immigrant groups have successively assumed control over the structure of organized crime,[19] a pattern that has been repeated in other societies.

Although (as will be discussed later) the immigrant population usually has a lower rate of criminality than the native population, organized crime is the one category of criminal behavior in which immigrants assume a significant role. The immigrant is often denied the possibilities for advancement in the highly bureaucratized contemporary society and, therefore, the less scrupulous among them sometimes resort to organized crime because it allows the offender to substitute the network of organized crime for the conventional business and social structure from which they are excluded.

The term white-collar crime was coined by the dean of American criminologists, Edwin Sutherland, who defined it as "a violation of criminal law by a person of the upper socio-economic class in the course of his occupational activities"[20] and included such offenses as price-fixing, fraud, embezzlement, tax evasion, violation of positions of trust, bribery, misrepresentation in advertising and salesmanship, and manipulation of the stock exchange.[21] Though the concept was conceived in the context of American society, it is a pervasive phenomenon common to all developed societies whose economies are based on cash and credit rather than the barter and exchange of preindustrial societies. The existence of large, complex, and bureaucratized business operations allows individuals to perpetrate these crimes and mask their activities. The impersonality of contemporary business makes these crimes difficult to detect, thereby encouraging their proliferation. All indicators suggest that the pervasiveness of white-collar crime in developed countries provides a major threat to the social order and the prosperity of the community.

Despite the social costs of these crimes, white-collar crimes are among the most underreported of all categories of criminal behavior in developed capitalist societies. Because the perpetrators of these crimes are typically established members of the business community who command respect from their fellow citizens, prosecutions for these crimes are infrequent and when they do occur, sentences imposed are generally lenient. In contrast, developed communist societies prosecute frequently and punish harshly those convicted of fraud and embezzlement because the victims of their criminal acts are not large corporations but socialist enterprises owned by the State.

Environmental crimes are primarily a problem in developed countries. Although 44 percent of the developed countries recognized these offenses as problems "only very few countries reported stringent ecological laws."[22] A study of perceptions of criminal behavior demonstrates that members of both industrialized and developing countries view pollution as both undesirable and criminal.[23] The United States, among the surveyed countries, showed the greatest concern with this form of illegal behavior and the most intense desire to punish offenders[24] A preoccupation with environmental crimes is naturally preeminent in developed countries because societies that are only now in the process of industrialization cannot afford to be greatly concerned with the social and environmental consequences of their current development.

It is these previously discussed offenses that differentiate the character of criminality in developed and developing societies. Though developing societies are not immune to these particular forms of criminal behavior, they are not as susceptible to the problems that result from the social and economic structure of modern societies.

Crime appears to be a major consequence of affluence. As society's material wealth increases so does the rate of crime, particularly that against property. This suggests that the motivation for crime in developed countries is not necessarily need but rather a consequence of the feelings of relative deprivation experienced more frequently by urban dwellers who are continuously exposed to the greater material possession of others. It is the process of development that results in more urbanization and, consequently, greater financial temptations.

Though the linkage between higher crime rates and economic development appears to be quite firmly established, there are certain important exceptions to this generalization. They must be examined to provide insights into the forces that counteract what otherwise seems to be the irrevocable link between crime and industrial development. The two consistent and major exceptions to the increasing crime rates of affluent developed countries are Japan and Switzerland. These two societies have both been studied to determine the national, political, social, and cultural characteristics that result in their distinctive crime rates.

Japan has industrialized and urbanized at a faster rate than many of the other developed countries included in this analysis; but despite the rapidity of this transformation, the nation has been spared major criminological consequences. The control of criminality has affected all major categories of property crime (theft, fraud, embezzlement, dealing in stolen property) as well as the violent crimes of homicide, robbery, and rape.[25] Between 1960 and 1975 crime rates for homicide, rape, robbery, and theft declined in Japan, while, except for rape (which remained constant in West Germany) the commission rates of the offenses have grown significantly in West Germany, England, and the United States.[26]

The only category of criminal behavior in which Japan has experienced growth is traffic offenses. This increase has occurred despite significant attempts by the authorities legislatively and judicially to control this type of illegal behavior. Nevertheless, the growth has not recently been disproportionate to the proliferation of automobiles and their increased use by inexperienced drivers.[27]

There are several explanations given for the dramatically different Japanese crime patterns. The first of these explains Japan's declining crime rates not in terms of the unique characteristics of Japanese society but in terms of the process of economic growth that the country has experienced in the postwar years. During the period of rapid economic expansion the United States and Great Britain underwent during the nineteenth century, criminality declined as the labor market grew.[28] According to this theory, the crime rates of Japan and West Germany in the postwar period (West Germany's overall crime rate increased insignificantly between 1960 and 1970) have been the beneficiaries of their rapidly expanded economies. The economic growth and prosperity of these societies in the postwar period provided a good and improved standard of living for most of the population and gave citizens legitimate opportunities of advancement, thereby reducing their need to turn to illegal means to achieve their goals.[29] Japan's crime rate will probably increase when the rate of economic and job expansion slows, social mobility is restricted, and existing income distributions are maintained.[30]

Other explanations for Japan's low crime rate stress the homogeneity of the country, its degree of centralization, and its common social and cultural heritage—all of which provide a cohesiveness not present in other developed countries.[31] The island status of the country and its consequent isolation helped preserve its traditions and ensure continuity within the society. Societal continuity is manifested in the preservation of informal social controls within the family, school, and community. Legal controls in many areas have also proven effective. For example, the inability to procure firearms has proven a great deterrent to those inclined to commit violent behavior. Lastly, the effectiveness of formal control through the criminal justice system has served as an excellent deterrent to criminal behavior. "Wide and strong public cooperation and participation has actually been seen in many aspects of criminal justice. Besides, Japan shows a higher percentage of police solution of crimes and convictions of criminals in comparison with other countries."[32] This supports Beccaria's contention that swift and certain apprehension and punishment have been effective in dissuading people from engaging in criminal activity.

Switzerland is another case of a developed country with a high degree of affluence but a low rate of crime commission. The country's crime rate is often compared with that of Japan and contrasted with that of Sweden. Sweden, another highly affluent neutral European country, has experienced significant and growing crime rates. Scholars explain this difference in terms of political structure, the operation of the criminal justice system, and the degree of urbanization. Sweden is more centralized and urbanized and thus allows less opportunity for community participation in the criminal justice system.[33]

Switzerland also differs from Japan, although it shares many common criminal characteristics. Unlike Japan, the country is neither centralized nor homogeneous as the country is divided up into many cantons that are highly independent. A culturally diverse native population has been even more greatly diversified by the influx of large numbers of migrant workers from Italy and other less developed countries.[34] These political and ethnic differences between the two countries demonstrate that Japan has not found the sole means to avoid what might otherwise seem to the inevitable link between urbanization and industrialization and high levels of criminality.

Japan and Switzerland do, however, share certain common characteristics. Citizens in both societies assume an important role in the operation of the criminal justice system and this assumption of "governmental responsibilities . . . by the citizenry [has] been unique in the western world and provide a certain counterforce to the development of criminality."[35] In both countries, the criminal justice system has been effective in controlling the problems of criminality and has not been conducive to the emergence or increase in certain forms of criminal behavior. Close family structure has been preserved in Switzerland, and recent research reveals that youths prefer to spend their time in the company of adults rather than with their peer group.[36] This finding appears to be unique to Swiss society.

Certain other factors in Swiss society also contribute to low rates of criminality. The phenomenon of urbanization has been linked internationally with the problem of increasing crime rates. Part of the reason that Switzerland has much lower rates of criminality than its neighboring countries may be the fact that it has had a slower and distinctive urbanization process. "While the country is highly industrialized, the growth of urbanization has been only moderate, due to the decentralization of industry into the rural and semirural areas."[37] Major urban centers have thus been spared the massive population influx that results in the overcrowding and decay of residential areas in unprepared cities. Slums, which have been seen as highly criminogenic by many analysts,[38] have never developed within Swiss society as they have in the centers of most European and American cities.

The absence of a tradition of violence has resulted in little use of firearms in crime commission even though these weapons are easily available to much of the Swiss population.[39] Though much of the crime problem, particularly offenses against property, remains the behavior of juvenile offenders, their delinquents have not formed a criminal subculture[40] that has proved so conducive to the perpetration and transmission of criminal behavior in other societies.

Although both societies have undergone urbanization and industrialization, Japan and Switzerland have been exempt from many of the crime problems that currently plague the other developed countries. The uniqueness of their developmental process, the preservation of a close family structure, and the participation of the citizenry in the fight against crime have served as powerful deterrents to increased frequency of crime commission.

Most other developed countries have considerably higher rates of crime commission than these two societies, but few developed countries have as high rates of crime commission as the United States. The crime patterns of the United States are unique among all developed countries in terms of the high rates of criminal behavior, the pervasiveness of the phenomenon, and the severity of crimes that are committed. The country has not benefited from the stabilization in crime patterns that appears to accompany the maturation of the developmental process. It is important for this analysis of developed countries to understand the factors contributing to this anomaly.

The problem of criminality in American society is pervasive and threatening to the lives of the general population and to the social order. The extent of the problem and its effect on society are reminiscent of the criminological consequences of the nineteenth-century developmental process in Europe. This analogy between the impact of crime on twentieth-century American society and nineteenth-century Europe is not as farfetched as it seems because some of the conditions that created these unfortunate effects at the beginning of the industrial revolution have been repeated recently in the United States and have contributed to the crime wave of the postwar period.

The analogy suggests that the United States, generally recognized as a developed country because of its social and economic position, bears characteristics representative of a society only now undergoing the process of industrialization. The evidence for this position is mixed. The high crime rate of contemporary American society is typical of a developing country, but the overall structure of its crime patterns resembles that of developed countries. Crime rates for property offenses outnumber those against the person but violence assumes a much more central role in overall criminality than in most other societies of comparable economic development.[41]

The reasons why American crime patterns are so distinctive arise from the social, cultural, and political history of the country as well as from recent demographic developments.

The characteristics that scholars claim are responsible for the low crime rates of Japan and Switzerland are absent from American society. The United States has both a tradition of violence[42] attributable to the presence of the frontier and to the slave-holding mentality, which holds that individuals are not equal and that violence against inferior individuals is all right, and ready access to firearms for most of the population. There has never been a tradition of cooperating with the criminal justice system and, in fact, the converse spirit of vigilantism has prevailed during much of American history[43] and is resurfacing in many American communities. The mobility of American society and the emphasis on independence and peer culture have resulted in a long-term weakening of the family structure and the emergence of highly atomized individuals. The ethnic diversity of the American population as well as the influx of immigrants has resulted in an extremely heterogenous population in sharp contrast to the regional homogeneity of the Swiss population or the national homogeneity of the Japanese population.

Neither the heterogenity nor the origins of the American population appears to be an adequate explanation of its observed rate of criminality. Australia and Canada, both settled by heterogeneous immigrant groups, have very different crime rates from the United States,[44] which suggest that factors other than origin of the population and the period of settlement are important in determining the character of a nation's criminality.

The previously named factors explain why the United States does not enjoy the low crime rates of Switzerland and Japan but it does not explain the distinctively high crime rates of the United States. The explanation for this alarming phenomenon appears to be quite similar to that used to explain the crime patterns of nineteenth-century Europe. The principal cause of crime at that time was the process of urbanization that dislocated traditionally rural members of society from the countryside to cities ill equipped to accept them. The United States, though urbanized at a much earlier period in history, has suffered from a new cycle of urbanization in the period since World War II.

The recurrence of urbanization can be explained in the following way. The city population, already accustomed to urban life, moved to the suburbs in large numbers in the postwar period. The urban exodus was in part a reaction against the movement into the city of large numbers of previously rural workers who were at first attracted by the employment of the wartime economy. Entire extended families followed the initial migrants resulting in an ever escalating exodus from rural areas. The core of American cities was thus filled by black rural workers from the South and white rural workers from Appalachia.[45] The already established cities were as unprepared for this major influx of humanity as these new settlers were unaccustomed to this new way of life. Slums developed and fostered conditions conducive to increased rates of criminality.

Thus, in the last several decades the United States has again experienced the process of urbanization, the effects of which are comparable to those observed in England, France, and other European countries during the past century. The disproportionately high rate of urban violence in contemporary American crime patterns, mentioned above, appears to be symptomatic of the traumatic transition from rural to urban life noted previously in studies of nineteenth-century Europe. American crime of the second half of the twentieth century is not the anomaly that it first seemed but is instead a comprehensible response to the problems of urbanization that affected the United States in the postwar period.

The previous case studies of the crime patterns of three developed countries show that certain social conditions or processes either contribute to or deter criminal behavior. The traditional process of urbanization and industrialization appears to be the factor most conducive to increased rates of criminality. Industrialization and urbanization do not, however, always lead to rocketing crime rates as the unusual developmental processes of Japan and Switzerland indicate. The social conditions that have been most successfull in controlling the rise in crime rates associated with modernization have been close family ties, ethnic homogeneity, and consensus and cooperation between the civilian population and the criminal justice system. As the analysis of countries with either extremely high or low crime rates shows, the physical size of the population, the total population, and the length of residence of a nation's population (colonization or long-term settlement) do not appear to be significant in explaining deviations in the crime patterns of developed countries.

THE CRIMINAL POPULATION

As in developing countries, the majority of offenders in developed societies are adult males. Adult male offenders have traditionally had both the highest rates of criminality and the most diversified criminal careers.[46] Adult males, unlike female and juvenile offenders, have committed the full range of possible crimes although their criminal behavior appears to taper off or become more specialized and less active as they advance in years.[47]

A significant share of the total criminality appears to be committed by a small group of repeat offenders. This idea has been corroborated by research in the United States, Scandinavia, and elsewhere in continental Europe.[48] The professional criminal who devotes his life to crime and develops specialized skills is characteristic of the criminal in developed societies. The appellation "the professional thief" was coined in the United States and the attributes ascribed to this individual were based on American experience.[49] Though little attempt has been made to establish the characteristics of this individual in other societies, the concept has been accepted as valid in other developed countries.

The adult male does not have a monopoly on crime commission in developed countries. Moreover, juveniles and females who already assume a much larger role in crime commission than their counterparts in developing societies have rapidly ascending rates of criminality. In fact, in many developed countries, adult males, who long epitomized the criminal offender, actually have declining rates of criminality while the commission rates of the other two groups are accelerating at unprecedented rates.

There are several explanations for the changing composition of the offender population. Though all of these reasons are rooted in the social change that accompanies modernization, different social conditions explain the increase in crime commission by juveniles and females. A brief analysis of the patterns of criminal behavior of these two groups is a necessary prerequisite to a critique of the forces affecting their criminal behavior.

Juvenile Delinquency

Evidence from both capitalist and socialist developed countries indicates that juvenile delinquency is an almost inevitable result of the developmental process. Even after the transition to development has already transpired, the problem of juvenile delinquency does not disappear or even stabilize but continues to grow. Juvenile delinquency in developed societies, unlike that of developing countries, is characterized by widespread acts of violence and wanton destruction that threaten the social order of individual communities and society in general.[50] "Everywhere the proportion of growth involved in property crimes is large."[51]

Juvenile criminality is a significant problem in industralized societies with both serious and less widespread crime problems. In countries with little crime, such as Switzerland and Japan, juvenile offense rates are rising while the crime rate of the adult population is declining.[52] The growth in juvenile crime has not been consistent for all age groups, but the composite effect has been an overall increase in youth crime. In England and Sweden, it is the violence rather than the crime rates of juvenile offenders that has been so alarming. Violent subcultures were established in the 1960s by the British teddy boys and the Swedish *raggare*.[53] In the United States, delinquents represent 40 percent of the arrests made, and juveniles commit many of the more serious and violent offenses. In the Federal Republic of Germany 25 percent of the reported crimes were committed by the 14–20 age group. Other societies report an even greater proportion of their criminality attributable to juveniles. Most European countries report a dramatic rise in the level of juvenile criminality since the late 1930s. The rapid increase reported in drug offenses has disproportionately affected juvenile delinquents by further aggravating their already rising crime rates. The collective nature of juvenile delinquency has made youths particularly susceptible to drug-related crimes as juveniles are introduced into the drug culture most often through the peer group.

Juvenile delinquency in developed countries as in developing societies is a bifurcated phenomenon consisting of both middle-class and lower-class delinquency. Middle-class delinquency is a more important component of total youth crime in developed than in developing countries, but both classes of delinquents are motivated by the affluence that surrounds them. In industrialized societies, neither group of delinquents is motivated primarily by need though their attitudes towards material possessions are, of course, influenced by their access to these goods.

Youthful offenders from less advantaged backgrounds generally commit more serious acts of violence. The delinquency of middle-class youths is more frequently directed towards property and is more transient than that of less affluent youths.[54] This results from the differential treatment by the criminal justice system of the two classes of offenders and the greater opportunities for legitimate social advancement available to members of the middle class.

The tendency for juveniles to be strongly influenced by their peers and to act collectively has made youth gangs a common phenomenon in developed countries throughout the world. In Switzerland group activity is not highly structured, but in some societies, such as Japan and the United States, gangs are closely associated with the world of organized crime. In societies such as Sweden and Finland the individual gangs act independently of adult criminals and do not serve to the same degree as training grounds for adult criminality.[55] Crimes committed by groups of juveniles generally tend to be more violent than those committed by individuals, as personal values and inhibitions cannot restrain collective activity to the extent that they do in the individual case.

The extent to which youths participate in gangs varies, and fluctuations in membership appear to be influenced by environmental conditions. The gang became a subject of significant media interest in the United States during the 1950s, but the level of gang activity at this time did not really merit the attention it received in the press. Gang activity increased during the early and mid-1960s, not only in the United States but in England, Sweden, Japan and other European countries as the postwar baby boom reached the teenage years. There was a recorded decline in some countries in the late 1960s, but gang problems reemerged during the 1970s.[56]

The fluctuations in gang participation and in youth crime, generally appear to be explained not only by the demographic characteristics of the population but also by law enforcement in the broadest sense and the stability of the general urban population. The influx of the labor force into cities during World War II, the postwar period of adjustment in Europe, an increasingly capital-intensive industrial technology that deprived less-trained youth of employment opportunities, the general social disruptions accompanying the Vietnam War, and the student protests in both Europe and the United States—all contributed to the increased participation of juveniles in criminal behavior.

Juvenile criminality is distinctive from that of adults not only because it is frequently committed in groups in many developed countries but also because it is confined generally to a much more limited number of offenses. Delinquents as a rule do not commit embezzlement or fraud, offenses that require positions of responsibility acquired only with maturity. Property crime is the primary form of youthful criminality, and certain property offenses are particularly characteristic of this age group. For example, theft of motor vehicles, shoplifting, and vandalism appear to be the typical offenses of this age group.[57] Much of the vandalism reported in the United States, Germany, and Sweden is directed against public property, and its increased frequency represents ever rising costs to local authorities.[58] Juvenile delinquents in many societies are also heavily represented in arrests made for robberies and burglaries but these crimes are not as clearly associated with this age group as the previously named crimes. Although many European countries report an increase in senseless violence committed by youths, this behavior is no where as troublesome as in the United States where youth gangs or offender groups often engage in extremely violent acts.

The explanations for the observed patterns of criminal behavior can be found both in the individual circumstances of each offender as well as in the general social and economic conditions of contemporary society. Many present-day delinquents have suffered the consequences of postwar mobility and the renewed urbanization that accompanied the war years. Scholars writing of black delinquents in the United States or Finnish and Japanese youthful offenders comment that these children of recent migrants to urban areas are a primary cause of the increased juvenile crime of the past 30 years.[59] The same forces of familial dislocation that are causing large-scale increases of criminality in the developing countries at the present time are also contributing to the pervasive problem of youth crime in developed societies.

It is the nature of adolescence and of family life in the urban environment that has made youths so prone to criminal behavior. The period of adolescence is prolonged in the technologically advanced societies as "the skills required for economic and social participation in the larger society also increase."[60] Therefore, it takes youths a longer time to reach the stage where they are self-supporting and able to command respect for themselves as individuals. "It is the lengthening period of ill-defined position and status that has made delinquency such a common characteristic of contemporary society."[61]

Youths in this transitional stage are not given as much support by the traditional family and social institutions that have in the past served to integrate the juvenile into his environment.[62] Both middle-class and lower-class delinquency are explained by the same social and economic factors of contemporary society that hinder the adjustment of youthful individuals to accepted role patterns. The mobility of modern society, particularly of families of delinquents, deprives juveniles of strong relationships with their extended families or even the community in which they are raised. The impersonality of the surrounding community and the tendency of juveniles to socialize primarily with their own age group have promoted the idolization of youths and, consequently, the reduction of controls over their behavior. This destruction of the sense of belonging that characterizes contemporary society in most developed nations is particularly conducive to the emergence of increased criminality.

Intimacy in the relationships of juveniles with members of their families is also reduced when both parents work outside the home, and youths spend the day away from their parents in the generally impersonal school environment. As adolescents spend less time with their parents, they are influenced more strongly by their peers and by the media. Personal worth is no longer determined by the values inculcated by the family, but juveniles are influenced instead by television and radio which disseminate the dominant social value of success through acquisition of material possessions. Contemporary youths in a dependent relationship for a prolonged period of time lack the means to obtain the trappings of achievement legitimately and, therefore, often resort to illicit means to secure them. The explanation of middle- and lower-class delinquency suggests why illegal acts in most developed countries are directed so often against luxury goods that impart social status to the owner.

The failure of juvenile offenders to gain success by traditional means promotes their drive to attain status through the commission of offenses. Criminals in developed countries are generally not achievers in any sense of the word and frequently their absence of achievements can be explained by the disadvantages of their home environment. In technologically complex societies, great emphasis is placed on academic performance but delinquents generally fail as students, often a result of a family life that is difficult and a household that is not conducive to study. Numerous research studies conducted in the United States, Canada, Europe, and Japan attest to the impact of broken homes, parental alcoholism, and the poor social and economic position of the parents on the origins of juvenile delinquency.[63] Juvenile delinquency is concentrated primarily in areas of community social disorganization where adolescents live in overcrowded housing, receive inadequate medical care, and reside in neighborhoods with minimal social stability and community cohesiveness.[64]

Juveniles raised in a disorganized community learn their criminal behavior by contact with peers already engaged in illegal activity. The theory of "differential association" or the idea that criminality is learned from individuals in close proximity explains the emergence of much lower- and middle-class delinquency as many youth offenses are committed in groups. Research in London, Paris, Berlin, and a Belgian city affirm the validity of this theory that was first developed to explain the origins of juvenile delinquency in American cities.[65]

Two factors, poor education and an absence of affluence, contribute more significantly to juvenile delinquency in developed countries than in those societies that are only now undergoing the process of development. As previously mentioned, in highly technologically advanced societies, education is the key to social advancement, and those who perform poorly in school are denied many legitimate opportunities for advancement. Unlike developing countries where general prosperity is uncommon, developed societies have attained an overall level of societal affluence that makes those members of society who lack the tangible signs of success more likely to resort to illegal means to acquire them. As one scholar explains the impact of affluence on crime causation in developed societies:

> Poverty cannot cause crime but resentment of poverty can, and, curiously enough, resentment of poverty is more likely to develop among the relatively deprived of a rich society than among the objectively deprived in a poor society. This is partly because affluent industrial societies are also secular societies; the distribution of goods and services here and now is a more important preoccupation than concern with eternal salvation. It is also because the mass media—to which television has

84

been a recent important addition—stimulate the desire for a luxurious style of life among all segments of the population. These considerations explain why the sting of socioeconomic deprivation can be greater for the poor in rich societies than for the poor in poor societies.[66]

Relative deprivation cannot explain the etiology of all forms of delinquency in developed societies but it does provide much insight into the external motivations for such behavior.

Female Criminality

An increase in female participation in criminality, particularly in certain forms of property crimes, appears to accompany the developmental process in almost all countries. Although the increase in criminality has not been as significant for females as for juveniles, the increased visiblity of the female offender has aroused the concern of scholars who have for too long neglected the criminality of this population group.

Before the advent of development, women in Europe were responsible for a small share of total crime, and their level of criminality was comparable to that of women in presently developed societies. At the turn of the century, women in Northern and Western Europe were responsible for approximately one-eighth of total criminality but their counterparts in the less technologically advanced Balkan societies like Bulgaria, Bosnia and Herzegovina, Serbia, and Greece contributed between 3 and 7 percent of all crimes.[67] The crime contribution of women in the developed countries of the world has remained remarkably stable during much of the twentieth century and woman have consistently committed between one-eighth and one-fifth of the total crimes in their societies.[68]

Many scholars have commented on the perceived increase in female criminality in developed countries since World War II and on the particularly noticeable rise in the last two decades.[69] The recent change in female criminality does not represent a doubling of the female commission rates such as occurred during the transition from developing to developed society, but it does represent the first major transformation in female crime rates in half a century. The greater criminality of women is indicative of a significant societal change that affects female behavior more directly than that of men. The international nature of this growth in female crime despite certain annual fluctuations suggests that a definite transformation in criminality has occurred rather than a change in law enforcement patterns.

85

Scholars have examined whether both the rates and forms of female criminality have changed. The most noticeable shift in female criminality has been the increase in their contribution to overall crime rates. Available Interpol crime data for 1960 and 1972 reveal increases in the amount of crime committed by women in seven out of the eight European countries for which there is data (with the exception of Austria) but a significant decline in the number of offenses committed by women in Japan.[70] (However, Japanese crime rates for women cleared by the police as suspects, once the perpetrator of the crime has been arrested, show an increase during the same time period.)[71] Comparisons of the increase in female offenders relative to males reveal that in many countries the rate of increase in criminality for women is greater than that for men. For example, in France, the relative frequency of female criminality increased by 155 percent during the 12-year period while that of men only by 51 percent.[72] When the decline of female criminality in Japan is analyzed in terms of the fluctuations in the national crime rate, it becomes apparent that women assumed a larger share of the nation's total crime rate during this period because the rate of crime commission among males declined even more dramatically.[73]

Contemporary scholars have not agreed whether the increase in female crime has occurred in all categories of criminal behavior or only in those traditionally associated with the woman offender. Assertions in the mass media and by certain scholars concerning the increasingly violent nature of the female offender do not appear to be substantiated by available data or analysis except in the case of some juveniles and youthful offenders. The criminality of women in most developed countries is still confined primarily to property crime, in which they predominate, while their rate of increase for violent offenses against the person is insignificant by comparison. Despite this fact, women have expanded their range of criminal activities and participate more actively in the more serious forms of property crime. Although women do not have as broad a criminal profile as men, their illegal activity is no longer confined to the crimes of purchase and sale of stolen goods, shoplifting, illegal abortions, and prostitution. The most noticeable expansion of female participation in crime has been directly related to the more active role of women in business and general economic affairs. Women in the United States and Western Europe are arrested with greater frequency for embezzlement, fraud, and other economic offenses[74] whose perpetration has only recently become feasible for women. In many developed countries women participate increasingly in major larcenies, an indication of the greater commitment by women to a professional criminal career.[75]

The criminality of women is a barometer of the extent of female participation in the society and the degree of their involvement outside the home. The diversification and increasing participation of women in criminal behavior can be correlated directly with the evolution in their societal role. Female criminality is one of the best comparative measures of criminal behavior because its minimal complexity in the past makes it possible to study clearly the impact of social forces and socioeconomic development on both rates and forms of crime commission.

Criminality of Migrants

Another group of offenders that has raised the interest of scholars in a number of developed countries is migrants. Concern for the impact of migrants on crime rates can be traced to early twentieth-century United States when isolationists tried to attribute much of the observed crime rate to the recent large influx of foreign immigrants. Research at that time showed that little of the crime rate could be explained by the behavior of recent settlers from abroad.[76] Although the criminological research failed to convince those who wanted to disparage the immigrants, it did provide a serious analytical base for future studies of the impact of migration on crime.

The contemporary studies of migration and crime affirm the fortunate relationship between criminality and international population movements observed 60 years ago. Recent studies on the criminal behavior of guest workers and foreign settlers show that these individuals have very different patterns of behavior from the migrants who move within their own country from the countryside to an urban area.[77] The reasons why internal and external migration have different criminological consequences help explain the relationship between crime and society and the impact of social conditions on the individual offender.

Migration has existed on a large scale in developed countries in the last few decades. The population movements have occurred in two patterns in industrialized societies: that is, migration from less developed countries to more developed countries as typified by the "guest workers" in Europe and the population movements from both developed and developing countries to such nations as Canada and

Australia that have sought to increase their populations. Both of these migrations are inspired by the desire for increased economic and social opportunity. The incentive for the move plays a very significant role in the limited contribution made by these groups to the crime rate of their new country of residence.

Criminological research in Australia, Canada, the United States, and much of Europe[78] demonstrates that both the guest workers and the recent but permanent settlers from abroad have lower rates of criminality than long-time residents of the nation. Although different ethnic groups show variations in their rates of commission,[79] the crime rates of all these different population groups are consistently below that of the native population. Even more remarkable is that traditional culture conflicts do not produce criminality in the new country of residence. "It is interesting to note that migrants' crime rates are lower even though there is rivalry between those who meet in Australia but whose countries of origin have been traditionally opposed—Turks and Greeks, for example."[80]

The low rate of criminality among migrants is remarkable on several counts. Firstly, the general hostility displayed by members of the criminal justice system towards foreign migrants results in a greater tendency to arrest those of foreign background and to sentence more harshly those convicted of crimes. Research in Italy, Switzerland, and Germany has shown that despite this tendency foreign workers have consistently had lower rates of criminality. Secondly, the migrants to most nations are disproportionately young males. The low crime rates of these migrants are doubly remarkable because "the age composition of the migrant group—gives an even more surprising value to the low criminal rates, which should ordinarily be higher for this age group."[81]

The sex of the migrants, their easy access to property through their jobs in hotels and as household servants,[82] and their difficulties of adjustment should all produce high rates of criminality; but, despite what are ordinarily contributory factors to high crime rates, the migrants have consistently lower commission rates than those who have less access to property and less material need to commit crimes.

The low rate of criminality among migrants is even more distinctive than the demographic characteristics of the migrant population might suggest because these individuals are exposed to residential, social, and employment conditions that appear to be conducive to criminality in most other population groups. Migrants live in overcrowded housing, often without their families, and work at the most undesirable of jobs. They perform jobs that in many cases no one else would choose to do and this provides them their only job security. Those employed in industry are more subject to economic oscillations and suffer from an uncertain employment situation.

The migrants, especially the guest workers, often live years abroad without their families and in that respect their life patterns do not differ from the rural migrants who arrive in cities unaccompanied. Despite the absence of the stabilizing influence of the family and the fact that the male migrants frequently reside in overcrowded conditions with other males, their social environment does not, however, produce higher overall rates of criminality.

Immigrant workers do not have consistently low rates of crime commission. Their low overall rate of criminality results from the fact that they commit certain relatively common crimes rarely while committing some generally infrequent crimes more often. Immigrants as a "rule do not commit infanticide, illegal abortion, forgery, fraud, arson and traffic offenses."[83] Theft rates sometimes fall above and sometimes below that recorded for the indigenous population. It is in the relatively rare crimes against the person—homicide, assault, and rape—that immigrants participate disproportionately in, owing to their overcrowded housing conditions and their cultural upbringing which approaches violence and sexual and personal honor differently, specifically among those from Turkey, the Balkans and Southern Italy. The relatively high rate of sexual criminality appears to be explained more by separation from family than by any innate sexual deviation.[84]

Slums have been shown to be conducive to criminality in both developed and developing countries, but the slum conditions in which most migrants reside have not produced these results among migrant workers or settlers. The reasons for this different pattern of behavior is explained not by the slum but by its inhabitants.

The crime patterns of migrants abroad are sharply differentiated from those who choose to migrate from rural to urban areas within their own countries. While the latter group has generally high rates of criminal behavior, the external migrants have rates that fall below the national average. Their low rate of criminality is explained by their motivations and expectations for life in their new country of residence. The tenuous legal status of the migrants as well as the fact that their residence abroad promises them increased opportunities is a sufficient deterrent to illegal conduct despite the difficulties encountered in their new residential environment.

The encouraging relationship between migration and crime

among the first generation of settlers from abroad is, unfortunately, not perpetuated into the second generation raised in the new country of residence.[85] These individuals raised in slum conditions suffer the stigma of foreign parentage and, unlike their parents, rarely perceive their new country to be a land of great opportunity. They often resort to illegitimate means to achieve goals that are otherwise unattainable to them. The increased criminality of the second generation of migrants, first observed in the United States at the beginning of this century,[86] has been replicated more recently in other industrialized societies. While the children of immigrants in the United States often directed their illicit activities through the structure of organized crime, in Europe where such networks are not as well developed, these children of migrants participate in more diversified criminal activities.

Recidivism

Developed nations, spared the crime problems that might be expected to accompany the disruptive process of migration, are not spared the activities of another category of criminal offender whose behavior is particularly destructive to the social order of the urban community. Recidivists, sophisticated criminals with a commitment to a criminal career, are increasingly a problem in many industrialized societies.[87] Their contribution to total criminality is so significant that along with juveniles they are responsible for the majority of crimes committed. Their sophistication and the inability of the society to cope with them through the criminal justice system makes recidivists more threatening than the casual offenders and youthful offenders, many of whom— will outgrow their criminal involvement.

The recidivism rate of most capitalist developed countries averages between 50 and 70 percent.[88] This level of repeat criminality is observed internationally regardless of the level of criminality present in the society, the quality of its penal institutions, or the percentage of the population incarcerated. The United States with its high crime rate[89] and Japan with its low crime rate[90] both have rates of recidivism that fall within this range. Switzerland, which uses prison far less frequently as a sanction than its European neighbors,[91] thereby confining its inmate population only to the most serious offenders, has a similar rate of recidivism. Sweden, with its very liberal penal institutions, has a recidivism rate of 80 percent,[92] exceeding the rates of almost all other industrialized countries. Only the developed countries that have followed the socialist form of development have been spared these recidivism rates. The reasons for this difference will be discussed in the following chapter.

The internationally consistent rates of recidivism among criminals in highly developed countries suggest that the structure of these technologically advanced society makes reintegration of former convicts into the economy and the law-abiding community difficult. The stigma of criminal conviction and the hiatus in employment that results from incarceration make reabsorption into society an insurmountable problem for most sentenced offenders.

In industrialized societies with a major organized crime problem and in countries generally spared this unfortunate phenomenon, recidivists either self-employed or in groups demonstrate the failure of the society to rehabilitate its criminal population, thereby ensuring that a younger generation of professional criminals will be educated by these mature offenders. The continuity of serious criminality in developed countries for years to come is thus assured.

Crime cannot be understood without an examination of the individuals responsible for all forms of criminality. An analysis of the dynamics of different offender groups does not fully explain the causation and perpetuation of crime in contemporary society, but it helps elucidate some of the motivation for criminal activity and the reasons why some crimes figure so prominently in overall commission patterns.

THE GEOGRAPHY OF CRIME

An analysis of the geographical distribution of crime in society is important because it illuminates the impact of such social forces as industrialization, urbanization, and community and familial structure on patterns of illegal behavior. Only by examining crime in terms of the context in which it is committed is it possible to explain how societal evolution and development affect both rates and forms of criminal behavior.

The geography of crime is different in developed and developing countries not only because of their different levels of economic development but also because of the different types of residential environments available to inhabitants of these two types of societies. Inhabitants of developing countries reside primarily in rural areas, towns, or cities. Suburbia, a type of community predicated on the automobile, is not the integral part of society in less developed countries that it is in the modern industrialized nations. The geography of crime in developed countries is more complex than that of developing nations because crime must be analyzed in terms of rural, urban, and suburban communities, each of which has its own patterns of behavior and social organization and, consequently, its unique criminal characteristics. Rural, suburban, and urban areas have differing rates of criminality, and each has certain offenses that dominate its overall crime rate.[93]

Development has not produced the same patterns of urbanization internationally. In the United States and England, for example, much of the population resides in medium to large cities; but in France, Sweden, and other Scandinavian countries significant proportions of the populations reside in small towns or rural areas.[94] This variation in the degree of urbanization of developed countries reduces the comparability of these societies. However, the geographical distribution of crime in developed nations is sufficiently different from that observed in developing countries that it is possible to make certain generalizations concerning the geography of crime in industrialized countries.

The study of the geographical distribution of crime has been of great interest to American researchers since 1942 when Shaw and McKay's pioneering work *Juvenile Delinquency in Urban Areas* was published.[95] Numerous ecological studies of crime and delinquency have followed examining the form and distribution of crime within urban areas and the relationship between different social variables and the recorded crime rates of existing neighborhoods. In addition, considerable attention has been paid by American researchers to the relationship between the level of urbanization and the rate of criminality.[96] This degree of concentrated interest in ecological and geographical studies of criminality has not been manifested by researchers in other developed capitalist countries. However, enough tangential references are made by foreign scholars to the subject that the geographical distribution of criminality can be studied in comparative perspective.

Researchers in several developed countries have established that significant regional differences exist in rates and patterns of criminality. Forty years ago a regional distribution of crime was established for the United States and more recently such research has been conducted in Europe and Canada.[97] These studies reveal particularly high rates of criminality in tourist and border areas and other regions with high traffic concentrations[98] or a high level of industrialization. For example, the northern regions of Germany and France, which rely on heavy industry, have higher overall crime rates and more property crime than the more southerly parts of their countries where more individuals are employed in agriculture.[99]

Crime in developed countries as in less industrialized nations is concentrated in cities. Urban criminality is not, however, a homogeneous phenomenon as city size and neighborhood characteristics affect the observed crime rates. The rate of criminality appears to increase directly with city size though researchers in the Netherlands have suggested that some middle-size cities in their country have higher rates of criminality than do the largest urban centers.[100] These results are tentative and certainly do not disprove the idea that large cities contribute disproportionately to their nation's criminality.

Community organization and its role in the etiology of criminality, once a subject of considerable interest to American researchers of criminality in poor urban areas, have been examined in a new context by European researchers. These scholars have focused their attention on the absence of community organization and stability in newly established towns as an explanation of the disproportionate rise in crime rates in these urban communities.

Researchers studying crime in urban areas have also examined the concentration of crime within particular sections of the urban environment. They have determined that crime, though not confined to one city region, is generally focused in certain neighborhoods of each city. Crime is most heavily concentrated in city centers and slum neighborhoods. City centers are magnets for criminals both in the United States, where the central core is often characterized by urban decay, and in Europe where the downtown area is distinguished by its popular and cultural attractions.[101] Slums and other less affluent city areas where crime rates are high are often populated by recent migrants from the countryside who contribute disproportionately to recorded crime rates.[102] Although patterns of law enforcement are usually biased against the less affluent members of society, thus exaggerating the crime rates of regions where indigent members of society reside, research in a number of industrialized societies has shown that poor urban residents do contribute disproportionately to total crime rates, though possibly not to the extent suggested by official police reports.

Poor regions do not have the monopoly on high crime rates for all forms of illicit behavior. As environmental opportunities for crime vary among urban neighborhoods, the frequency of crime commission for particular categories of crime reflects the feasibility of crime commission.[103] Offenses associated with affluence such as bank robberies, burglaries, and white-collar crimes are most frequently committed outside of slums and working-class districts. Violent crimes, often accompanying alcohol consumption, and the more common forms of property crimes are characteristic of slums and working-class neighborhoods.

Researchers have attempted to understand the social conditions responsible for the observed variations within and among cities. Urbanization has been used as a primary explanation of high crime rates. Observers have commented that the initial period of adjustment is the most traumatic for recent arrivals and, consequently, crime rates of areas populated by these individuals are exceedingly high. Research has shown that some highly urbanized areas have low rates of crime commission while others have correspondingly higher ones,[104] thereby suggesting that urbanization only partially explains the crime rates of a particular community. Instead, it is the whole structure of modern life that elucidates the observed crime phenomenon. Therefore, social, political, religious, and cultural traditions, the geographic location of the city, and the qualifications and honesty of the local criminal justice system become of paramount importance in determining the degree and severity of observed crime patterns after the initial transformation to urbanization has transpired.

To evaluate the impact of individual variables on urban life, criminologists have correlated the crime rate with such social factors as level of industrialization, population density, standard of living, number of children, divorce and illiteracy rate, and the frequency of mental illness, alcoholism and infant mortality.[105] The early theories that explained the disproportionate criminality of cities as a consequence of their dense population of urban areas have been increasingly called into question. Consistent research results have not been obtained, but increasingly evidence indicates that the number of people employed in industry, the divorce, and the infant mortality rate correlate with as much or more of the observed criminality than the degree of urbanization or the physical environment of cities.[106]

Certain explanatory factors are more difficult to quantify such as the impact of historical tradition, social upheaval, and the tenacity of religious values. These influences along with the more measurable variables explain much about the ability of a community to control the problems of criminality. Though it is possible to identify and evaluate the impact of individual characteristics that will influence the crime patterns of a given urban area, it is not always easy to predict what will be their composite effect on the criminality of a metropolitan area.

Numerous social forces interact in a complex way to deter or reinforce illegal behavior. Though the prosperity of the community may provide an incentive for crime commission, strong religious traditions may prevent high rates of criminality. For example, though the cities of Switzerland are among the most affluent in Europe, the population stability and the perpetuation of strong Calvinistic traditions result in low rates of criminal activity.[107] Hamburg, Germany, a port city with a highly transient population and a long-established tradition of illegal conduct does not benefit from the social and political controls that suppress the crime rates of other parts of contemporary Germany.[108]

The conditions of city life and the process of urbanization explain the uniquely high crime rates of urban areas as well as the distinctive crime patterns of individual cities. These social forces affect the crime patterns of cities and of their adjoining suburban areas.

Despite their relatively recent appearance, suburbs have become widespread around major cities in most developed western countries, but the exodus by the middle class from urban centers to these communities has been nowhere as extensive as in the United States. The suburban communities have expanded particularly after World War II, because members of the middle class seek acceptable housing which enables them to support a life-style centered on the family. Suburbs are an integral part of contemporary society and their patterns of criminality should not be ignored.

Surprisingly little attention has been paid by researchers to the crime patterns of suburbs in developed countries and only recently has American criminological research discussed the influence of this form of settlement on the crime patterns of greater metropolitan areas.[109] The general economic and community stability of the suburban way of life does not lead to the commission of the more traditional forms of property and violent crimes by adult members of the community. Adult suburbanites, if they commit crimes at all, are most likely to perpetrate white-collar offenses, crimes that are infrequently detected and prosecuted. Although certain recent studies suggest that suburban residents venture into the city to commit crimes,[110] the force of most research has been that offenders commit crimes in their own towns and to a significant extent in their own communities.[111] The general affluence of suburban communities makes it unlikely that residents would venture far from their homes to commit crimes when the suburb itself is a natural target for perpetrators of property crimes. There is some evidence that the sophisticated professional criminal in the United States is venturing increasingly from the city to the suburbs to commit property crimes.[112] This development has not been observed on a mass scale in many other industrialized societies but it can be expected that criminals elsewhere will soon learn of the material advantages to be gained from traveling to the suburbs.

The major offenders in suburban communities are middle-class delinquents. The criminality of these delinquents, discussed earlier in this chapter, is often not minor as their absence of respect for property often results in much wanton destruction. The increasing prevalence of drug use among middle-class youths has increased this problem of already significant proportions.

The overall crime rate of suburban areas, like its population density, lies between that of urban and rural areas. The explanation for its level of criminality is complex, resulting more from its community structure than from the relative lack of population density. In terms of their degree of family and community integration, homogeneity, and social and economic stability—elements of social structure that affect crime rates—suburbs lie between city and country. Suburbs lack the impersonality of the modern city but do not share the family and community cohesiveness known in rural areas.

Rural areas are characterized by distinct crime patterns regardless of the state of development of the rest of society. The criminal behavior characteristic of the rural environment both before and during economic development is similar to that which currently exists in rural areas of industrialized societies. Rural areas are still characterized by a high level of homicide.[113] Homicide and assault, although not as frequent as in urban areas,[114] assume a larger share of total criminality than in cities where theft, the crime that epitomizes modernization, predominates. The preeminence of violence in rural communities may be receding because of a recent growth in property crimes attributable, in part, to increasingly mobile urban inhabitants. Although the possible financial rewards derived from these crimes may be less than in the city environment, the lack of sophistication of the criminal justice system reduces the certainty of arrest. The increased frequency of property offenses provides the first notable change in the previously static patterns of rural criminality. Despite this increase in criminality, crime rates in the rural areas of industrialized societies are still less than in other parts of these countries.

The perpetuation of traditional rural patterns of criminality is explained by the structure of rural society and the lessened impact of modernization on the rural community. Family stability, the perpetuation of a traditional way of life, and the high level of community integration are all responsible for generally low rates of crime. Rural areas have not been immune to the forces of industrialization but their effect on criminality in the countryside has in some ways been positive rather than disruptive. The youthful male exodus to urban areas, though a destabilizing influence on family life, has reduced the most crime-prone age group in the countryside, thereby deflating their possible crime rates. Rural areas therefore retain the traits that contribute to low rates of criminality without suffering from the forces that are conducive to increased criminal activity. As rural areas become more modernized, they will probably assume the characteristics of urban communities. At that time the crime rates of rural areas will rise above their presently depressed level.

It is not a coincidence that a common geography of crime exists for developed countries. The existence of distinct crime patterns associated with the rural, urban, and suburban ways of life demonstrates that crime trends are a reflection of social structure and societal evolution. As Tarde commented nearly a century ago, changes in observed criminal behavior reflect significant changes in social structure and community organization.[115] Therefore, the impact of industrialization and urbanization is manifested not only in the crime rate but in the structure and distribution of criminality in modern developed society.

FUTURE CRIME TRENDS

There are three fundamental questions concerning future crime patterns. How much crime will there be? What kinds of crime will there be? Who will be committing these crimes? The answers to these questions are much more difficult to predict for developed than for developing countries. The history and current crime patterns of developed countries provide a likely model for the future crime trends of developing nations but, unfortunately, no such model exists to aid predictions of the future state of criminality in already developed nations. The future of crime in developed countries thus remains highly speculative.

Predictions can be made by using the factors shown in the past to be effective in explaining the nature of crime commission. These factors are the process of social and economic development, the degree of social control exercised in society, and the values and aspirations of the population. These closely interrelated factors will be used to develop answers to basic questions concerning future patterns of crime commission in the developed nations of the world.

The prime concern of most observers of criminality is the overall level of crime. The populations of most developed countries presently feel threatened by the level of criminality in their countries, but it is unlikely that the future will bring significant reductions in current crime rates. The best that can be hoped is that the annual rate of increase in criminality will stabilize once the transition to development is completed,[116] while the worst possible scenario is that crime rates will grow at an even faster rate than at the present time. There is little likelihood that crime rates will decline because in the last 50 years crime rates have been increasing in almost all developed nations and those countries that have had steady or declining crime rates have recently experienced growth as a result of the increased participation of juvenile offenders.

The process of development has been shown in this and the previous chapter to be of primary importance in explaining the quantity and forms of criminality. Therefore, future crime rates will be determined primarily by the forces of social and economic development. Speculation on future crime rates hinges on the question whether the conditions of modernization are conducive to high crime rates or the transition to full social and economic development. The previous discussion suggests that crime rates are highest during the transition to modernization and that the rate of increase in criminality decelerates or declines once society is already embarked on its course of development. Present crime rates support this position as the developed countries now have a 1 percent annual increase in their crime rates while the developing countries have an annual increase two and a half times as great.[117] Some, however, might protest that these different rates of increase in criminality are not a function of the stage of historical development but are merely a reflection of the differential rate of population increase of developed and developing societies. But rates of population growth are also a function of the stage of societal development, thus deflating the argument against the association of crime rates and development.

The future rate of criminality will also be influenced by the dominant societal values and the criminal justice system. The present emphasis on secular values that place possessions over spiritual qualities has made property crimes the hallmark of modernization. Violent crimes against the person, once the predominant forms of criminal behavior, have become less frequent. The relationship between the commission rates for these two categories of offenses should be sustained as the desire for more property will not abate in a society where individual worth is increasingly measured by the quantity of personal possessions.

This future crime trend should be evaluated in terms of the seriousness of the offenses as well as the quantity of crime. Property offenses are generally perceived by most individuals as less serious than crimes against the person. Provided that property crimes are not accompanied in the future by increased violence, the increased frequency of these offenses might mean that, although crime is more pervasive and absolute crime rates are higher, the crime problem might not have become more threatening to the social order of the community.

Crime trends will also be influenced by the existing criminal justice systems—their quality and sophistication and the cooperation provided them by the general population. The research examined indicates that in few cases has the criminal justice system been instrumental in controlling the phenomenon of crime as it is social forces that have been most decisive in determining the level of criminality that exists in society. The criminal justice systems of Switzerland and Japan have been most effective in limiting crime commission because there the communities cooperate with the police and courts. In the United States where the spirit of vigilantism prevails the criminal justice system has been less able to control criminality. Unless general societal attitudes towards law enforcement change in developed nations, it can be expected that the criminal justice system of these countries will fail to have a significant impact on their future level of criminality.

In the future, the traditional forms of property and violent crime should still comprise the majority of all offenses. Simultaneously, crimes facilitated by the interrelationship of countries and the advent of modern technology should proliferate. This means that the drug trade should continue to grow as well as other forms of illegal international commerce. Computer crimes and other property crimes made possible by new technology should become more frequent as the needed technology becomes more accessible to the general population.

Some change should also be expected in the structure of the offender population. Adult male offenders may cease to be the largest contributors to total crime commission as juveniles and women become more actively involved in criminal activity. Juvenile crime is greatest in urbanized areas and is increasing internationally even in such countries as Japan, where commission rates for other categories of offenders are declining. These two trends together suggest that juveniles in developed nations will assume an ever larger share of total crime commission. The process of development is associated in most societies with an increase in female criminality, particularly in the area of property crimes, explained primarily by their increased access to goods. As more women join the work force, it can be postulated that their crime rates for property crime will continue to rise. Whether such a transformation will also occur in their commission rates for violent criminality remains a matter of conjecture.

In conclusion, it would seem that as societies continue to modernize, crime rates will increase slightly but not to the extent known at earlier stages of the developmental process. The increases in crime will continue to be primarily in the area of property crime, the offenses most associated with the present level of societal development. Violence will continue both in crimes against the person and maybe more frequently in association with property crimes as individuals will seek to acquire property by any possible means. The character of the offender population will also greatly influence the number and types of crimes committed. Juvenile offenders may cease to contribute as large a percentage of total crime, if the birthrate drops or greater social control is exercised by family, school, and other social institutions over the behavior of youths. As there is no indication that the increased property crimes of women replace those committed by men, the further emergence of the female offender will merely supplement the crime rates already recorded for men. The criminal justice systems of the developed nations, in the future as in the past, will be generally ill prepared and too isolated from their nation's populations to control these new crime trends.

PART THREE

CRIME UNDER SOCIALISM

5

Crime in Socialist Countries

This chapter analyzes the claim of socialist countries that their form of economic development has made them exempt from many of the crime problems associated with the developmental process in capitalist societies. It examines this claim in terms of the crime rates, the forms of crimes committed, the geographical distribution of offenses, and the nature of the offender population. The analysis determines that in certain respects the crime problems of socialist societies are innately different from those of capitalist societies. It explores the extent of this difference attributable to the socialist form of economic development and the degree to which these differences are ascribable to controls exercised over the population, the extent of community involvement in the criminal justice system, and the values fostered by the society.

Socialist societies exist in Europe, Africa, Asia, and Latin America. Because data sufficient to analyze their crime problems are, however, available almost exclusively from the Soviet Union and Eastern Europe, this discussion of crime in socialist countries will focus primarily on the Soviet Union and its sphere of influence in Eastern Europe. In addition, the Soviet Union, as the first socialist society, has had a significant influence in the rest of the socialist world on the legal definitions of criminality, the means taken to control the phenomenon of crime, and the theories used to explain the existence of criminal behavior.

The crime patterns of socialist societies must be analyzed differently from those of the developed and developing capitalist countries, discussed in the previous two chapters. As crime data are absent or frequently suspect and criminological research is often highly influenced by ideological considerations, all available research from socialist countries should not be accepted at face value. The research of scholars in Eastern Europe and the U.S.S.R. must, therefore, be evaluated in terms of its academic merit and the degree to which the research findings and conclusions reflect ideological demands. These caveats concerning the limitations of the research are more applicable to the Soviet Union where greater restrictions are placed on intellectual freedom of criminological researchers than in other socialist countries.

The problems of criminological data are most acute for the Soviet Union and its faithful follower Bulgaria, but, in general, less is known about the entire crime picture in socialist countries than in other nations of a comparable level of economic development. While other nations may not be able to provide accurate or comprehensive crime statistics because of problems of collection, absence of personnel to compile them, or a general lack of sophistication in the criminal justice area, socialist countries like the Soviet Union, China, and Cuba are the only ones which consciously withhold their crime figures from international organizations and fail to disseminate this information through their own publications and to their own people. Nevertheless, these data are made available to a select group of scholars who use them for administrative and planning purposes. Such "liberal" socialist countries as Poland, Hungary, and Yugoslavia publish some of their crime figures, but they omit arrest and conviction rates for political crimes and certain other offenses.

The absence of comprehensive data is deliberate and the reasons for this secrecy is primarily ideological. As socialist ideology proclaims that crime will wither away under socialism and disappear under communism, the persistence of crime under socialist conditions is both an embarrassment and evidence of weakness in the ideology. Authorities in socialist societies, who not only have failed to eliminate their crime problems, but also face growing rates of juvenile delinquency, choose to suppress their crime data rather than admit their failures.

Despite the absence of published Soviet crime data and of comprehensive criminological statistics for the rest of the socialist countries of Eastern Europe, it is still possible to study the crime patterns of these nations. While the actual crime data used for planning purposes may not be available to foreigners, the analysis made of these data by criminologists are published in readily available journals and books.

By piecing together evidence from different available sources it is possible to construct a picture of the patterns of criminality and the nature of offender populations.

This analysis focuses on the impact of the modernization process on the character of crime in socialist countries. The impact of socioeconomic development on crime has been a subject of considerable interest to scholars in Eastern Europe and certain consequences of the modernization process have been of consistent concern to Soviet scholars. Therefore, a considerable body of research from diverse socialist countries exists that examines the impact of industrialization, urbanization, and intense population migration as well as other factors associated with modernization on the crime patterns of these nations.

The previous two chapters divided the world's capitalist nations into those that were "developing" and those that were already "developed." This distinction can also be made in this chapter because Romania and Bulgaria are at a much lower level of socioeconomic development than the more industrialized socialist countries of East Germany, Poland, and Czechoslovakia. The U.S.S.R. is not, however, the highly developed country that many consider it to be because of its industrial and military might, since many of the Asian regions are still undergoing development.

It must be remembered that the distinction between the developed and developing countries of Eastern Europe is not as great as the differences established among the countries discussed in chapters 3 and 4. Many of the socialist countries had achieved some industrial development by the beginning of this century, years before they became socialist. "Socialist modernization, then, had as its base point not the relatively undifferentiated, tribalistic social and economic structure of many contemporary Afro-Asian modernizing states, but an already fairly high degree of institutional development."[1] The intense industrialization and urbanization that have occurred in Eastern Europe since World War II are an attempt to catch up with the United States and Western Europe.

PATTERNS OF CRIMINAL BEHAVIOR

It is difficult to make generalizations about the crime patterns of the socialist countries because they are characterized by such diversity. Despite the difficulties involved in such a survey, the following analysis focuses on the rates and trends in crime commission as well as on the geographical distribution of criminality in these societies.

Socialist countries pride themselves on the fact that, unlike the rest of the world's nations, they have succeeded in reducing their national crime rates. Soviet criminologists compare their recent crime statistics with those of the postrevolutionary period and Eastern Europeans make comparisons with the pre-World War II years. In both cases criminologists maintain that a significant decline in criminality has occurred since their socialist revolutions. This assertion, though possibly technically correct, does not, however, reveal the entire picture. First, the periods chosen for comparison in the U.S.S.R. are not representative as the years following a war are usually ones characterized by abnormally high rates of crime. Second, the decline observed has not been consistent as some forms of criminality have increased, others have declined, and still others have stabilized. Third, although the rates of criminality may have declined for adult offenders, most socialist countries have an increasing problem of juvenile delinquency, a serious problem for the present and an even more threatening one for the future. These other considerations suggest that even if a decline in criminality has occurred there is little chance it could be sustained in the future.

The Polish crime statistics for the 1970s reveal that crime rates have remained relatively constant during this period. The total crime rate has fluctuated around 1,000 crimes per 100,000 population.[2] There are strong indications that many categories of criminality remain very much underreported. For example, the number of arrests and prosecutions for currency violations is rather limited while even the most casual tourist in Warsaw will report on the extensive opportunities for illegal exchange of foreign currency. This suggests that the constancy of the Polish crime rates may be attributable more to the readiness of the Polish police to ignore certain crimes than to the success of the state in controlling the problems of criminality.

Property crimes in Poland comprise a very significant share of total criminality. In 1975, crimes against socialist and personal property amounted to 210,492 reported crimes out of a total number of 340,423 or 62 percent of total criminality.[3] Crimes against life increased approximately 250 percent between 1954 and 1963[4] and declined nearly to 1950s levels by 1975 at which time crimes against the person represented less than 6 percent of total crime commission.[5] This relationship between crimes against property and offenses against the person conforms to the crime patterns of a developed country.

The overall crime rates of Hungary, in contrast to those reported by Poland, have been rising gradually since the mid 1960s when 1,540 crimes were recorded per 100,000 as compared to the comparable rate of 1,697 recorded in 1965.[6] The relationship between overall rates of property crime and crimes of violence is similar to that observed in Poland. Property crimes represented between 57 and 60 percent of all criminality in Hungary in the mid-1970s,[7] and 40.5 percent of the theft was committed against socialist property.[8] The proportional contribution of crimes of violence is harder to calculate because significant fluctuations exist in the arrest rates reported for "threats while performing professional duties." When arrest rates were low for this offense, crimes against the person accounted for less than 8 percent of total crime commission, but during the early 1970s when many offenses were reported in this category, the amount of crime attributable to offenses against the person more than doubled.[9] Much of this temporary increase was blamed at the time on an increase in alcohol use, an explanation that loses its validity in retrospect because alcohol use among perpetrators of crimes against the person has continued to rise all through the 1970s.

The crime rates recorded for East Germany during the same period were much lower than those recorded for Hungary. East German criminologists generally more ideological than their Eastern European counterparts, claim that the country is experiencing a generally declining crime rate.[10] In 1963, in East Germany there were 956 reported crimes per 100,000, one-third the rate reported in West Germany.[11] The relationship between the crime rates of the two Germanys was even more pronounced in regards to Berlin in the late 1960s. The unique geographical position of West Berlin and its difficulties in attracting a work force are used to explain its rate of 5,475 offenses per 100,000, almost five times the rate recorded for East Berlin. Property crimes account for approximately half the offenses committed in East Germany, and crimes against the person are declining with particular rapidity, another indication of the impact of the developmental process.[12]

The number of individuals charged and convicted in Yugoslavia had declined since the 1950s although the conviction rate has increased since the 1960s.[13] Yugoslavia has a generally higher crime rate than that reported by East Germany but one roughly comparable to that observed in Hungary. Crimes against the person have declined significantly since the 1960s. From 1960 through 1969 between 48,000 and 60,000 individuals were accused annually of crimes against life and limb while the corresponding figure for 1976 was around 38,000. Crimes against the person represented a larger share of total crime commission in Yugoslavia than in most socialist countries as nearly 25 percent of all reported crimes were attributable to this group of offenses.[14] As in East Germany and Bulgaria, nearly half of the crimes committed are against private and social property.

Because limited crime statistics are published in Bulgaria, it is hard to know much about the actual rates of crime commission in that country. Newspaper reports, however, reveal a significant increase in crime commission in such categories as theft of socialist property, currency violation, and crimes committed by juvenile offenders. The general trend in criminality has been upward since 1962, although the present national commission rate of approximately 400 offenses per 100,000 is approximately 20–25 percent less than the rates recorded during certain war years and in the period immediately following the war when socialism was first introduced in Bulgaria.[15] Crimes against the person have oscillated from a high in 1960 to a rate half that in the mid-1960s, back to the present rates that nearly reach the high of two decades ago. Rates recorded for premeditated murder have generally followed the patterns observed for other violent offenses. The trend in property crimes has generally been upward. Open stealing, one of the most serious property crimes, has increased over fivefold during the period from 1959 to 1973.[16] Crimes against the person represent over a quarter of all offenses and another half are comprised of political crimes, misappropriation, and economic offenses.[17]

Czechoslovakia, like Bulgaria, reports an increased rate of criminality since 1968. The number of convictions rose from 83,941 in 1968 to 149,981 in 1970. Such a rapid rate of growth is probably a reflection both of increased social tensions leading to higher rates of deviant behavior and of the increasingly harsh attitude displayed towards offenders by members of the criminal justice system. These differential patterns of law enforcement have also affected the crime rates observed for different categories of criminal activity. From 1958 through 1967 crimes against property represented between one-fifth and one-third of all offenses, only to rise slightly in 1968 and decline after that. The growth in violent crimes against the person has been significant but not consistent as crimes against the person reached a nadir in 1968.[18]

The Soviet Union makes fewer crime statistics available than any of the socialist countries previously discussed. Soviet authorities vehemently contend that the rate of crime commission in their country is declining; but they provide no hard evidence to substantiate their claim, and much other evidence points to the fact that their crime rates are actually increasing, particularly in certain categories. Some of the evidence indicative of a growing crime rate are newspaper reports and criminological commentaries on the increasing problem of juvenile crime, increased criminal justice efforts to prevent and apprehend criminals, and a growing problem of uncontrollable behavior associated with ever larger rates of alcohol consumption. Secret Soviet crime statistics for 1976 published in the West reveal a total rate of 1,064 convictions per 100,000 for both serious and minor forms of criminality.[19] The discrepancy that exists almost universally between crimes reported and actual convictions suggests that the Soviet Union has a crime problem at least comparable if not greater than that of Hungary.

Statistics on the distribution of criminal offenses in the late 1960s and the late 1970s show little change in the proportion of crimes committed against property and the person. At both times, crimes against the person represented 17 percent of all criminality, a figure much higher than that given for all other socialist societies and a strong indication that the Soviet Union has still not reached an advanced state of socioeconomic development. The total number of property offenses were almost equally divided between crimes against personal and public property. In the 1960s and 1970s, these crime categories together represented just a third of total crime commission.[20] The Soviet Union, therefore, had proportionately less property crime than its socialist neighbors.

Significant differences, as previously mentioned, are found between the crime patterns of the European and Asian parts of the Soviet Union. For example, some of the country's highest crime rates are found in the urbanized Baltic republics. There the majority of offenses are property crimes committed in urban areas. Juvenile crime is particularly threatening in this region of the country and in some parts of the Baltics, juveniles account for over half the arrests made,[21] a greater proportion of crime attributable to youth than in some of the most crime-prone cities of the United States. An examination of police reports from Georgia, a highly rural southern republic still dominated by traditional values, reveals very different patterns of criminal behavior and generally lower rates of crime commission from that in the Baltic republics. In the Georgian countryside, most crimes are against the person while in cities more diverse forms of property crime coexist with the usual violent offenses. In the republic as a whole, violent crimes assume a more important role and crimes against property a less central position than in the more economically developed Baltic republics.[22] The contrast in crime patterns between the two republics of the Soviet Union is a reflection of the level of socioeconomic development of these two regions.

This review of national crime trends in the Soviet Union and Eastern Europe reveals that significant variations exist in both the amounts and types of crime commission. The crime rates range from a low in Bulgaria to a high in the Soviet Union and Hungary. The reported rates of criminality in the developing and developed socialist countries are lower than the average rates of criminality reported by capitalist societies at comparable levels of economic development.

There are several reasons that authorities in socialist countries have been able to suppress the level of criminality. Large police forces in each country patrol urban areas and restrict the internal mobility of the population. Strong institutional controls are exercised by the school, the work place, and the party apparatus. All of these factors help reduce the likelihood of crime commission. The socialist countries have succeeded partially in averting the spiraling crime rates that have often accompanied industrialization by encouraging citizen participation in the criminal justice system as is done in Japan and Switzerland.[23] While the cooperation in the latter two countries is entirely voluntary, participation in and with the police and judiciary in socialist countries is both voluntary and coerced. The voluntary cooperation is, however, inspired by the same motives as in Japan and Switzerland—the shared values of the citizenry with those who enforce the laws. The communality of values among the enforcers of the law and the public is a result of the repugnance of the population towards certain categories of criminality as well as extensive propaganda that extols citizens who uphold socialist legality.

Although societal controls have helped suppress the overall level of criminality in socialist societies, they have not transformed the patterns of crime commission. In all socialist countries examined, with the exception of the Soviet Union and Czechoslovakia, property crimes represented at least half of total crime commission. Violent crimes against the person represented a relatively small share of total crime commission except in the U.S.S.R., Bulgaria, and Yugoslavia where the tendency towards violence was more pronounced. The high rate of violence in these societies can probably be explained by the significant rural populations in areas of lesser economic development.

The information on the level of crime and the relationship between rates of violent and property crime in Eastern Europe makes it possible to differentiate crime patterns in terms of the level of economic development. As explained previously, developed countries are those in which crimes against property occur much more frequently than those against the person. The present analysis suggests that Poland, Hungary, and East Germany should be classified as developed nations while Bulgaria, Yugoslavia, and the Soviet Union need to be considered as countries in the transitional stage of development. The latter three countries are, however, generally more developed than those classified as "developing" in chapter 3.

These tentative classifications can be more closely examined as a result of recent research conducted by Eastern European criminologists within their countries. Researchers in Hungary, Poland, and Yugoslavia have coordinated their research efforts in studying the relationship between the developmental process and criminality.[24] In analyzing this relationship they have surveyed numerous indicators of development such as the national distribution of the population, the age and educational structure, the means of mass communication, the standard of living and the gross national product, medical care, level of industrialization, and geographical mobility of the population. Studies in all three countries concluded that, despite internal differences in the process of modernization, the crime patterns of these nations have been significantly affected by the course of societal transition.[25]

In Hungary, the industrialization process has been more intensive rather than extensive, resulting more in increased productivity than in an increase in the number of enterprises.[26] Despite differences in the quality of development, the developmental process has had an impact on Hungary very similar to that observed elsewhere as offenses against both personal and social property increase in frequency with increased development.[27]

In Yugoslavia, research on the relationship between development and crime reveals that delinquency is greatest where the population is urban, employed outside the agricultural sector, benefits from a high standard of living, and is strongly influenced by mass communication. As in Hungary, the impact of development is most evident in crimes against property. Delinquency is lowest where the level of education is low and the population is old, both indicators of a low level of economic development.[28]

The Polish research studies on the relationship between crime and development support the findings made in Hungary and Yugoslavia. The researchers established a very strong relationship between the level of development and the level of juvenile delinquency.[29] The problems of delinquency in urban areas are augmented by the recent arrival of rural emigrants whose adjustment problems further accentuate the disproportionate urban criminality.[30] The impact of the developmental process was most pronounced on crimes against property that increased at a greater rate than it was on other categories of criminality. The demographic factors most strongly correlated with rates of criminality are the percentage of the population residing in urban areas, employment in industry, transport, and communication, and the relative prosperity of the community.[31]

These analyses of the relationship between crime and development in three Eastern European countries indicate that property crime increases with the level of development. Indicators of development are also correlated with higher levels of juvenile delinquency. In Yugoslavia, which has not reached the level of economic development achieved by Poland and Hungary, many less developed regions still manifest the crime patterns associated with developing nations.

CRIMES UNIQUE TO SOCIALIST SOCIETIES

There are several different kinds of criminality that exist only in socialist societies and are unique to the socialist process of modernization. Many of these crimes result directly from the fact that land, natural resources, and the means of production are owned either entirely or primarily by the state. Others result from the requirements of a planned economy that necessitates a degree of control over individual citizens known in almost no other societies. The crimes unique to socialist society are those related to the government monopoly over the exchange of goods and services and those related to the political control exercised over the population. All of the major socialist countries have some kinds of crime that conform to the previous description, but none of them appear to have as many unique proscriptions on human behavior as the Soviet Union.

These crimes created by socialist societies represent only a small proportion of total crime commission in these countries. Precise statements as to the percentage contribution of these crimes to total criminality are difficult to make because of the absence of complete crime statistics. The available statistics from several socialist societies in Eastern Europe suggest that in none of these countries do these distinctive crimes, excluding the category of crime against socialist property, contribute more than 10 percent of total convictions.[32] The inclusion of theft of socialist property would increase considerably the percentage of crime commission unique to socialist countries, but as most of the crimes included under this heading are nothing other than theft, robbery, and embezzlement, their inclusion would distort the overall crime picture. In each of the socialist countries, the share of criminality ascribable to these distinctly "socialist" crimes differs, but in none of the nations have prosecutions for these crimes even approached the rates recorded for the more conventional property offenses and crimes against the person.

The majority of crimes unique to socialist societies are those resulting from state ownership of land and the means of production. In some socialist countries, like the Soviet Union and China, the means of production are totally owned by the state, while in Poland and Yugoslavia, for example, it is possible to be self-employed or to work for a small-scale private enterprise. Despite these differences in economic structure, the state in socialist countries remains the largest employer and the primary owner of property. There are several principal forms of criminality in socialist countries that stem from this system of property ownership and employment: crimes against socialist property, economic crimes, and parasitism.

Crimes against socialist property encompass a full range of property crimes such as theft, burglary, and embezzlement in which the victim is not a private individual but the state. Crimes related solely to the state ownership of property, as defined by the Soviet criminal code, are negligent destruction of state property such as forests, careless maintenance of agricultural equipment, and unconscientious attitude toward protection of state property.[33] Although such crimes are not innately socialist, the near or total state monopoly on ownership of land and the means of industrial production gives these crimes additional salience within the socialist context.

The easy access to state goods in societies frequently threatened by shortages makes all forms of theft from the state common. "The 'socialist consciousness' is as yet only a distinct goal, whereas corruption is seemingly endemic to varying degrees in the socialist countries of Eastern Europe."[34] In the Soviet Union, for example, over 17 percent of all convictions are for crimes against socialist property, slightly more than the contribution of crimes against personal property to the total crime picture. In the more industrially developed countries of Poland and Hungary where property crimes are much more frequent than crimes against the person, crimes against socialist property comprise approximately 25 and 20 percent of all crimes, respectively, and are exceeded in frequency only by crimes against personal property.[35]

The types of crime included under theft of socialist property range from the theft of a few pair of rubber boots from a factory all the way up to large-scale embezzlement from a government enterprise. The reason that these crimes against socialist property are so pervasive is not only their frequency of commission but the readiness of the state to prosecute offenders. While enterprises in the West are frequently reluctant to press charges against employees whose hands are found in the till and expect a certain amount of petty thievery of office supplies, authorities in socialist countries show no such hesitation to press charges against a large number of offenders in this category. Not only is the state willing to try such individuals, but in the Soviet Union, several hundred individuals are executed annually for large-scale embezzlement of socialist property.[36] The number of individuals prosecuted in socialist countries for crimes against public or social property represents only a fraction of the possible defendants.

Another form of criminality related to the state's partial or total monopoly on the means of production and consequently on employment is parasitism. This crime is a direct outgrowth of the ideological belief "to each according to his needs, from each according to his labor." Translated into specific terms, all are required to work unless in ill health or supported by their husbands.

The parasite law was first introduced in the Soviet Union in 1961 and was subsequently introduced in Hungary, East Germany, Bulgaria, and Czechoslovakia. In some of the criminal codes, the crime of parasitism is grouped under the same article with prostitution and procuring. In some socialist countries, such as Hungary, the existence of parasite laws has always been controversial, but in the Soviet Union the controversy surrounding this law has centered primarily on its application. The potential for misuse of the law through its application to politically undesirable elements is possible in all socialist countries, but the threat posed to individuals by the parasite laws is greatest in the Soviet Union because there are almost no possibilities for employment outside of state enterprises.

Few individuals outside of the Soviet Union have been affected by the parasite laws. Despite the fact that two other crimes are grouped under this article, no more than a few hundred individuals have been prosecuted for these offenses in the countries of Eastern Europe. In the Soviet Union, in the early 1970s, more arrests were made for parasitism, when calculated on a per capita basis, than in all the other socialist countries. A massive Soviet police study of the application of the parasite laws in the late 1960s showed that in a 10-month period over 6,000 individuals were processed nationwide under this act and many were sent into exile as a result of convictions.[37] More recently this penalty imposed on parasites has had unforeseen consequences for the social order of the rest of the country, which has led to its less diligent application by the police.

Probably the most important crimes resulting from the existence of a socialist economy are the "economic crimes," which include a wide range of offenses linked to the abolition of the capitalist system and the management of a state-run economy. In the Soviet Union and in many other socialist countries, the following crimes are included under this heading: issuance of poor quality goods, distortion of accounts concerning the fulfillment of the plan, misappropriation of goods for resale, private entrepreneurial activity, speculation, damaging of crops, and violation of mining and forestry regulations. Differences exist in the definition of these offenses among socialist countries dependent on the extent of capitalist activity permissible. For example, the total ban on private enterprise is confined to the Soviet Union and other entirely socialized economies, i.e., China, Cuba, and Bulgaria, and speculation is defined differently in Poland than in the U.S.S.R. because of allowances made for limited capitalist activity.

This group of crimes is essential to the preservation of the socialist economy. For without the application of sufficient penalties to curtail the profit-seeking motive in human beings, it would be difficult to sustain the total or partial ban on private industrial production and on speculation (the purchase and resale of goods at a profit). The criminal code, therefore, assumes a central function in the socialist system by assuring that criminal sanctions are applied to those who fail to fulfill national economic objectives or who seek to engage in private entrepreneurial activities prohibited by the government.

In none of the socialist countries do these crimes represent a large share of total criminality but in many of the countries the volume and scale of the illegal operations represent a substantial financial loss to the centralized economy. The socialist countries differ in their readiness to prosecute economic crimes. In the Soviet Union and Yugoslavia, convictions for these crimes are several times more frequent than in Poland and Hungary. For contrasting reasons, both Yugoslavia and the Soviet Union may both feel especially vulnerable to economic infractions against their regime. Both Poland and Hungary maintain a middle position in regards to the extent of permissible capitalist activity and, therefore, may not feel as threatened by economic crimes as liberal Yugoslavia and the socialistically orthodox Soviet Union. Yugoslavia and the U.S.S.R. both believe they must work harder to maintain the economic systems they presently have.

The conditions of socialist society make both large-scale theft of socialist property and economic crimes nearly inevitable. The problems inherent in running a large-scale centralized economy make the problem of shortages nearly chronic. The emphasis in these highly militarized states on hardware rather than consumer durables further compounds the constant problems of short supply of goods sorely desired by the public. These conditions lead to the "second" or parallel economy where needed goods and services are furnished illegally to the general population.

The corruption in Eastern Europe and the Soviet Union is "not of the same sort as that in African and Asian nations,"[38] but it is surely as pervasive as that discussed in chapter 3 in reference to developing countries. In both socialist and developing societies the extent of corruption now known is associated with the process of modernization, but in the case of developing countries it results from a historical tradition whereas in most socialist countries it has risen anew as a necessary response to the economic rigidity of the present regimes.

The third area of criminal law that can be classified as distinctly socialist is the laws governing travel both within and outside socialist countries. Socialist countries justify the significant controls they maintain over the movements of their populations as necessary for the operation of a planned economy which requires control over human as well as material resources. Socialist countries are the only societies in the world to circumscribe the movement of their population both within and outside their countries. The controls are achieved through provisions in the criminal code as well as by other published and unpublished legal acts.

The laws controlling internal and external population mobility in most socialist countries are included in sections of the criminal code devoted to crimes against the state and the system of administration.

Provisions are made in these sections of the criminal code not only for such internationally recognized offenses as treason and illegal dealings in hard currencies but for such crimes as illegal exit abroad, failure to return to the homeland, illegal entry into border areas, and violation of external and internal passport rules. Not all of the socialist societies, however, have provisions for all of these offenses in their criminal codes. For example, Hungary makes it a crime to fail to denounce an individual who intends to cross the border illegally, a provision absent from the Soviet criminal code.

These political laws and their enforcement help shape the distinctive character of socialist criminality. Even though socialist authorities try their best to mask the extent of criminal activity in these areas, it is possible to obtain some fragmentary evidence of the contribution of these crimes. The majority of the offenders in the Soviet Union convicted of crimes against the state have not been accused of treason or anti-Soviet agitation and propaganda. Instead they are convicted of currency violations and illegal attempts to cross the border. There is substantial evidence that the passport laws are applied, in the U.S.S.R. and to a lesser extent in other socialist countries, in a selective way. For example, thousands of individuals reside illegally in major cities without ever being prosecuted for their violations of the passport laws. It is violations of the passport laws, however, rather than new acts of criminality that return many ex-offenders to prison. The passport laws governing those released from corrective labor institutions are even stricter than those for the general population.[39] Thus, they provide increased options for local Soviet police authorities who want to revoke the freedom of those who they believe have returned to a criminal way of life but against whom there is insufficient evidence to press for criminal convictions.

It is this sweeping authority granted to law enforcement officials in socialist countries that helps make the crime patterns of socialist countries distinctive from those of other societies at a comparable level of development.

The socialist countries have both created and abolished forms of criminal behavior. While the new forms of criminality were created by means of legal sleight of hand, the reduced frequency of certain forms of criminality is both a consequence of the conditions of socialist society and intense law enforcement efforts. Socialist societies have succeeded in substantially reducing the level of organized crime and such "victimless crimes" as large-scale gambling, pornography, houses of prostitution, and organized vice rings.[40] The success of the socialist countries in controlling all but limited incidences of these previously common forms of behavior is explained not by the unique conditions of socialist society but by the distinctive abilities of these highly centralized societies to summon and coordinate all possible resources in order to suppress these forms of criminal activity. By the time of Stalin's death, the Soviet Union had rid itself of the problem of organized crime by physically eliminating a generation of such offenders. The purge destroyed both the existing ranks and the teachers of a future generation of organized criminals.

Another group of crimes whose commission rates have been significantly reduced by the conditions of socialist society are those related to the economic operation of the capitalist system. Representative offenses in this group are tax evasion, loan sharking, and fraudulent statements and forging of signatures in order to acquire loans.[41] In socialist societies where tax payments are automatically deducted from paychecks and loans are almost unknown, except among friends, the financial incentives necessary for the commission of these crimes are absent.

Socialist societies have created distinctive patterns of criminality within their societies. Although the observed crime patterns for property offenses and for crimes against the person resemble those of capitalist societies at similar levels of economic development, these societies have nearly eliminated certain forms of criminal activity prevalent in capitalist societies and have created other forms of criminal behavior unique to their societies.

GEOGRAPHY OF CRIME

The geography of crime in socialist countries reflects both the level of socioeconomic development of these nations and the controls exercised over the populations of socialist societies. The following discussion of crime within socialist countries addresses the national distribution of criminality, the differences between crime rates and offense types in urban and rural areas, and the distribution of crime within urban areas. This analysis reveals that the Soviet Union and Bulgaria, because of their unique population controls, have a distribution of criminality very different from that of both developing and developed countries. Many of the other socialist countries share several, though not all, of these distinctive geographical features.

From their teenage years, members of all socialist countries (except for collective farm workers in the U.S.S.R. who have only recently become eligible for passports) are required to possess internal passports that establish their places of residence and control their movements within their countries. The passports, issued by the police, must be carried at all times. The passports control not only travel but permanent movement between cities because no individual can move to a new place of residence without police permission and the entry of a change of address on their internal passport by the police authorities.[42] All violators of the passport laws are subject to the imposition of criminal sanctions.

In some of the socialist countries such as the Soviet Union and Bulgaria, these passport regulations concerning individual movement are supplemented by significant controls over movement into cities. As no individual is able to move to another city without the permission of police authorities, the existence of approximately 25 *rezhimnyi* cities (closed to future settlers) in the U.S.S.R. and 16 in Bulgaria prevent the entry into cities of masses of rural emigrants. Thus, rural emigrants are forced into areas that cannot afford to be selective about the individuals they choose to register in their communities.

Crime in the Soviet Union and Bulgaria, as in most nations, is greatest in urban areas. Urban crime in the U.S.S.R. exceeds rural criminality by as much as 40 percent,[43] but in Bulgaria such a significant difference exists solely in regard to juvenile criminality. Surprisingly, in Bulgaria commission rates for adults in urban and rural areas are much less differentiated than for juveniles.[44] This suggests that effects of industrialization, urbanization, and lessened social control are experienced more by juveniles than by adults.

As demonstrated in the previous chapters, rates of criminality in most countries ascend with degree of urbanization. This relationship does not exist in the Soviet Union and Bulgaria as the highest rates of criminality are not found in the largest cities of Moscow, Leningrad, and Sofia but in smaller urban communities. In the Soviet Union, the crime rate is highest in Vladivostok, the Far Eastern port city, and the recently developing cities of the Far Eastern and the Far Northern Russian Soviet Federated Socialist Republic (RSFSR).[45] In Bulgaria, the highest crime rates are reported in Lowec, a recently developed urban center and in two cities with traditionally high crime rates: Ruse, the Danube port city, and Sliwen, at the juncture of several major national highways.[46] Both of these older cities have criminal traditions that predate the socialist period. The major cities and recently developed urban centers in Bulgaria have somewhat lower rates of criminality than the three cities previously mentioned. Therefore, in Bulgaria as in the Soviet Union, the highest rates of criminality are not recorded in the largest cities but in areas of rapid development and in areas with highly transient populations.

The current distribution of crime in the U.S.S.R. and Bulgaria is different from that of both capitalist and socialist industrialized and industrializing countries as a result of the degree of control exercised by the governments of these two countries over their domestic populations. The controls maintained by the more orthodox socialist societies over the course of their internal development differentiates their crime patterns from those of societies which permit modernization to progress without significant governmental interference.

The demographic policies implemented through the internal passport and registration system have prevented convicted offenders and the youthful work force from congregating in cities. As a result of these controls, youthful males and recidivists, the most crime-prone groups, have been unable to settle in the largest cities. They have instead settled in recently developed urban centers, in smaller cities with highly transient populations, and in towns on the perimeters of major urban centers. For this reason the highest rates of criminality in the U.S.S.R. are found in those urbanizing and newly developed cities where the planned economy has resulted in the isolation of young men from women, the concentration of recidivists, and a generally unstable population.[47] Similar laws and social policies have spared the largest Bulgarian cities of Sofia and Plovdiv the very high rates of criminality associated with the largest cities of Western industrialized countries.[48]

As laws prohibit additional settlement in the largest cities of Bulgaria and the U.S.S.R., migrants from rural areas are forced to settle in the smaller, presently industrializing cities. These cities are, therefore, attracting a youthful, primarily male urban work force that is unaccustomed to the conditions of urban life. These individuals who frequently migrate on their own without their families, benefit from none of the stabilizing influences that tend to reduce the likelihood of deviance in a recently settled urban area.

The youthful work force, denied entry to major Bulgarian and Soviet cities, settles instead in the towns that surround the major urban centers. Unlike the suburbs of the United States and Western Europe these fringe communities are not the protected preserve of the affluent from urban problems. But in the Soviet Union and Bulgaria, as in

South America, the population residing outside the city limits is the source of a large proportion of urban crime.[49] In these two socialist countries, unlike Latin America, the contribution of the commuting criminals does not result in exceedingly high urban crime rates because individuals residing within the confines of the largest Bulgarian and Soviet cities have artificially low crime rates.

Migrants from rural areas contribute to an increase in criminality in cities, in areas of recent settlement, and in areas inhabited by individuals culturally different from the immigrants. The newly established Bulgarian cities, created by youthful workers in the post-World War II period, have some of the highest crime rates recorded within Bulgaria. Soviet crime statistics suggest a similar relationship between migration and crime.

Soviet researchers studying crime in the Russian republic have learned that a region with a high coefficient of migrants is characterized by a higher coefficient of crime. Research first conducted between 1963 and 1965 demonstrated the relationship between rural to urban migration and crime.[50] A later study conducted in 1968 revealed that seven of the eight *oblasts* with the greatest number of migrants, many of them inhabited by non-Slavic peoples (Tiumen, Magadan, Kamchatka, Yakutsk, Tuva, Komi, Krasnoyarsk, and Primorskii) had the highest recorded rates of criminality. In the 20 oblasts with the least influx of population, 13 of the 20 regions were in the lower half of all RSFSR oblasts in terms of their rates of criminality.[51]

These analyses of the impact of migration on crime both confirm and refute some of the conclusions reached in the previous two chapters. In both developed and developing capitalist countries, researchers discerned an increase in criminality among recent arrivals in urban areas emigrating from rural areas of the same culture, whereas migrants from a different culture usually have lower rates of criminality than the resident population. The Soviet Union differs from these internationally observed crime patterns because both types of migrants in the U.S.S.R. are responsible for more crime than the indigenous population.

The reason that the Soviet migrants to areas with cultures different from their own have such high rates of criminality, unlike the experiences of most other societies, may be explained by the fact that the migrants are still residing within their country. Migrants and foreign workers in Europe, Australia, and Canada may feel compelled to behave because they are not citizens or can easily lose their residence rights. However, the Soviet migrants who move to a culturally distinct area within or outside their republic, are frequently Russians who are not moving to a foreign country and who may feel superior to the native population.

The crime patterns of rural areas in both Bulgaria and the Soviet Union do not differ significantly from those of other nations. In both countries rural areas have very low rates of criminality. In Bulgaria, in 1973, only 37 percent of adult criminals and 31 percent of juvenile offenders committed their crimes in rural areas at a time when the country was 44 percent rural.[52] In the U.S.S.R. urban crime rates are a full 40 percent higher than in rural areas.[53] The contrast in these two societies between the crime rates of both urban and rural areas may be even more marked than in many other nations previously discussed. Urban residents in these two countries do not venture into rural areas, an increasingly common phenomenon in many other societies,[54] because of the poverty and inaccessibility of the countryside. The same conditions have also produced the mass exodus of the youthful work force from the rural areas of the western U.S.S.R. and Bulgaria, leaving the countryside to elderly women unlikely to perpetrate many offenses apart from bootlegging.

The distinctive geography of crime observed in Bulgaria and the U.S.S.R. is a consequence of the socialist form of economic development where the state maintains ownership over the means of production and organizes its economy through centralized planning and controls over the movement of the labor force. In other socialist countries, where not as many controls are placed over the movement of the population within the country and state ownership of the means of the production is not total, the internal distribution of criminality resembles more closely that of capitalist developing and developed nations where no constraints are placed on the process of urbanization.

The relationship between population migration and the general geographic distribution of criminality has been studied in Poland, Yugoslavia, and to a lesser extent in Hungary. In these three countries, the distribution of crime among cities and between urban and rural areas resembles the patterns of criminality discussed in the previous chapters. Only in the case of the newly industrialized cities of these nations do the crime patterns observed conform to the "socialist" model of criminal distribution observed in Bulgaria and the Soviet

Union. Most of the research on the geography of crime in these three Eastern European nations has been conducted in reference to juvenile offenders, the group of criminals most affected by the destabilizing influences of the modernization process.

In Poland, the level of juvenile delinquency is correlated both with the degree of urbanization and the level of industrialization of a particular region. In almost all the 16 districts of the Gdansk *voivodship* (a geographical region similar to a province), the higher the level of urbanization and the greater the percentage of the population employed in industrial rather than agricultural production, the higher the coefficient of criminality recorded for the region.[55]

Between 1946 and 1960, three and a half million Poles left their original rural residences and moved to cities.[56] These rural emigrants moved not only to established urban centers but also to recently founded communities. The adjustment problems of these migrants were manifested in criminality and in other forms of social deviance. Pathology such as alcoholism and family disorganization are more pronounced in the cities experiencing their initial growth than in cities with more established social organizations.

A Polish study that compared rates of juvenile crime in both an older established city and a newly established town found very different rates of criminality for juvenile offenders of all age groups. The new town of Nowa Huta had a rate of 21.2 delinquents per 1,000 for the 10–17 age group while the established city of Sosnowiec had a comparable rate of 13.9. The two cities were comparable in both population size and level of industrialization. Although the female offenders were responsible for only a small share of all criminality, the differences in the proportional contribution of the female offender population was even more pronounced in these two cities. In Sosnowiec there were 0.9 female delinquents per 1,000 while the comparable figure was 2.6 in the new town of Nowa Huta.[57]

A more extensive study of delinquency in "new" as opposed to well-established provinces in Poland concluded that the higher level of criminality observed in these recently settled areas was a consequence both of intense geographical mobility as well as of their more advanced economic development. The former factor explained why even in the eastern provinces with a lower level of economic development, the level of juvenile delinquency is still quite high.[58]

Research on the relationship between migration and crime also demonstrated the negative effect of recent population influx from the countryside on rates of criminality in Yugoslavia. In Yugoslavia the greatest growth in urban populations, a result of rural emigration in the period 1953 to 1961, was observed in the smaller cities with population of 20,000 to 50,000 rather than in the larger urban centers. As in the U.S.S.R., it was in these smallest cities where new migrants represented a significant share of the population that crime increased most significantly. In almost all the cities studied, regardless of size, the proportional contribution of delinquent immigrants was higher than that of the native population,[59] providing further evidence to support the thesis that the adjustment problems accompanying rural emigration all too frequently produce criminality.

The high rates of criminality associated with the new and expanding towns and cities of Poland and Yugoslavia recall the experience of the Soviet Union and Bulgaria rather than the crime patterns of western countries. The distinctive ability of socialist countries to organize both economic and human resources for the creation of new urban centers is a feat not possible in societies where the economy is not centralized and the government has no control over the movement of the population. These aspects of socialist society have created a distinctive geography of crime that differentiates socialist from capitalist countries. In Poland, Bulgaria, the U.S.S.R., and Yugoslavia alone no correlation exists between the level of urbanization and criminality as the highest crime rates in these countries are in the smaller burgeoning cities.

The crime rates of urban and rural areas are also sharply differentiated in Poland. In 1960, Polish nationwide conviction statistics for the 17-to-20 age group showed an average of 47.3 convictions per 1,000 males; but the rural rate was only 40.7 while the urban rate was 55.6. Female offenders demonstrated even more pronounced differences in their rates of urban and rural criminality though their commission rate was less than one-fifth of that for males in the same age group. The conviction rates for females in 1960 were 10.6 and 5.1 convictions per 10,000 in cities and the countryside, respectively.[60] The urban-rural difference in female criminality may be explained by the more active role of women in the economies of urban communities, a role that subsequently provides them with more opportunities to commit crimes.

Research conducted in the same year revealed that similar urban-rural differences exist for commission as well as conviction rates. Polish research reveals that the rate of delinquency in a city may be two or three times higher than the rate recorded in the surrounding area. Despite the differences in rates, urban and rural areas in the same region are both affected similarly by the forces that either suppress or contribute to criminality. Therefore, the rural areas surrounding cities with high rates of criminality are also plagued by disproportionately high crime rates.[61]

In Poland, a disproportionate number of sentenced individuals resides in cities. In 1973, 53.1 percent of the total population lived in towns but 64.3 percent of those sentenced resided in urban areas. Those who reside in cities are more likely to commit financial crimes or crimes against personal dignity and personal inviolability, while rural offenders more frequently commit crimes against the person, the public, and traffic safety.[62]

Another important factor to be considered in the geography of crime in socialist countries is the impact of seasonal tourism. Each year Yugoslavia, Romania, and Bulgaria receive large numbers of both foreign and domestic tourists at their many beaches and other resort areas. This large population influx from both socialist and capitalist countries has resulted in an increasing problem of criminality in these areas and generally high rates of criminality in areas where the native population contributes little to the total crime rate.[63]

Extensive research in Yugoslavia on the relationship between the tourist season and vacation spots on the level and distribution of criminality reveals a significant increase in criminality in the summer months as well as a significant annual increase in the number of tourists annually arrested while visiting the resort areas of Yugoslavia. In 1969, nearly 6,000 arrests were made of tourists in Yugoslavia, nearly double the overall rate for 1959 and triple the summer rates recorded during the same year.[64] The criminality of tourists in rural areas provides the only exception to the generalization that higher crime rates are observed in urban rather than rural areas.

Crime in socialist societies as in capitalistic developing and developed societies is concentrated most heavily in particular areas of the urban environment. These regions are characterized by both high levels of property crime and crimes of violence. These high rates of criminality exist despite the fact that the government in socialist societies exercises significant control over the nature of the urban population and the physical structure and settlement patterns within the confines of the city.

As was discussed in the previous chapters, the concentration of criminality in particular urban regions has been explained by the social disorganization of ghetto life deemed conducive to the proliferation of illegal activity. Another explanation of high city crime rates attributes the intensity of criminality in certain urban neighborhoods to the population density of a particular region. Neither of these theories serves to explain criminality in socialist societies. The government, through its intense involvement in community organizations and its control over the resident population and over the extent and type of construction in each neighborhood should produce a more uniform distribution of urban crime commission.

All the evidence points to the contrary. Socialist societies, as a result of historical traditions and contemporary conditions, have also produced neighborhoods with excessive criminality. Research in many of the Eastern European countries and the Soviet Union has shown that in most major cities, areas of the city inhabited primarily by workers who have recently emigrated from the countryside as well as areas with long-standing reputations for criminality have disproportionately high rates of criminality.

Research in Poland provides strong evidence of the detrimental impact on crime of large-scale migration to particular urban areas. An analysis of the crime coefficients of established communities in contrast to those settled by new migrants (those arrived since 1945) reveals very great differences in rates of criminality. The more complete the transition in the post-1945 period in a particular town or city, the higher the recorded rate of criminality. This study, isolating the impact of the recently arrived urban work force from that of the more permanently settled urban population, reveals that changes in social structure that have reduced community stability and integration among the urban population have been particularly conducive to high rates of urban crime commission.[65]

Studies in Moscow and Orel revealed very much the same findings as the Polish research. In Orel, one area of the city was found to have a particularly high index of crime, recidivism, dangerous criminality, and retention rate of individuals on charges of petty hooliganism, while another region of the city had much lower indices of criminality than average.[66] In Moscow, recent studies have shown that crime is concentrated in the older sections of the city that have traditionally had high rates of criminality and in new regions of the city that house workers who have only recently emigrated from the countryside.[67] Crime rates are also higher in the areas surrounding train stations—locations with highly transient populations.[68]

Research on the spatial distribution of crime in Ljubljana, Yugoslavia, reveals that 25 percent of all known offenses were committed in 0.9 percent of the total land area of the city. The area of the city where these crimes were committed was not the area of residence of the offenders but the center of the city that housed the bus and railroad terminals, markets, and entertainment areas. The majority of the criminal offenders were lower-class individuals who came to the city center because of the services it provided.[69]

The urban criminological research of Poland, the Soviet Union, and Yugoslavia suggests that, despite the controls that the government has over settlement patterns and services within the urban community, the centralized authorities have not been able to prevent the localization of criminality in particular urban areas. Crime rates are greatest in areas inhabited or frequented by lower-class individuals often recently emigrated from the countryside.

The geography of criminality reveals the difference between socialist and capitalist countries in the effect of the developmental process. The unique ability of authorities in socialist countries to maintain some control over the internal movements of their populations has resulted in a geographical distribution of criminality different from that in many capitalist societies, but the controls and planning mechanisms are not strong enough to prevent the concentration of crime in certain urban areas or the differentiation of crime patterns and rates in urban and rural areas.

THE CRIMINAL POPULATION

The criminal population in socialist countries resembles that of capitalist societies at comparable levels of socioeconomic development. In these countries as elsewhere, criminality is primarily a male activity. Available statistics from the socialist countries demonstrate that in no country do women represent more than a sixth of all apprehended criminals. In the Soviet Union, women commit one-sixth or one-seventh of all crimes and their criminality is concentrated primarily in embezzlement, theft, and speculation.[70] In Poland, Yugoslavia, Hungary, and Bulgaria the sexual differences in commission rates are just as pronounced. In Yugoslavia in 1976, 113,576 men were convicted while 17,163 women were sentenced.[71] Hungarian juvenile crime statistics for the period 1963–1967 reveal that of the 17,938 individuals convicted during that period, only 2,300 were girls.[72] In Poland in 1970 less than 8 percent of convicted juveniles were female while the comparable figure for adults was slightly over 10 percent.[73]

In Bulgaria in the period 1959 to 1973, women were responsible for between 9.3 and 16.6 percent of all crimes but their total contribution to criminality was declining in relationship to men.[74] There is no indication that women in other socialist countries contribute to any greater or lesser extent to crime commission.

In all the countries mentioned women contribute approximately one-sixth or one-seventh of all crimes. This proportional contribution of the sexes to criminality corresponds to that observed in other developed countries. Only less economically developed Bulgaria shows adult female offenders committing less than 10 percent of total crime, a characteristic of criminality previously observed in the chapter on developing countries. Polish research indicates that female commission rates rise in relation to males in the urban environment.[75] More recent research in Poland[76] and Yugoslavia[77] demonstrates that the level of socioeconomic development is closely correlated with the rate of female delinquency. This research supports the observation made in capitalist developed societies that increased female criminality is a consequence of the modernization process.

With increasing development, juveniles as well as females contribute increasingly to total criminality. In the socialist countries, as elsewhere, juvenile crime is primarily an urban problem and its increase is very closely associated with the growth of cities. In Bulgaria, for example, in the years 1965 to 1973, between 61 percent and 73 percent of all convicted juveniles committed their crimes in urban areas during a period when no more than 62 percent of convicted adults perpetrated their offenses in cities.[78] The urban character of juvenile delinquency is equally or more pronounced in the Soviet Union as "seventy-five percent of juvenile violations are said to take place in cities, demonstrating an overrepresentation of urban youth in such offenses by one and one-half."[79]

Polish research on juvenile delinquency has focused on the relationship between urbanization and the increase in youth crime.[80] Extensive research in 1957–1961 in the 16 districts of the Gdansk *voivod* found that delinquency was greatest where the level of industrial development and urbanization was highest and where there had been the greatest displacement of the population since World War II.[81] Parallel national research in the same period demonstrated that in rural areas, where significant numbers of individuals are employed outside of the agricultural sector, higher rates of juvenile delinquency are observed.[82]

The Gdansk research has some broader implications for the examination of the impact of the modernization process in socialist countries on patterns of criminality. The positive correlations that were established between delinquency rates and the percentage of the population residing in urban areas, working outside of the agricultural sector, and employed in industry have been observed in countries undergoing the capitalist form of economic development.[83] Under both socialist and capitalist modernization the greatest increase in crime and juvenile delinquency occurs in the initial stages of the urbanization process. As the Gdansk research indicates, when new social and community ties develop, the growth of crime and other forms of social pathology is arrested.[84]

The Gdansk research, however, provides some evidence of the distinctive effects on criminality of the socialist process of modernization. The researcher found that delinquency rates were correlated with the percentage of arable land in the socialist rather than in the privately owned sector.[85] "The socialization of agriculture . . . can be seen as part of the extension of urbanism or 'modernity' in the countryside—a process which apparently has some implications for deviant behavior. Poland, with its large private agricultural sector for 'contrast,' provides the clearest illustration of this." The impact of modernization in the Polish countryside, Connor suggests, may be so significant because modern technology, communication, and transportation have accompanied the advent of socialism in this area.[86] According to this observation, the more economically developed countries of Czechoslovakia and Hungary should follow the Polish pattern. In contrast, Bulgaria and the U.S.S.R., which have completely socialized agriculture without the benefits of advanced technology, should not adhere to the correlation between modernization and rural crime observed in Poland.

This discussion of the offender in socialist societies has focused on the demographic characteristics of the criminal population but has provided little information about the social, educational, or familial backgrounds of the individual criminals. In almost all the socialist societies for which there is available information, all indicators point to the fact that the criminal is at a disadvantage compared to the general population in terms of almost every available indicator. The criminal population, as a group, has not benefited to the extent of the rest of the population from the improved standard of living and the social advantages that have accompanied the process of industrialization under socialism.

In socialist countries, as in other societies examined in this book, the criminal population is not drawn from the educated or bureaucratic elite or from the peasant population; instead, the majority of criminals are youthful male workers. Although socialist societies do not like to admit that criminality is most concentrated among the group that should have benefited most from the advent of socialism, certain scattered data from these societies point to the heightened criminality of these individuals.

Research and crime reports from the Soviet Union demonstrate that although criminals are drawn from all social strata of the population, the preponderance of criminals comes from the urban working class.[87] This is true both for the Russian republic and the highly urbanized Estonian republic[88] as well as for the much less developed Georgian republic in the Caucasus.[89] Bulgarian crime rates seem to confirm this trend as most of the criminal population is drawn from the youthful urban work force.[90]

Yugoslavia and Poland are most open about the contribution of lower working-class individuals to their nation's criminality. Yugoslavian researchers even investigated the reasons that street crime has been the prime form of illegal activity of members of the working class.[91] The Poles, in their studies of crime and development, provide data on the social position of the delinquents' families. Between 1953 and 1960, 60 to 62 percent of the juveniles processed through the criminal justice system had parents who were manual workers, and an additional 4 to 5 percent had parents on welfare. Less than 10 percent of the delinquents had parents employed in office or professional positions.[92] A smaller scale study of juvenile delinquents and young adult offenders in the new town of Nowa Huta in the early 1960s reveals that nearly three-fourths of the offenders were workers whose parents were small-scale farmers.[93] It seems that this group of workers of recent peasant origins is the one that suffers most severely from the adjustment problems associated with modernization.

Although little data is available from other socialist countries on the social origins of the criminal population, the preponderance of criminality in the urban areas of those nations suggests that there, too, manual workers are disproportionately represented in the criminal population. The advantages that supposedly accrue to workers under the socialist system do not include a dispensation from criminality.

The difference between the educational level of criminals and the general population is in all cases significant. Strong evidence from all socialist countries for which data are available suggests that the criminal population does not take advantage of the educational opportunities made available to them. Researchers in the U.S.S.R. point out repeatedly that criminals have a low educational level particularly those residing in rural areas.[94] Certain categories of criminals such as murderers, hooligans, and recidivists have especially low levels of educational attainment.[95] In the 1960s 67.8 percent of murderers had only a seventh grade education while the comparable figure for the general population was 59.5 percent in 1959.[96] In Bulgaria, the Sliwen *okrug* (district), one of the regions with the highest rates of criminality, is a food and textile producing area where little incentive exists for educational attainment; and consequently, a significant number of criminals were school dropouts. The rest of the Bulgarian criminal population has also been characterized as possessing limited education or the specialized skills required for advancement in industrial society.[97] Polish research also attests to the low level of educational attainment among the delinquent and young adult criminal populations. Research in Nowa Huta reveals that 40 percent of those arrested there had caused serious problems in school.[98] Truancy among delinquents is a particularly severe problem which may help contribute to the fact that 50 percent of the juvenile offenders were required to repeat a grade in school while the comparable figure for their age group was 10 to 15 percent. A very significant share of the delinquents were three or more years behind in their grade level. Youthful offenders are also more likely to drop out of school and among this group, 20 to 25 percent of them left school before the minimum leaving age of 14.[99]

The poor home environment of criminal offenders may help explain why criminals are so educationally disadvantaged. Studies throughout the Soviet Union support the findings of research conducted in Moscow in the 1960s showing that as many as half of the delinquents did not have both parents at home. Not only are delinquents disproportionately victims of broken homes but there are many indications that their parents generally had a lower level of educational attainment than the national average.[100] Polish research demonstrated that in that country as well a significant share of the delinquents grew up in homes without both parents. Between 1953 and 1956, one-third of the delinquents were orphans or came from one-parent homes, but by 1960 that figure had declined to slightly less than one-quarter.[101] Although these figures are considerably lower than in the Soviet Union, it must be remembered that in Catholic Poland, divorces and separations are less frequent than in the U.S.S.R.

The available data from different socialist countries suggest that, despite significant governmental intervention in the child-rearing process, the demographic characteristics of offenders in these countries differ little from their counterparts in capitalist societies. Convicted juveniles and adults are more than likely to be young urban males of working-class background, often recent migrants from rural areas, from broken homes, and with a lower than usual educational level.

RECIDIVISM

Does the extent of governmental control over the lives of citizens of socialist countries have an effect on later stages of the criminal career? While all societies have control over the offender during the period of institutional confinement, socialist authorities have more control over the convicted criminal. This control is achieved by means of the internal passport and registration system and in some socialist countries, the settlement patterns of released convicts. Has this degree of governmental intervention been successful in averting recidivism?

The answer is a qualified yes. Several of the socialist countries for which statistics are available tend to show a lower rate of recidivism than the rate of at least 50 percent reported by most capitalist societies. The Soviet Union reports an average rate of recidivism among all convicted offenders of 30 to 35 percent. Recidivism among violent offenders has increased dramatically while the level of recidivism among property offenders has consistently remained at 33 percent. Men are more frequently recidivists than women.[102] In the years 1963 to 1967, only 5.7 percent of the women in labor camps were returnees to institutional confinement[103] while the corresponding figure for men was 30 to 50 percent. In Bulgaria, the level of recidivism has been rising almost annually between 1959 and 1973. The overall level of recidivism is around 25 percent for all offenders; approximately 42 percent of all recidivism is in the category of crimes against property while about 27 percent is for crimes against the person. The disparity between recidivism for property and violent crimes is similar to that of the Soviet Union; recidivism for crimes against the person is increasing at a faster rate than that against property. In Poland in 1962, 18 percent of the young male adult population (17-to-20 age group) were recidivists while, among those aged 20 to 25, the rate of recidivism had risen to 25 percent.[104] The research indicates that the recidivists came overwhelmingly from urban areas,[105] and their home life was much more disagreeable than that of first offenders as many of their parents were alcoholics who paid less attention to them than did the parents of first time offenders.[106] Hungary also reported a recidivism rate of approximately 20 to 35 percent in the 1960s.[107]

Do the rates of recidivism in Bulgaria, the U.S.S.R., Hungary, and Poland, which are lower than in most capitalist countries, indicate that socialist societies have discovered the key to rehabilitation or do they instead suggest that increased use of repression both within and outside of institutional confinement is conducive to less repeat criminality? The fact that both Bulgaria and the Soviet Union are encountering increased problems of repeat criminality among those who commit violent crimes against the person, a group with generally low rates of recidivism in other societies, suggests that the key to reforming criminals has yet to been found. Instead, several pieces of evidence suggest that the level of societal control exercised over released offenders explains the reduced level of recidivism in several socialist countries. Both Poland the Soviet Union are known to have a rate of institutional confinement several times higher than the United States which has the highest known rate of incarceration per capita in the western world.[108] Therefore, the socialist countries are not imprisoning just the hardcore offender population that would in all probability become recidivists. They are also confining a large number of petty criminals who are not confirmed offenders and, consequently, are unlikely to return to crime after their release. The surveillance of released convicts and the requirement in the Soviet Union and Bulgaria that serious offenders not return to their original place of residence curtail the opportunity to commit crimes. By broadening the base of the prison population and restricting the opportunities to return to criminality, socialist authorities have succeeded in lowering their recidivism rates in a way that societies that refuse to restrict personal freedom to such an extent have failed.

CRIME AND MODERNIZATION IN SOCIALIST SOCIETIES

The research discussed here indicates that, contrary to ideological expectations, the advent of socialism has not brought a diminution in criminality. Instead, development in socialist countries, like that in capitalist societies, has led to increased rates of property crime, a reduction of violent crimes relative to those committed against property, and an increase in criminality among juveniles and females. The majority of criminals, however, remain youthful male workers who have often only recently emigrated from the countryside. In both types of societies, crime is primarily an urban phenomenon and cities are characterized not only by proportionately more property crime but by the concentration of crime in particular urban neighborhoods. These similar effects of development on crime in both socialist and capitalist societies should not suggest that the two diverse forms of development have produced homogeneous crime patterns. With modernization, very great differences prevail in the crime rates, forms of crimes committed, and geographical distribution of criminality between both developing and developed capitalist and socialist societies.

The observable differences in the crime patterns of the two types of societies as a result of the modernization process are attributable both to the advent of a socialist economy as well as the level of social control necessitated by a centralized planned economy. The most direct impact of the socialization of the means of production on criminality has been the creation and the elimination of certain categories of crime. Controls in socialist societies over population migration and the construction and settlement of new urban centers have made socialist societies the exception to the internationally established correlation between the level of urbanization and criminality. The unique controls exercised by socialist societies over the mobility of their populations and the distribution of human and economic resources within their countries have produced very different rates of crime and patterns of recidivism from capitalist societies at comparable levels of economic development.

Despite the fact that socialist societies have been able to alter what were seemingly international patterns of criminality, they have been unable to realize their ideological prophecy that crime will wither away under socialism and disappear under communism. By means of ideological exhortation and coercion, socialist societies have been able to foster close citizen involvement in the criminal justice system; this action has served to suppress but not eliminate the crime problem. Socialist development has changed the quantity and quality of criminality but it has provided no panacea for the world's crime problem. Under socialism as under capitalism, crime is one of the major costs of modernization.

6

Conclusion: Modernization and Crime

This book examines the impact of modernization on crime in a historical and in a global context. It attempts to synthesize a heterogeneous body of literature on crime patterns and criminal offenders during the past two centuries. I do not confine the analysis of development and crime to just one aspect of criminality or to one region or transitional period, but try to show the extent to which the developmental process has a unifying or differentiating effect on world crime problems.

The project is by definition ambitious. No attempt has been made to provide exhaustive treatment of the subjects discussed. Instead, I survey those salient criminal characteristics and crime patterns that will reveal most successfully the impact that the transition to modernization has had on extremely diverse societies.

No previous book has attempted to examine globally the impact of the process of development upon crime. Several excellent studies have analyzed the impact of modernization on crime in selected geographical regions, nations, or time periods, but no serious attempt has been made to examine the composite implications of all of these studies except in survey articles. Researchers in the past two decades have made an increasing body of information available concerning the impact of modernization on crime during the past two centuries in different parts of the world, but these research findings have never previously been synthesized. This work is an effort to piece together information from scholars of many different cultural, national, and educational backgrounds. Publications from a number of countries have been studied, and I have used my travel experience to clarify some of the observations in the literature.

The book is different from much of contemporary sociological research because no effort has been made to collect massive data, to conduct extensive survey research, or to perform elaborate statistical analyses of available data. I have instead followed the methods of nineteenth-century sociologists who relied on previously collected data to determine the impact of the process of development on crime and the criminal population. The conclusions of this book are based on the analysis of the research findings of an international body of scholars and of national and international crime statistics. The internal reliability of much of the statistical data and the general consistency of the research findings of numerous scholars have made possible some definitive statements concerning the consequences of modernization for contemporary criminality.

The general interest in the problem of crime and the ability of even the most unsophisticated observer and international traveler to make perceptive observations concerning the impact of modernization on crime removes the novelty from much that has been discussed here. In fact, many of the points made may appear to be academic illustrations of the obvious. But it is their very "obviousness" as well as the interest of individuals everywhere in crime problems that makes the previous neglect of the composite picture of the relationship between development and crime more curious.

The value of the research conclusions in this book is not their novelty but the fact that what has for so long seemed to be the evident effects of the developmental process on crime are part of a general international and historical pattern that has broader implications for the understanding of the impact of both socialist and capitalist development on human behavior. The previous chapters provide the historical, contemporary, and international framework necessary for understanding the complex relationship between social change and criminality. Examining capitalist and socialist societies within one context makes it possible to analyze the impact that both forms of socioeconomic development have had on crime and the criminal. Only by examining cross-culturally and historically the evolution of development in diverse societies is it possible to reach conclusions that have international validity.

The previous chapters have provided ample evidence that crime patterns observed in many nations during the past two hundred years show a generally consistent response to the process of development. Present world crime patterns are not an inexplicable and unfathomable problem but an understandable reaction to the rapid social changes that have affected diverse societies in similar ways.

The changes in criminality that were observed in Britain two centuries ago with the advent of the industrial revolution have been repeated time and time again as other societies have undergone similar transitions to modernity. Modern technology, which has facilitated increased mobility and communications, has made the present-day transition qualitatively different from what it was in the first half of the nineteenth century in Western Europe, but these technological differences have failed to alter the seemingly unavoidable consequences for criminality of the process of development.

The developmental process has elevated the crime problem from that of an isolated social concern affecting primarily urban centers to a major problem of modern society. As societies have become increasingly urbanized, what was once a problem that affected the lives of the limited number of urban residents has become a problem that affects the very nature of modern existence and impedes the future course of development of many nations. Crime has become one of the most tangible and significant costs of modernization.

The universality of the crime problem in modern societies suggests that both the process of development and the achievement of development are conducive to criminality. This raises the central questions: Why is it that modernization has such a generally homogeneous effect on crime? And why is crime the barometer of this massive social change? Some would deny that development has inevitable consequences for the crime patterns of modernizing countries, by citing Japan and certain Middle Eastern countries where crime is not the problem that it is in rest of the world. The individual nations that do not conform to contemporary world crime patterns have not achieved this distinction as a result of their intentional actions, but generally because they have managed to preserve many elements of their traditional way of life in the face of encroaching modernization. The implications of this finding will be discussed more fully in the final analysis of modernization theory at the conclusion of the chapter. These nations do not then refute the thesis that development has an almost inevitable and unfortunate effect on crime patterns.

The previous chapters have shown that as the process of development has affected new nations and new regions of the world, crime patterns have repeated the transformation in criminality first observed in England two centuries ago. Neither socialist nor capitalist countries in their efforts to develop their economies have avoided the criminogenic consequences of modernization.

The changes in crime patterns observed first in England, Germany, and France as a result of the industrial revolution have accompanied modernization elsewhere. The process of urbanization accompanying industrialization has had a rapid and direct impact on crime in urban and rural areas in the nineteenth and twentieth centuries in both capitalist and socialist countries. During the initial transition to modernization, commission rates for property offenses and crimes against the person increase in urban areas, while rural areas experience a drop in criminality as a result of the population exodus to the burgeoning cities. While the level of criminality changes in rural areas, the crime patterns of agricultural areas are still characterized by higher rates of violent crime.

It is the initial phase of the transformation to a modern society that brings the most traumatic problems for the urban areas of these developing societies. In Europe during the initial phase of the industrial revolution, in the socialist countries of Eastern Europe during the postwar period, and in the developing countries of Asia, Africa, and Latin America today, the highest rates of criminality have been experienced with the convergence of urban and rural patterns of criminal behavior. Traditionally, higher urban rates of criminality have been further augmented at this stage of the developmental process by the arrival of rural migrants whose traditional patterns of rural violence have accompanied them and whose usual violent response to social tensions has been aggravated by their difficult adjustment to unfamiliar circumstances. The always difficult adjustment to a new environment has become more pronounced because of the size and the intensity of the urban migration. The cities, the recipients of this massive influx of population, have been ill prepared and unable to assimilate this massive new work force. Even in socialist countries where provisions have been made for the accommodation of new urban residents, one observes the formation of slums or the congregation of recent migrants in urban areas with inferior housing.

The new urban residents, in a state of deprivation compared to the more established inhabitants and surrounded by a level of material possessions they had never previously known, seek the fruits of the process of modernization. Theft, therefore, motivated in part by their unfulfilled desires and in part by actual need (in countries developing now) leads to new levels of property crime that supplement the usual level of violence of these recently rural residents. Therefore, cities during the initial phase of urbanization experience increased rates of violence simultaneously with new levels of property crime. Only as urbanization progresses, as migration into urban centers subsides, and as the newly arrived urban inhabitants adjust to city life, does the total crime rate decline. Crimes of violence cede their once preeminent place to offenses against property.

In terms of crime the hallmark of modernization is the transition from a society dominated by violent crime to one characterized by increasing property crime. Property crime is the dominant form of criminality in all modernized societies because tangible goods in societies increasingly dominated by secular rather than religious values assume a previously unknown significance. In the increasingly mobile modern society, position becomes determined by possessions rather than by birth. In this context, the acquisition of goods becomes not only a fulfillment of tangible needs but a means of acquiring status. The acquisition of property, particularly among juveniles in modern societies through legal or illicit means, becomes a way of proving one's individual worth. Violent crimes against the person, associated primarily with the conditions of rural life, decrease in signifirance in urbanized societies. Violence in modern societies is, however, increasingly associated with the commission of property crimes as individuals are willing to resort to whatever means necessary to secure desired goods.

Modernization produces changes in the type as well as in the level of crime commission. Increased criminality is not, however, as universal a phenomenon as the change in the relative frequencies of crime against property and the person. The crime rates of urban areas have consistently been higher than those of rural areas, but increasing urbanization has not resulted internationally in higher overall reported commission rates. Although property crimes are more frequent now in most developing and developed societies than they were before the onset of modernization, this increase has not always been sufficiently large to offset the decline in crimes against the person. The number of countries that have been spared the spiraling crime rates of the contemporary period is small, but their presence is sufficient to suggest that the development of national economies does not necessarily ensure that the societies will suffer the unfortunate consequences of societal modernization. While the vast majority of the world's nations report an increase in their total crime rates, the level of increase is not consistent in all societies. The crime rates of developing capitalist or socialist societies are increasing at a greater rate than those of nations that have already achieved a degree of development. This suggests that the maturation of the developmental process brings a stabilization in the recorded crime rates. A slower rate of increase in criminality was first noticed in the latter half of the nineteenth century in Europe and the differential growth rates of criminality in developing countries (2.5 percent annual increase for developing nations versus 1 percent for developed) today suggest that the attainment of development has permanently slowed the rate of increase in crime in most developed nations.

The increasing urbanization of modern society produces higher crime rates and the distinctive crime patterns associated with urban life. The level of urbanization in both capitalist developing and developed societies is correlated with the crime rate and the highest crime rates are concentrated in certain urban regions.

The capitalist societies with uncontrolled population mobility have the highest crime rates in the most urbanized metropolitan areas. While this does not mean that each large city necessarily has a very high crime rate, as an aggregate the largest cities have higher crime rates than medium-size cities. Suburbs have crime rates generally equivalent to those of small cities or large towns whereas rural areas have the lowest composite rates of criminality. The generally universal correlation in the capitalist world between urbanization and crime is not, however, valid in the socialist world. Controls over internal population migration in some of the socialist countries have made the largest population centers relatively safe havens while the burgeoning industrializing centers are the crime capitals of these nations.

While the regions of maximum criminal activity in socialist and capitalist countries differ, no such differences exist in regard to the dispersion of crime within cities. In developed and developing countries regardless of their form of economic development, crime rates are highest in the urban core as well as in slum areas often populated by migrants from rural areas. Not all forms of criminality are necessarily predominant in these areas, but the aggregate crime rate for serious offenses appears to be greatest in these urban neighborhoods.

The process of development has a significant effect not only on the level, type, and location of criminality but also upon the nature of the offender population. Increasing development has resulted in a universal increase in rates of juvenile and female crime commission. Before the advent of the industrial revolution when youths were watched over by their extended families, adults were the principal perpetrators of criminal offenses. With increasing development, delinquent juveniles, primarily male, assume a noticeable share of total criminality, and the amount of crime ascribable to them increases as the society becomes more industrialized. Theft is the archetypal offense of youthful males, but many nations report increasingly violent acts perpetrated by juveniles either in conjunction with their property offenses or as wanton acts of violence against the person.

Economic development also results in an increased commission rate for female offenders. Before the industrial revolution in Europe, women were responsible for a limited number and range of criminal offenses. As societies modernize, women commit both a larger share of total criminality and a greater range of criminal offenses. Women in developing nations rarely commit more than 10 percent of all crimes while their counterparts in the developed countries contribute up to one-sixth of their country's total crime rate. The crimes of women are confined primarily to property crimes and to violent offenses perpetrated against individuals with whom they are intimately involved.

The developmental process has been shown to have a consistent effect on socialist and capitalist societies both in the initial stage and after the industrialized society has matured. The most common effects of development can be summarized as an increase in the frequency of property crime, a general growth in the overall crime rate, and the emergence of two new categories of criminal offenders—juveniles and females.

What do the similar effects of the modernization process suggest concerning the impact of economic development on criminal behavior? Do the similar effects suggest that crime is an index of modernization or are the observed changes a consequence of societal development? Do the similar changes observed in crime patterns in socialist and capitalist societies suggest that there is a convergence between the two systems or does it suggest that class and income distribution may not be as significant as modernization in explaining the etiology of criminal behavior? Are established criminological theories adequate to explain the impact of development on crime or are new explanations of criminal behavior necessary? What do the trends in criminality over the last two hundred years suggest for future patterns of criminal behavior?

The evidence presented in the preceding chapters suggests that only the changes accompanying the developmental process are great enough to explain the enormous changes that have occurred in international crime patterns in the last two centuries. It is no coincidence that the crime patterns that characterize the contemporary period emerged at the initial stages of the industrialization of England. Ample evidence is provided in the previous chapter from many dispersed societies to suggest that the transformation in criminality occurred as a result of the process of urbanization and industrialization.

Only political, religious, and economic controls exercised by the society over its members appear sufficiently strong to avert the consequences of modernization. When societies enforce deliberate social policies that prevent or control the seemingly inevitable urbanization accompanying economic development, then the consequent growth and transformation of criminality that accompanies modernization may be partially voided. When political regimes such as Stalin's in the Soviet Union and Franco's in Spain maintain strict control over the criminal population through long prison terms or by annihilation, then even a modernizing society can contain some of its crime problems. The endurance of traditional religious values or of societal traditions associated with the religious heritage make societies at least partly immune to some of the destabilizing criminogenic consequences of modernization. Japan and the countries of the Middle East, which have preserved their traditional cultural values in the face of modern technology, increasing industrialization, and societal prosperity, have crime rates well below those of nations at comparable levels of social and economic development. A society may also avert the disorienting and criminogenic consequences of modernization by means of economic controls. For example, in the socialist countries of Eastern Europe where controls are placed over the distribution of wealth, employment is guaranteed, and the fruits of material success are hidden from the general public, crime rates are much lower than in most developing nations. The crime problem is aggravated where the financial gap between rich and poor is enormous or, as in the United States, where advertising through the mass media fosters the feeling of deprivation among large numbers of less affluent members of the population.

Religious, social, economic, and political controls can mitigate the effects of the modernization process for a significant period of time. These controls are more successful in averting the rise of crime than in preventing the transformation in criminality that accompanies the process of economic development. The nations of the Middle East, Japan and the socialist nations of Eastern Europe have avoided the high crime rates found in technologically advanced Western countries, but they have failed to avert the growth of female criminality, juvenile delinquency, and the growth of property crime relative to crimes of violence. Strong social controls can forestall or lessen the impact but cannot prevent what appears to be the almost inevitable transformation of crime in modern society.

Students of modernization concerned primarily with the overall effects of societal change will examine the new perspectives this study gives on the process of modernization and conclude that crime can be used only in a general sense as an index of modernization because crime is not now a sufficiently refined measure of the level of modernization attained in a developing or a developed society. As yet no exact correlation has been established between the crime rates or commission patterns for particular offenses and the level of societal industrialization. Increasing crime and, in particular, commission rates for property offenses can be used only as general indicators to show that the process of modernization has commenced.

The similar crime patterns of modernizing socialist and capitalist societies suggest that the two diverse forms of economic development have very similar criminogenic consequences. Students of convergence would cite the parallel evolution of criminality as evidence that the process of industrialization makes the two types of societies alike. While the similarities in crime patterns may provide evidence for the convergence theory, conversely, it may be argued that the processes of urbanization and industrialization, the forces primarily accountable for the changing crime patterns, are not really different under capitalism and socialism. This is why such similar transformations in criminality occur in both societies. Moreover, the fundamental differences between crime patterns in capitalist and socialist societies are explained by the strong controls exercised over the populations of socialist countries, an effect attributable more to the political system than to the form of economic development chosen by these societies.

This brief discussion of the book's implications for modernization and convergence theory suggests that the analysis of crime in modern society may provide broader insights into the contemporary world than many expect from the problem of crime. This book has been devoted, however, more to the impact of the societal transformation of the last two hundred years on the problems of crime than to the state of crime as an indicator of the nature of contemporary society. No matter how tantalizing it is to speculate about the broader implications of this study, such analysis is really outside the capabilities of this book. The final pages of this conclusion is to place the new insights concerning present-day criminality in the context of contemporary criminological theory and use the recent history of crime to provide insight into the future state of criminality.

The theories discussed in the first chapter of this book have been used to explain many of the criminological phenomena associated with the process of development. These theories have not been entirely successful in explaining the evolution of criminality in the last two centuries because none of these theories is sufficiently broad to subsume all the effects of the processes of industrialization and urbanization into its conceptual framework. All the major twentieth-century criminological theories dealt with either the adult or the juvenile offender or the impact of the environment on criminal behavior, and all failed to consider that the behavior observed might be explained by the large-scale phenomenon of modernization.

The preceding chapters provide strong evidence for the theory of modernization as an important explanation of the etiology and proliferation of criminality in contemporary society. Modernization theory alone analyzes crime in terms of the effects that urbanization, industrialization, the breakdown of the traditional way of life and the nuclear family, and the growth of literacy and prosperity have had on the development of criminal behavior. Other explanations of criminal behavior have been tied too closely to a particular region, nationality, or brief historical period. They are, therefore, incapable of explaining the proliferation of crime or the international repetition of the crime patterns first observed in industrializing England and in many other nations in the past two centuries. This book surveys the changes in crime patterns that have occurred internationally since the advent of industrialization, providing ample support for the assertion that certain common societal forces associated with modernization account for the increasingly pervasive problem of criminality in the contemporary period.

Only the modernization theory of criminality is capable of explaining the changes in criminal behavior discussed in the previous chapters. Property crime increased relative to violent crime because rural life characterized by relatively frequent crimes against the person declined in prominence while simultaneously urban life that promotes the rise in property crime became more pervasive. The general rise in the crime rate and its concentration in the urban environment are explained by other aspects of modernization. Increasing urbanization and prosperity contribute to the greater availability of goods, the increased feasibility of crime commission, and the increased likelihood of feelings of relative deprivation. The growth in female and juvenile participation in crime is explained by the changing roles of these two groups in modern society—by the increased participation of women in activities outside the home and by the decline of an established role for juveniles in society. These conditions of modern society have contributed to the transformation in quality and quantity of crime commission internationally in the last two hundred years.

Can we expect crime patterns to evolve further in a manner dictated by modernization theory? The answer is a qualified yes. Those societies that are only now developing can be expected to follow, to some extent, the previously observed evolution of criminality. The degree of social control exercised by each society will influence the extent to which its future crime trends conform to previously established patterns. Modernization theory has less explanatory capabilities for those societies that have already achieved a high degree of development because it is more a descriptive rather than a predictive theory. If precedent can be applied with validity in the future, two strong but opposing forces will compete. The general trend of decelerating crime rates with further development will be counteracted by the inceased participation of youthful and female offenders. With a more diverse criminal population, crimes may not be so localized as at the present time and the frequency of violent crimes may rise relative to property offenses.

Modernization theory has been shown to explain the evolution of criminal behavior in culturally, politically, and economically diverse and geographically separated nations. While predictions of future crime trends based on contemporary experience are always risky, the broad based body of data that has been used to establish the validity of modernization theory suggests that it may have greater explanatory powers than other contemporary theories. The theory of crime and socoeconomic development may prove to be as applicable to future developments in criminality as it has been to the explanation of the recent international history of crime patterns.

NOTES
SELECTED BIBLIOGRAPHY
INDEX

NOTES

INTRODUCTION

1. Émile Durkheim, *Suicide: A Study in Sociology;* Gabriel Tarde, *La criminalité comparée;* William Adrian Bonger, *Criminality and Economic Conditions.*

2. Clifford R. Shaw and Henry D. McKay, *Juvenile Delinquency and Urban Areas;* Ted Robert Gurr, "On the History of Violent Crime in Europe and America"; Hugh Davis Graham and Ted Robert Gurr, eds., *Violence in America Historical and Comparative Perspectives;* Ted Robert Gurr, *Rogues, Rebels and Reformers: A Political History of Urban Crime and Conflict; La délinquance juvénile en Europe;* and Yves Chirol, Zarco Jasovic, et al., eds., *Délinquance juvénile et développement socio-économique* (The Hague: Mouton, 1975).

3. Marshall B. Clinard and Daniel J. Abbott, *Crime in Developing Countries: A Comparative Perspective.*

4. Walter D. Connor, "Deviance, Stress and Modernization in Eastern Europe", in *Social Consequences of Modernization in Communist Societies*, ed. Mark G. Field, p. 181.

5. For other definitions see also S. N. Eisenstadt, *Tradition, Change and Modernity,* pp. 22–29; and Alex Inkeles and David H. Smith, *Becoming Modern.*

6. Johannes Andenaes, "Negligent Homicide in Some European Countries—A Comparative Study," in *Crime and Culture,* ed. Marvin Wolfgang, pp. 221–44.

I. CRIME IN THEORETICAL PERSPECTIVE

1. Marvin E. Wolfgang, "Cesare Lombroso," in *Pioneers in Criminology,* ed. Hermann Mannheim (Montclair, N. J.: Patterson Smith, 1972), pp. 232–91.

2. Sir Leon Radzinowicz, *Ideology and Crime* (New York: Columbia University Press, 1966), pp. 33–34.

3. Ibid., pp. 31–37.

4. Friedrich Engels, *The Position of the Working Class in England;* and Karl Marx and Fredrich Engels, *Sobranie Sochineniia,* vol. 5, p. 332.

5. Sir Leon Radzinowicz and Margaret S. Wilson Vine, "Gabriel Tarde," in Mannheim, *Pioneers in Criminology,* pp. 292–303.

6. John Vincent Barry, "Alexander Maconochie," in Mannheim, *Pioneers in Criminology,* p. 88.

7. Walter A. Lunden, "Emile Durkheim," in Mannheim, *Pioneers in Criminology*, pp. 385–98.
8. Radzinowicz, p. 89
9. Robert K. Merton, *Social Theory and Social Structure*, pp. 131–40.
10. Don C. Gibbons, *The Criminological Enterprise* (Englewood Cliffs, N. J.: Prentice-Hall, 1979), p. 67.
11. Thorsten Sellin, *Culture Conflict and Crime.*
12. Gibbons, pp. 53–54.
13. Edwin H. Sutherland and Donald R. Cressey, *Principles of Criminology*, 5th ed., pp. 77–80.
14. Clifford R. Shaw and Henry D. McKay, *Juvenile Delinquency and Urban Areas.*
15. Albert K. Cohen, *Delinquent Boys;* R. A. Cloward and L. E. Ohlin, *Delinquency and Opportunity;* and Walter B. Miller, "Lower Class Culture as a Generating Milieu of Gang Delinquency," pp. 5–19.
16. David Matza, *Delinquency and Drift.*
17. Cloward and Ohlin.
18. See Jackson Toby, "Affluence and Adolescent Crime," pp. 132–94.
19. Richard Quinney, *Critique of Legal Order* (Boston: Little, Brown & Co., 1974).
20. David M. Gordon, "Capitalism, Class and Crime in America," *Crime and Delinquency* 19 (April 1973):163–86.
21. Steven Spitzer, "Toward a Marxian Theory of Deviance," *Social Problems* 22 (1975):638–51.
22. David F. Greenberg, "Delinquency and the Age Structure of Society," *Contemporary Crises* 1 (April, 1977):189–223.

2. INDUSTRIAL DEVELOPMENT AND CRIME

1. Michel Foucault, *Discipline and Punish: The Birth of the Prison*, p. 75.
2. Louis Chevalier, *Laboring Classes and Dangerous Classes.*
3. Theodor Hampe, *Crime and Punishment in Germany.*
4. Ibid., p. 50.
5. John Bellamy, *Crime and Public Order in England in the Later Middle Ages*, p. 3.
6. Gamini Salgado, *The Elizabethan Underworld*, p. 15.
7. Foucault, p. 75.
8. Ibid., p. 75.
9. Salgado, p. 13.
10. Salgado, pp. 27–30; Hampe, p. 41.
11. Hampe, pp. 39–56.
12. Bellamy, p. 69.
13. Salgado, p. 45.
14. J. J. Tobias, *Crime and Industrial Society in the 19th Century*, pp. 31–32.
15. E. J. Hobsbawm, *Primitive Rebels*, p. 13.
16. Ibid., pp. 26–27.
17. Foucault; and Ted Robert Gurr, *Rogues, Rebels and Reformers: A Political History of Urban Crime and Conflict.*
18. Foucault, p. 75.
19. Hobsbawm, p. 5.
20. Denis Szabo, *Crimes et villes: études statistiques de la criminalité urbaine et rurale en France et en Belgique*, p. 119.

21. Gerhard Lenski, *Power and Privilege,* p. 65.
22. Howard Zehr, *Crime and the Development of Modern Society Patterns of Criminality in 19th Century Germany and France,* p. 20.
23. Lenski, p. 281.
24. Ibid., pp. 282–83.
25. Hobsbawm, p. 19.
26. Lenski, p. 283.
27. Tobias, p. 37.
28. Zehr, *Modern Patterns of Criminality,* p. 20.
29. Friedrich Engels, *The Position of the Working Class in England,* p. 105.
30. Ibid., pp. 167–68.
31. Karl Marx and Friedrich Engels, *Sobranie Sochineniia* vol. 5, p. 332.
32. Anthony Giddens, *Capitalism and Modern Social Theory,* pp. 71–72.
33. This belief is still widely held by many scholars. See Paul H. Shapiro, "Social Deviance in Eastern Europe: On Understanding the Problem," in *Social Deviance in Eastern Europe,* ed. Ivan Volgyes, p. 13. This work, however, tries to provide a more comprehensive view of modernization.
34. Lenski's *Power and Privilege* is an exception in that crime is integrated into his analysis of social structure and mobility.
35. The discussion of industrialization is conceived for the purposes of this chapter in terms of the nineteenth century and thus excludes questions of social change addressed in works such as Seymour M. Lipset and Reinhard Bendix, *Social Mobility in Industrial Society* (Berkeley and Los Angeles: University of California Press, 1959).
36. Hobsbawm; A. Q. Lodhi and Charles Tilly, "Urbanization, Crime and Collective Violence in Nineteenth Century France," pp. 296–318; Charles Tilly, Louise Tilly, and Richard Tilly, *The Rebellious Century: 1830–1930*; and Ted Robert Gurr, Peter N. Grabosky and Robert C. Hula, *The Politics of Crime and Conflict: A Comparative History of Four Cities.*
37. Gabriel Tarde, *La criminalité comparée.*
38. Louis Wirth, "Urbanism as a Way of Life."
39. Szabo, pp. 42–43.
40. Chevalier, pp. 437–39.
41. Ibid., pp. 12–18.
42. Ibid., p. 440.
43. Ibid., p. 32.
44. Philippe Ariés, *Centuries of Childhood: A Social History of Family Life.* The type of childhood experienced is a reflection of the social and cultural life of the period.
45. I am indebted to Steve Crawford for his suggestion on the novelty of the contribution of teenagers as a separate entity to the community of the period.
46. Steven Marcus, *Engels, Manchester and the Working Class,* p. 223.
47. Zehr, *Modern Patterns of Criminality,* p. 141.
48. Zehr, *Modern Patterns of Criminality,* p. 142.
49. See Lenski for example.
50. Although the Lodhi and Tilly study disagrees with some of the findings discussed in the following section on case studies, they are in general agreement that the social structure of an industrialized society has an impact on patterns of criminality.
51. Zehr, *Modern Patterns of Criminality,* p. 138.
52. Tobias, pp. 37 and 45.
53. Chevalier, pp. 120–21.

54. Tilly, Tilly, and Tilly, p. 11.

55. V. A. C. Gattrell and T. B. Hadden, "Criminal Statistics and Their Interpretation."

56. Zehr, *Modern Patterns of Criminality*, p. 118.

57. Ibid., p. 120.

58. Howard Zehr, "The Modernization of Crime in Germany and France, 1830–1913."

59. Chevalier.

60. Lodhi and Tilly.

61. The theft to violence ratio compares the relative frequency of violent as compared to property crimes:

$$TVR = 100 \times \frac{\text{homicide} + \text{assault}}{\text{homicide} + \text{assault} + \text{theft}}$$

62. Zehr, "Crime in Germany and France," p. 123.

63. Ibid., p. 126.

64. Lodhi and Tilly, pp. 300–301; Zehr, *Modern Patterns of Criminality*, p. 146, comments on similar conclusions made in the Tillys' book: "In their recent *The Rebellious Century* [they] find that assize records show a massive fall in serious property crimes during the nineteenth century, and thus conclude that the present century is more disorderly than the previous one. The error here is serious. . . . Besides the increasing number of property crimes which were simply dropped, more and more cases were sent to lower courts during the century."

65. Lodhi and Tilly, p. 308.

66. Zehr, "Crime in Germany and France," p. 128.

67. Lodhi and Tilly, pp. 300–301.

68. A more dramatic statement is made in regard to homocide rates by Rosemary Gartner in "Urbanization, Urban Growth and Homicide: A Comparable Analysis," presented at the American Sociological Association meeting in Boston, 1979. She finds that homicide rates decline during urbanization and urban growth both in developing and developed countries and at earlier and later stages of urbanization.

69. See, for example, Allan Silver, "The Demand for Order in Civil Society, A Review of Some Themes in the History of Urban Crime, Police and Riot."

70. E. P. Thompson, *The Making of the English Working Class*, pp. 59–61.

71. Sir Leon Radzinowicz, *History of the English Criminal Law and Administration from 1750*, vol. 1 (London: Stevens, 1948).

72. Tobias, p. 122–25.

73. Gurr, Grabosky, and Hula, p. 66.

74. Marcus, p. 4.

75. Malcolm I. Thomis, *The Town Labourer and the Industrial Revolution*, p. 48.

76. Marcus, pp. 19–27.

77. Gurr, Grabosky, and Hula.

78. Ibid.

79. Ibid.

80. Tobias, p. 213.

81. M. N. Gernet, *Moral'naia Statistika* (Moscow: Central Statistical Administration, 1922).

82. *Prestupnyi mir Moskvy,* (Moscow: Law and Life, 1924).

83. M. N. Gernet, *Prestupnost' samoubiistva vo vremiia voiny i posle nee* (Moscow: Central Statistical Administration, 1927).

84. See Lenski, p. 419, for a further discussion of this point of view.

3. CRIME AND DEVELOPING COUNTRIES

1. Jean Pinatel. *La Société Criminogène*, pp. 21–32; Marshall B. Clinard and Daniel J. Abbott, *Crime in Developing Countries: A Comparative Perspective*; William Clifford, *Introduction to African Criminology*, pp. 1–2; R. E. S. Tanner, *Three Studies in East African Criminology*, pp. 51–66.
2. Clinard and Abbott, *Crime in Developing Countries*, p. 35.
3. General Assembly, "Crime Prevention and Control," United Nations, Report of the Secretary General, 22 September 1977.
4. Ibid., p. 12.
5. Ibid., p. 15.
6. Ibid., p. 11.
7. Ibid., Paul Bohannan, ed., *African Homicide and Suicide:* Tibamanya Mushanga, *Criminal Homicide in Uganda;* Clinard and Abbott, *Crime in Developing Countries.*
8. Mushanga, p. 165; A. C. Emovon and T. A. Lambo, "Survey of Criminal Homicide in Nigeria," p. 55.
9. Clinard and Abbott, *Crime in Developing Countries*, p. 58; and Jacqueline H. and Murray A. Straus, "Suicide, Homicide and Social Structure in Ceylon," p. 468.
10. Clinard and Abbott, *Crime in Developing Countries*, p. 58.
11. Tanner, pp. 63–67.
12. Marvin E. Wolfgang and Franco Ferracuti, *The Subculture of Violence.*
13. Thorsten Sellin's theory of culture conflict is applicable here.
14. G. Mangin, "La délinquance juvénile en Afrique noire Francophone," p. 225.
15. S. P. Tschoungui and P. Zumbach, "Diagnostic de la délinquance au Cameroun," p. 43; and Manuel Lopez-Ray, "Economic Conditions and Crime with Special Reference to Less Developed Countries," p. 35.
16. L. A. Kayiira, "Violence in Kondoism—The Rise and Nature of Violent Crime in Uganda."
17. Paul Raymaekers, "Predélinquance et délinquance juvénile à Leopoldville".
18. Tschoungui and Zumbach, p. 37; and Evelyne Pierre, J. P. Flamand, and H. Collomb, "La délinquance juvénile à Dakar," p. 29.
19. Lois B. DeFleur, "A Cross-Cultural Comparison of Juvenile Offenders and Offenses: Cordoba, Argentina and the United States."
20. Gunnar Myrdal, "Corruption: Its Causes and Effects"; Manuel Lopez-Ray, *Crime: An Analytical Appraisal;* and David Bayley, "The Effects of Corruption in a Developing Nation."
21. Clinard and Abbott, *Crime in Developing Countries*, p. 752.
22. For example see Dae H. Chang ed., *Criminology: A Cross-Cultural Perspective*, vol. 2, p. 786.
23. United Nations, p. 10.
24. Kettil Bruun, Lynn Pan, and Ingemar Rexed, *The Gentlemen's Club: International Control of Drugs and Alcohol*, p. 233.
25. Ibid., p. 232.
26. United Nations, p. 15.
27. R. S. Cavan and J. Cavan, *Delinquency and Crime: Cross-Cultural Perspectives.*
28. Tschoungui and Zumbach, p. 44; and Clinard and Abbott, *Crime in Developing Countries*, p. 67–68.
29. Chang, pp. 675–76.
30. Clinard and Abbott, *Crime in Developing Countries*, pp. 42–43.

31. Ibid., pp. 257–58.
32. See National Criminal Justice Reference Service, *International Summaries.* Vol. 3 is devoted to terrorism.
33. Conversations with Yugoslav scholars.
34. Yonah Alexander, ed., *International Terrorism* (New York: Praeger, 1976).
35. S. Rizkalla, "Crime and Criminal Justice in the Developing Countries."
36. Kayiira.
37. *World Almanac and Book of Facts* 1979 (New York: Newspaper Enterprise Association, *1979*), pp. 513–79.
38. United Nations, pp. 24–25.
39. "Changes in the Forms and Dimensions of Crime in Iraq," (New York: United Nations, 1975).
40. Fahad Al-Thakheb, "Crime in Kuwait," paper read at International Crime Symposium, 1978, in Stockholm, Sweden. Mimeographed.
41. Israeli scholars have produced a sophisticated and multifaceted body of criminological research as exemplified in *Israel Studies in Criminology.*
42. Shlomo Shoham and A. Abd-el-Razek, "Immigration, Ethnicity and Ecology as Related to Juvenile Delinquency in Israel", pp. 406–7.
43. United Nations, p. 31.
44. Marshall Clinard, "The Problem of Crime and Its Control in Developing Countries," in *Crime in Papua, New Guinea,* ed. David Biles.
45. Preben Wolf, "Crime and Development: An International Comparison of Crime Rates."
46. United Nations, p. 28.
47. Sir Leon Radzinowicz and Joan King, *The Growth of Crime,* p. 13.
48. Mangin; Luis R. Manzanera, *La Delincuencia de Menores en Mexico;* U. N. Lynn, "Backgrounds of Crime and Delinquency", United Nations Asian and Far East Institute for the Prevention of Crime, Series No. 14, 1978.
49. Menachim Amir and M. Hovav, "Juvenile Delinquency in Israel," *Israel Annals of Psychiatry and Related Disciplines* 14(1976): 161–72.
50. Mangin; Tschoungui and Zumbach; Henri Tarniquet, "Note sur la criminalité en milieu urbain à industrialization rapide"; and Herman Venter, "Urbanization and Industrialization as Criminogenic Factors in the Republic of South Africa."
51. A. Peillad, "Criminologia del minor delincuente"; A. Sanchez Galindo, "El perfit del delincuente en el estado de Mexico"; Pierre, Flamand, and Collomb; and K. C. Kowk, "Juvenile Delinquency in Hong Kong," United Nations Asia and Far East Institute for the Prevention of Crime. Resource Material Series No. 14, 1978.
52. Mangin.
53. "Quelques considerations sur la prévention de la délinquance juvénile dans les pays africains subissant des changements sociaux rapides," *International Review of Criminal Policy;* and Olufunmilayo Oluruntimehin, "A Study of Juvenile Delinquency in a Nigerian City."
54. Tschoungui and Zumbach; Lopez-Ray, *Crime: An Analytical Appraisal.*
55. Franco Ferracuti, S. Dinitz, and E. Acostade Brenes, *Delinquents and Nondelinquents in the Puerto Rican Slum Culture.*
56. Tschoungui and Zumbach; Manzanera.
57. Ferracuti, Dinitz, and Acostade Brenes; Abdellatif El Bacha, "Quelques aspects particuliers de la délinquance juvénile dans certaines villes du royaume du Maroc"; S. Kirson Weinberg, "Juvenile Delinquency in Ghana: A Comparative Analysis of Delinquents and Non-Delinquents."
58. Tsung-Yi Lin, "Two Types of Delinquent Youth in Chinese Society."
59. Ibid.

60. DeFleur, "Cross-Cultural Comparison."
61. Clinard and Abbott, *Crime in Developing Countries.*
62. Ibid.
63. El Bacha.
64. Bohannan.
65. United Nations, p. 12.
66. Radzinowicz and King, p. 16.
67. See, for example, R. Ahuja, *Female Offenders in India* (Meerut: Meenakshi Prakashan, 1969).
68. Sanchez-Galindo.
69. Mangin; Tschoungui and Zumbach; Tarniquet; and Venter.
70. Clinard and Abbott, *Crime in Developing Countries.*
71. Clinard and Abbott, *Crime in Developing Countries.*
72. "Quelques considerations sur la prévention de la délinquance juvénile dans les pays africains."
73. Clinard and Abbott, *Crime in Developing Countries,* p. 78.
74. Ibid., p. 85.
75. Ibid., pp. 209–10.
76. Brian J. L. Berry, *The Human Consequences of Urbanization,* pp. 78–79.
77. Lois B. DeFleur, "Ecological Variables in the Cross-Cultural Study of Delinquency," p. 566.
78. Marshall B. Clinard and Daniel J. Abbott, "Community Organization and Property Crime: A Comparative Study of Social Control in the Slums of an African City."
79. Clinard and Abbott, *Crime in Developing Countries,* pp. 109–10.
80. Ibid., pp. 119–27, 142–65.
81. Ibid., pp. 48–49.
82. Lopez-Ray, *Crime: An Analytical Appraisal.*
83. Dane Archer et al., "Cities and Homicide: A New Look at an Old Paradox," *Comparative Studies in Sociology* 1 (1978):73–95.
84. Clifford, *Introduction to African Criminology.*
85. Radzinowicz and King.
86. Ted Robert Gurr, Peter N. Grabosky, and Robert C. Hula, *The Politics of Crime and Conflict: A Comparative History of Four Cities.*
87. Émile Durkheim, *The Rules of Sociological Method.*
88. Gabriel Tarde, *La criminalité comparée;* and Sir Leon Radzinowicz, *Ideology and Crime* (New York: Columbia University Press, 1966), pp. 31–37, 82–83.

4 . CRIME IN DEVELOPED COUNTRIES

1. Gerhard Lenski, *Power and Privilege* pp. 243–96 and 346–409.
2. Philip M. Hauser, Introduction to *The Study of Urbanization,* ed. Philip M. Hauser and Leo F. Schnore, p. 24.
3. Preben Wolf, "Crime and Development. An International Comparison of Crime Rates," pp. 107–20.
4. Ted Robert Gurr, "The Criminal Ethos"; idem, "On the History of Violent Crime in Europe and America."
5. Dane Archer and Rosemary Gartner, "Violent Acts and Violent Times: A Comparative Approach to Postwar Homicide Rates."
6. Gurr, "The Criminal Ethos."
7. E. L. Gaier, "Shifts in Delinquent Behavior, 1951–1973"; Karl O. Christiansen and S. J. Jensen, "Crime in Denmark," p. 92; Jean Pinatel, *La Société Criminogène,* p. 76.

8. United Nations General Assembly, Report of the Secretary General, "Crime Prevention and Control," September 22, 1977, p. 13.

9. Ibid.

10. Ibid., p. 15.

11. Ibid., p. 13.

12. Ibid., p. 13.

13. Ibid., pp. 11 and 13.

14. Wolf, pp. 118–19.

15. Ibid., p. 11.

16. William Clifford, "New Dimensions in Criminality—National and Transnational," p. 69.

17. United Nations General Asembly; and H. J. Kerner, *Professionelles und Organisiertes Verbrechen* (Weisbaden: Bundeskriminalamt, 1973).

18. Marvin E. Wolfgang and Franco Ferracuti, *The Subculture of Violence,* p. 273.

19. Hermann Mannheim, *Group Problems in Crime and Punishment,* p. 196; R. S. Cavan and J. Cavan, *Delinquency and Crime: Cross-Cultural Perspectives,* p. 207.

20. Edwin H. Sutherland, "Crime and Business," *Annals of the American Academy of Political and Social Science* 217 (September 1941):112–18.

21. Gilbert Geis and Robert F. Meier, eds., *White Collar Crime,* rev. ed. (New York: Free Press, 1977).

22. United Nations, p. 15.

23. Graeme R. Newman, *Comparative Deviance,* p. 166.

24. Ibid., pp. 304–5.

25. For a general discussion of this phenomenon, see David H. Bayley, *Forces of Order: Police Behavior in Japan and the United States;* William Clifford, *Crime Control in Japan;* David H. Bayley, "Learning About Crime—The Japanese Experience." *Public Interest,* 44 (Summer 1976), pp. 55–68; T. Matsushita, "Crime in Japan—A Search for the Causes of Low and Decreasing Criminality," *UNAFEI Resource Material Series,* no. 12 (October 1976), pp. 36–48; R. A. Ross, "Criminal Justice from East to West," *Crime and Delinquency,* vol. 25, no. 1 (January 1979), pp. 76–86; W. A. Lunden, "Violent Crimes in Japan in War and Peace, 1933–1974," *International Journal of Criminology and Penology,* vol. 4 (1976), pp. 349–63; R. Evans, Jr., "Changing Labor Markets and Criminal Behavior in Japan," pp. 477–89; Karl O. Christiansen, "Industrialization, Urbanization and Crime," pp. 51–57; *Summary of the White Paper on Crime,* 1977.

26. Clifford, *Crime Control in Japan,* pp. 1–2.

27. Ibid., p. 3; *Summary of the White Paper,* pp. 47–49.

28. Evans, p. 487.

29. *Summary of the White Paper,* p. 19.

30. Evans, p. 489.

31. Bayley, "Learning About Crime," pp. 55–68.

32. *Summary of the White Paper,* p. 20; Matsushita, pp. 36–48.

33. Marshall B. Clinard, *Cities with Little Crime,* p. 16.

34. P. Pradervand and L. Cardia. "Quelques aspects de la délinquance italienne à Genève." *Revue internationale de criminologie et de police technique,* vol. 20, no. 1 (1965), pp. 43–58.

35. Clinard, *Cities with Little Crime,* p. 103.

36. Edmund W. Vaz and John Casparis, "A Comparative Study of Youth Culture and Delinquency: Upper Middle-Class Canadian and Swiss Boys," pp. 1–26.

37. Clinard, *Cities with Little Crime,* p. 104.

38. *The Challenge of Crime in a Free Society: A Report by the President's*

Commission on *Law Enforcement and Administration of Justice* (New York: Avon Books, 1968); and Marshall B. Clinard, *Slums and Community Development: Experiments in Self-Help* (New York: Free Press, 1966), pp. 9–17.

39. Clinard, *Cities with Little Crime*, p. 103.

40. Ibid., p. 122.

41. Andrew F. Henry and James F. Short, Jr., *Suicide and Homicide: Some Economic, Sociological and Psychological Aspects of Aggression*. The authors show that, though homicide rates are high in rural areas, American urban counties also display high rates of homicide contrary to international expectations. In contrast, see Ragnar Hauge and Preben Wolf, "Criminal Violence in Three Scandinavian Countries."

42. Fred P. Graham, "A Contemporary History of American Crime," pp. 371–85.

43. Richard M. Brown, "The American Vigilante Tradition," in *Violence in America—Historical and Comparative Perspective*, ed. Hugh Davis Graham and Ted Robert Gurr vol. 1 (Washington, D.C.: U. S. Government Printing Office, 1969), 1:121–70.

44. W. J. McGrath, *Crime and Its Treatment in Canada;* Duncan Chappell and Paul Wilson, *The Australian Criminal Justice System.*

45. Mannheim, *Group Problems*, p. 198.

46. Sir Leon Radzinowicz and Joan King, *The Growth of Crime*, p. 13.

47. Manuel Lopez-Ray, *Crime: An Analytical Appraisal* pp. 212–15.

48. See Marvin E. Wolfgang, *Delinquency in a Birth Cohort* (Chicago: University of Chicago Press, 1972), and replications of this study.

49. Edwin H. Sutherland, *The Professional Thief.*

50. Cavan and Cavan, p. 216.

51. Clinard, *Cities with Little Crime*, p. 123.

52. Clifford, *Crime Control in Japan*, p. 111; Clinard, *Cities with Little Crime*, pp. 122–23.

53. Jackson Toby, "Affluence and Adolescent Crime," app. H, pp. 132–44.

54. Graeme S. Fraser, "Parent-Adolescent Relationships and Delinquent Behavior: A Cross-National Comparison," pp. 505–13; David Matza, *Delinquency and Drift.*

55. Clifford, *Crime Control in Japan*, pp. 118–19; Clinard, *Cities with Little Crime*, p. 127. Patrik Tornudd, "Crime Trends in Finland, 1950–1977"; James F. Short, Jr., "Gangs, Politics and Social Order," in *Delinquency, Crime and Society*, ed. James F. Short, Jr., p. 145.

56. Walter B. Miller, "Youth Gangs in the Urban Crisis Era," in Short, *Delinquency, Crime and Society*, p. 95.

57. Wolf Middendorf, "New Forms of Juvenile Delinquency: Their Origin, Prevention and Treatment"; R. Loitz, "Shoplifting, *Kriminalistik*, vol. 19, no. 10 (1965), pp. 509–12; Clinard, *Cities with Little Crime*, p. 125.

58. Clinard, *Cities with Little Crime*, p. 125.

59. Barbara N. McLennan and Kenneth McLennan, "Public Policy and the Control of Crime," in *Crime in Urban Society*, ed. Barbara N. McLennan p. 134.

60. Paul C. Friday and Jerald Hage, "Youth Crime in Postindustrial Societies," p. 353.

61. Ibid., p. 353.

62. Ibid., p. 366.

63. For example, see W. Stelling, *Youth Between Guilt and Destiny* (Hanover: National-Verlag, 1972); McGrath; Toby; and Short, *Delinquency, Crime and Society.*

64. See the discussions of the theories of Shaw and McKay's work in Short, *Delinquency, Crime and Society.*

65. Peter Scott, "Gangs and Delinquent Groups in London," pp. 4–26; Hermann Mannheim, "Juvenile Delinquency," pp. 148–52; Middendorf, "New Forms of Juvenile Delinquency"; Edmund W. Vaz, "Juvenile Gang Delinquency in Paris," *Social Problems* 10 (Summer 1962): 21–23; Josine Junger-Tas, "Hidden Delinquency and Judicial Selection in Belgium," in *Youth Crime and Juvenile Justice— International Perspectives,* ed. Paul C. Friday and V. Lorne Stewart.

66. Toby, p. 143.

67. M. N. Gernet, "Prestuplenie i bor'ba s nim v sviazi s revoliutsiei obschestva," in *Izbrannye Proizvedeniia,* ed. M. M. Babaev (Moscow: Juridicial Literature 1974), p. 250.

68. Radzinowicz and King, pp. 13–16; and Manuel Lopez-Ray, pp. 197–98.

69. See Freda Adler, "The Interaction Between Women's Emancipation and Female Criminality: A Cross-Cultural Perspective"; Lee Bowker, "Women and Crime: An International Perspective"; and Rita J. Simon, "American Women and Crime."

70. Simon, pp. 40–41.

71. Clifford, *Crime Control in Japan,* p. 130.

72. Bowker, p. 6.

73. Clifford, *Crime Control in Japan,* pp. 128–30.

74. Radzinowicz and King, p. 15.

75. Simon, p. 46.

76. William S. Bennett, "Immigrants and Crime," *Annals of the American Academy of Political and Social Science,* July 1909, pp. 117–24.

77. Mannheim, *Group Problems in Crime and Punishment,* p. 195.

78. McGrath; Robert A. Silverman and James J. Teevan, Jr., *Crime in Canadian Society;* Franco Ferracuti, "European Migration and Crime," in *Crime and Culture,* ed. Marvin E. Wolfgang, pp. 189–219; Courtlandt C. van Vechten, "The Criminality of the Foreign Born," *Journal of Criminal Law and Criminology* 32, no. 2 (July–August 1941):137–38; Duncan and Chappell, pp. 209–12.

79. Duncan and Chappell, pp. 209–12; and McGrath, pp. 83–85.

80. Duncan and Chappell, p. 208.

81. Jurgen Neumann, *Die kriminalitat der italienischen Arbeit-krafte im Kanton Zurich* (Zurich: Juris Verlag, 1963); J. Graven, "Le Problème des travailleurs étrangers délinquants en Suisse," *Revue Internationale de Criminologie et de Police Technique* 19, no. 4 (1965):265–90; Stephen Castles and Godula Kosack, *Immigrant Workers and Class Structures in Western Europe,* pp. 341–56.

82. Castles and Kosack, pp. 345–47. According to the authors, employees of hotels steal more than other groups of migrants.

83. Ibid., p. 347.

84. Ibid., p. 350.

85. Duncan and Chappell, p. 208; and Ferracuti, p. 211.

86. Harold Ross, "Crime and the Native-Born Sons of European Immigrants," *Journal of Criminal Law and Criminology* 28 (1937):202–9.

87. John P. Conrad, *Crime and Its Correction* (Berkeley and Los Angeles: University of California Press, 1970); and Denis Szabo, *Crimes et villes: études statistiques de la criminalité urbaine et rurale en France et en Belgique,* p. 131.

88. Clinard, *Cities with Little Crime,* p. 120.

89. Daniel Glaser, *The Effectiveness of a Prison and Parole System* (New York: Bobbs-Merrill Co., 1964), pp. 504–31.

90. *Summary of the White Paper on Crime,* p. 27.

91. Clinard, *Cities with Little Crime,* p. 116.

92. Ibid., p. 120.

Notes to pages 92–96

93. McLennan, *Crime in Urban Society;* Marvin E. Wolfgang, "Urban Crime" in *The Metropolitan Enigma,* ed. James Q. Wilson (Cambridge, Mass: Harvard University Press, 1968), pp. 246–81; Karl O. Christiansen, "Industrialization and Urbanization in Relation to Crime and Juvenile Delinquency," p. 5.

94. Szabo, *Crimes et villes;* Ted Robert Gurr, Peter N. Grabosky, and Robert C. Hula, *The Politics of Crime and Conflict: A Comparative History of Four Cities,* pp. 232–34.

95. Clifford R. Shaw and Henry D. McKay, *Juvenile Delinquency and Urban Areas.*

96. See, for example, Sarah Boggs, "Urban Crime Patterns," pp. 899–908; Richard Quinney, "Structural Characteristics, Population Areas and Crime Rates in the United States," pp. 46–52; and Calvin F. Schmid, "Urban Crime Areas: Part II."

97. Stuart Lottier, "Distribution of Criminal Offenses in Metropolitan Regions," *Journal of Criminal Law and Criminology* 29(1938):37–50: Larry K. Stephenson, "Spatial Dispersion of Intra-Urban Juvenile Delinquency," pp. 20–26; McGrath; and *Research Bulletin of the Ministry of Justice of the Netherlands,* pp. 82–83.

98. C. Amelunxen, "Kriminologie der Grenze," *Archiv für Kriminologie* 156, no. 5–6 (1975):129–40; J. Hellmer, *Kriminalitatsatlas der Bundesrespublik Deutschland and West Berlins* (Wiesbaden: Bundeskriminalamt, 1972).

99. Hellmer, p. 87; and Szabo, *Crimes et villes,* pp. 63–73.

100. F. H. McClintock and N. Howard Avison, *Crime in England and Wales.*

101. Wolfgang, "Urban Crime"; V. V. Stanciu, *La criminalité à Paris;* Schmid. See also John Charles Tachovsky, "Crime in New Castle County, Delaware: A Multivariate Analysis of the Geographic Distribution of Crime Occurrence Rates."

102. McLennan and McLennan, "Public Policy and the Control of Crime," p. 134.

103. Boggs, p. 899.

104. Szabo, *Crimes et villes,* pp. 70–75; James V. Bennett, "Criminality and Social Change," in *Critical Issues in the Study of Crime,* ed. Simon Dinitz and Walter Reckless (Boston: Little, Brown & Co., 1968), pp. 17–18.

105. A. M. Guerry, *Statistique morale* (Paris: Crochard, 1833) was the first student of the impact of population density on crime. He has been followed by such scholars as Denis Szabo, *Crimes et villes;* A. H. Bloemberger et al., "Criminality and Macro-Social Characteristics: A Report of Trial and Error," in *Criminology between the Rule of Law and the Outlaws,* ed. C. W. G. Jasperse, K. A. V. Leeuwen-Burow, and L. G. Toornvliet. (Deventer, Netherlands: Kluwer, 1976), pp. 217–38.

106. Vincent Peyre, "La comparaison internationale," in Yves Chirol, Zarco Jasovic, et al, eds. *Délinquance juvénile et développement socio-économique* (The Hague: Mouton, 1975), pp. 295–301.

107. Clinard, *Cities with Little Crime.*

108. Hellmer, p. 87.

109. Jack P. Gibbs and Maynard Erickson, "Crime Rates of American Cities in an Ecological Context," *American Journal of Sociology* 82 (1976):605–20; and Wesley Skogan, "The Changing Distribution of Big-City Crime: A Multi-City Time Series Analysis," *Urban Affairs Quarterly* 13 (1977):33–48.

110. Gibbs and Erickson.

111. Donald Capone and Woodrow Nichols, "Urban Structure and Criminal Mobility," *American Behavioral Scientist* 20 (1976):199–213; John E. Farley and Mark Hansel, "The Ecological Context of Urban Crime: A Further Exploration."

112. Farley and Hansel, pp. 7–8.

113. Dane Archer et al., "Cities and Homicide: A New Look at an Old Paradox," *Comparative Studies in Sociology* 1 (1978):93–94.

114. Ibid., p. 75.

115. Gabriel Tarde, *La criminalité comparée.*

116. Gurr, "On the History of Violent Crime in Europe and America."

117. United Nations, "Crime Prevention and Control," p. 13.

5. CRIME IN SOCIALIST COUNTRIES

1. Walter D. Connor, "Deviance, Stress and Modernization in Eastern Europe," p. 182.

2. Ibid., p. 186; and *Rocznik Statystyczny* (Warsaw, 1976), pp. 523 and 529; Lucjan Czubinski, "Crime Problems in Present-Day Poland," p. 15.

3. *Rocznik Statystyczny,* p. 523.

4. Ibid., p. 523 and Connor, "Deviance," p. 187.

5. Calculated from *Rocznik Statystyczny,* p. 523, using their total figures for crimes against life and health as the total for all categories of offenses.

6. Miklos Radvanyi, "Die Kriminalitat in Ungarn," p. 109.

7. Calculated from tables given in Radvanyi, pp. 114–17.

8. Radvanyi, p. 106; see also Ivan Volyges, "Social Deviance in Hungary: The Case of the Private Economy," in *Social Deviance in Eastern Europe,* pp. 75–77, edited by Ivan Volgyes (Boulder, Colorado: Westview, 1978).

9. Radvanyi, p. 118.

10. John Lekschas, "On Some Aspects of Criminality in Socialist Society," p. 16; and Erich Bucholz, et al., *Socialist Criminology—Theoretical and Methodological Foundations.*

11. *Kriminologiia,* p. 85.

12. J. Hellmer, *Criminality in Berlin,* p. 3.

13. *Statisticki Godisnjak Jugoslavije* (Beograd: Savezni, 1978), pp. 394–97.

14. Connor, "Deviance," p. 187.

15. Veselin Karakashev, *Problemi na prest'pnostta i neinata struktura,* pp. 185–86.

16. Ibid., p. 191.

17. Ibid., p. 231.

18. Connor, Deviance," p. 187.

19. Calculated from a table given in Frederick Neznansky, "Statistika prestupnosti v SSSR," *Posev* 5 (1979):47.

20. Ibid., p. 47; *Kriminologiia,* pp. 118–19.

21. Private conversations with Soviet scholars.

22. Louise Shelley, "Criminality in Soviet Georgia," *Papers on Soviet Law* 3 (1981), pp. 5–15.

23. *Summary of the White Paper on Crime,* p. 19; Clinard, *Cities with Little Crime,* p. 156.

24. See the two volumes produced in collaboration with western researchers: *La délinquance juvénile en Europe* from L'Institut de Sociologie de l'Université de Bruxelles, and Yves Chirol, Zarco Jasovic, et al., eds., *Délinquance juvénile et développement socio-économique.*

25. Vincent Peyre, "La comparaison internationale," in *Délinquance juvénile,* ed. Chirol, Jasovic, et al., pp. 281–301.

26. Andras Szabo, "Délinquance juvénile et développement socio-économique en Hongrie," in *Délinquance júvenile,* ed. Chirol, Jasovic, et al., p. 143.

27. Ibid., p. 147.

28. Desanka Lazarevic and Zarco Jasovic, "Délinquance juvénile et développement socio-ecónomique en Yugoslavie," in *Délinquance juvénile,* ed. Chirol, Jasovic, et al., p. 253.

29. Bolestaw Maroszek, "Délinquance juvénile et développement socio-économique en Pologne," in *Délinquance juvénile,* ed. Chirol, Jasovic, et al., p. 192.
30. Ibid., p. 200.
31. Ibid., p. 213.
32. See Radvanyi, pp. 109–17, *Rocznik Statystyczny;* and *Statisticki Godisnjak Jugoslavije.*
33. Harold Berman, *Soviet Criminal Law and Procedure,* 2nd ed. (Cambridge, Mass: Harvard University Press, 1972).
34. Connor, "Deviance," p. 190.
35. See Radvanyi, p. 109–17; and *Rocznik Statystyczy.*
36. Konstantin Simis, "The Position of the Death Penalty in the USSR" *Research Bulletin Radio Liberty* 103 (1978).
37. L. N. Gusev and A. A. Bakhitov, "O resultakh sotsiologicheskikh issledovaniia o retsidivistov i drugikh otkloniashikh ot sotsial'nogo poleznogo truda," *Informatsionnye soobshcheniia VNIIOP pri MOOP,* 35 (1971).
38. Connor, "Deviance," p. 192.
39. Leon Lipson and Valery Chalidze, Collected Documents, *Papers on Soviet Law* 1 (1977):173–85.
40. Wojciech Michalski, "The Effect of Social Changes on Crime in Poland in Light of Research by Criminologists," pp. 203–4; A. Stromas, "Crime, Law and Penal Practice in the U.S.S.R.," p. 301.
41. Michalski, "The Effect of Social Changes." p. 204.
42. Mervyn Matthews, *Class and Society in Soviet Russia* (New York: Walker & Co., 1972), pp. 53–57.
43. Walter D. Connor, *Deviance in Soviet Society: Crime, Deliquency and Alcoholism,* pp. 174–75.
44. Evident from tables given by Karakashev, p. 188.
45. M. M. Babaev, "Kriminologicheskaia otsenka sotsial'no-ekonomicheskikh i demograficheskikh faktorov," *Sovetskoe gosudarstro i pravo,* 6 (1972):97–102.
46. Karakashev, p. 98.
47. Babaev, "Kriminologicheskaia otsenka."
48. Karakashev, pp. 98–99.
49. O. V. Derviz, "Rabota ili ucheba vne mesta postoiannogo zhitel'stva-odin iz faktorov prestupnosti nesovershennoletnikh," in *Prestupnost' i ee preduprezhdenie,* ed. N. P. Kan and M. D. Shargorodskii (Leningrad: Izd. Leningradskogo Universiteta, 1971), pp. 64–70; Karakashev, pp. 198–99.
50. M. M. Babaev, "Kriminologicheskie issledovaniia problem migratisiia naseleniia," *Sovetskoe gosudarstvo i pravo* 3 (1968):86.
51. Ibid.
52. Karakashev, pp. 96–99; 188.
53. Connor, *Deviance in Soviet Society,* pp. 174–75.
54. The article by Derviz indicates the reverse phenomenon is the problem in Soviet society. Commuters are a source of urban crime as Skogan has suggested in the U. S.
55. B. Maroszek, "Développement économique, structures sociales et délinquance juvénile dans certaines régions de Pologne," in *La délinquance juvénile en Europe,* pp. 18–22.
56. Jerzy Jasinski, "La délinquance des mineurs et des jeunes adultes en Pologne de 1951 à 1962," in *La délinquance juvénile en Europe,* p. 60.
57. H. Kolakowska, "La délinquance juvénile dans une ville industrielle ancienne et dans une nouvelle cite d'habitation," in *La délinquance juvénile en Europe,* pp. 91–92.

58. Maroszek, p. 202.

59. A. Todorovic, "Croissance des villes et délinquance juvénile," in *La délinquance juvénile en Europe*, pp. 95–100.

60. S. Batawia, "La délinquance des mineurs et des jeunes adultes en Pologne d'après les recherches criminologiques," in *La délinquance juvénile en Europe* p. 131.

61. Jasinski, p. 61.

62. Wojciech Michalski, "Phenomena in the Field of the Dynamics and Structure of Crime in Poland," pp. 130–31.

63. United Nations, "Crime Prevention and Control," Report of the Secretary General, 22 Sept. 1977, p. 29.

64. Male Kalanj and Anton Lukezic, *Organizacija suzijanja kriminaliteta u turistickoj sezoni i turistickim mjestima,"* p. 154.

65. Maroszek, pp. 22–24.

66. R. S. Mogilevskii and Iu. A. Suslov, "Gorodskaia prestupnost' kak ob'ekt kriminologicheskikh issledovanii," *Pravovedenie* 5 (1973):114.

67. N. F. Kuznetsova, ed., *Sravnitel'noe kriminologicheskoe issledovanie prestupnosti v Moskve v 1923:1968–1969gg.* (Moscow: Moskovskii Universitet, 1971).

68. Effektivnost' bor'by s khuliganstvom i dinamika nekotorye tiazhkikh prestuplenii," *Informatsionnye soobshcheniia VNIIOP pri MOOP* 6 (1966).

69. Janez Pecar, "Vloga privlacujoah objektov v prostorski poraz delitvi odklonskosti," *Revija za kriminalistiko in kriminologijo* 26 (1975):186.

70. *Lichnost' prestupnika* (Moscow, 1971), p. 85.

71. *Statisticki Godisnjak Jugoslavije*, pp. 394–97.

72. Andras Szabo, "Délinquance juvénile en Hongrie," p. 140.

73. Connor, "Deviance," pp. 192–93.

74. See table in Karakashev, p. 195.

75. Batawia, p. 131

76. Maroszek, p. 212.

77. Lazarevic and Jasovic, p. 253.

78. Karakashev, p. 188.

79. Connor, *Deviance in Soviet Society, p.* 93.

80. Andrzej Mosciskier, "Delinquency in Poland and the Processes of Industrialization and Urbanization"; Jerzy Jasinski, "Juvenile Delinquency in Poland 1961–1967"; Andrzej Mosciskier, Delinquency in Regions under Intensified Industrialization and the Relationship between the Dynamics of Delinquency and the Dynamics of Socio-Economic Processes."

81. Maroszek, pp. 18–24.

82. Jasinski, "La délinquance des mineurs," pp. 61–62.

83. Maroszek, p. 21.

84. Ibid., p. 35.

85. Ibid., p. 35.

86. Connor, "Deviance," p. 194.

87. *Lichnost' prestupnika*, p. 75.

88. Connor, *Deviance in Soviet Society*, p. 92.

89. Shelley.

98. Karakashev, pp. 188–95.

91. Pecar.

92. Jasinski, "La délinquance des mineurs," p. 50.

93. P. Zakrzewski, "Recherches sur la délinquance juvénile à Nowa Huta," in *La délinquance juvénile en Europe*, p. 76.

94. *Lichnost' prestupnika*, p. 98.

95. Ibid., p. 65.

96. Ibid., p. 100.

97. Connor, "Deviance," p. 193.

98. Zakrzewski, p. 77.

99. Jasinski, "La délinquance des mineurs," pp. 51–52.

100. Connor, *Deviance in Soviet Society,* pp. 88–90.

101. Jasinski, "La délinquance des mineurs," p. 49.

102. Peter Juviler, *Revolutionary Law and Order,* p. 152; Iu. V. Solopanov and V. E. Kvashis, *Retsidiv i retsidivisty* (Moscow: Ministerstvo vnutrennykh del SSSR, 1971).

103. *Lichnost' prestupnika,* p. 59.

104. Batawia, p. 132.

105. S. Walczak, "La délinquance juvénile et le développement économique: remarques concernant l'objet et les methodes de recherches," in *La délinquance juvénile en Europe,* p. 145.

106. Batawia, pp. 129–30.

107. Radvanyi, p. 104; and M. Vermesh, "O nekotorykh kriminologicheskikh issledovaniiakh v Vengrii," p. 144.

108. Neznansky, p. 51, and tacit admission by Polish scholars at the World Congress of Sociology, Uppsala, Sweden, 1978.

SELECTED BIBLIOGRAPHY

ABRAMS, CHARLES. "City Planning and Housing Policy in Relation to Crime and Juvenile Delinquency." *International Review of Criminal Policy* 16 (1960):25–28.

ADLER, FREDA. "The Interaction Between Women's Emancipation and Female Criminality. A Cross-Cultural Perspective." *International Journal of Criminology and Penology* 5 (1977):101–12.

———. *Sisters in Crime: The Rise of the New Female Criminal.* New York: McGraw-Hill, 1975.

ADLER, FREDA, and MUELLER, G.O.W., eds. *Politics, Crime and the International Scene: An Inter-American Focus.* South Hackensack, N. J.: Fred B. Rothman, 1972.

ALBINI, J. L. "Mafia as Method—A Comparison Between Great Britain and USA Regarding the Existence and Structure of Types of Organized Crime." *International Journal of Criminology and Penology* 3 (1975):295–305.

ANDENAES, JOHANNES. "Negligent Homicide in Some European Countries—A Comparative Study." In *Crime and Culture,* edited by Marvin E. Wolfgang. New York: John Wiley & Sons, 1968.

ANDERSON, F. *Changes in the Distribution of Population and Its Effects Upon Arrest.* Richmond, Virginia: Virginia Division of Justice and Crime Prevention, 1976.

ANDRY R. G. "Juvenile Delinquency in Developing Countries." *Annales Internationales de Criminologie* 1 (1964):87–92.

ANTILLA, INKERI. "Crime Trends in Finland." Paper read at ISA Research Symposium on Crime, August 1978, in Stockholm, Sweden. Mimeographed.

ARCHER, DANE, and GARTNER, ROSEMARY. "Homicide in 110 Nations: The Development of the Comparative Crime Data File." *International Annals of Criminology* 16 (1977):109–42.

———. "Violent Acts and Violent Times: A Comparative Approach to Postwar Homicide Rates." *American Sociological Review* 41 (1976):937–63.

ARIÈS, PHILIPPE. *Centuries of Childhood: A Social History of Family Life.* Translated by Robert Baldick. New York: Alfred A. Knopf, 1962.

ASUNI, T. "Focus of Social Defense Research in the Developmental Context." *International Review of Criminal Policy* 29 (1970):28–32.

BACON, MARGARET; CHILD, IRVIN L.; and BARRY, HERBERT, III. "A Cross-Cultural Study of Correlates of Crime." *Journal of Abnormal and Social Psychology* 66 (1963):291–300.

Selected Bibliography

BALDWIN, J. "British Area Studies of Crime: An Assessment." *British Journal of Criminology* 15 (July 1975):111–227.

BAUR, E. J. "Statistical Indexes of the Social Aspects of Communities." *Social Forces* 53 (October 1954):64–75.

BAYLEY, DAVID H. *Forces of Order: Police Behavior in Japan and the United States.* Berkeley and Los Angeles: University of California Press, 1976.

———. "The Effects of Corruption in a Developing Nation." In *Political Corruption* edited by Arnold Heidenheimer, pp. 521–33. New York: Holt, Rinehart & Winston, 1970

BELLAMY, JOHN. *Crime and Public Order in England in the Late Middle Ages.* London: Routledge & Kegan Paul, 1973.

BERRY, BRIAN J. L. *The Human Consequences of Urbanization.* New York: St. Martin's Press, 1973.

BIANCHI, H.: SIMONDI, M.: and TAYLOR, I. *Deviance and Control in Europe—Papers from the European Group for the Study of Deviance and Social Control.* New York: John Wiley & Sons, 1975.

BILES, DAVID, ed. *Crime in Papua, New Guinea.* Canberra: Australian Institute of Criminology, 1976.

BOGGS, SARAH. "Urban Crime Patterns." *American Sociological Review* 30 (1965):899–908.

BOHANNAN, PAUL. "Cross-Cultural Comparison of Aggression and Violence." In U.S. Task Force on Individual Acts of Violence, *Crimes of Violence,* vol. 13, pp. 1189–239. Washington, D.C.: U.S. Government Printing Office, 1969.

———. ed. *African Homicide and Suicide.* Princeton, N. J.: Princeton University Press, 1960.

BONGER, WILLIAM ADRIAN. *Criminality and Economic Conditions.* Boston: Little, Brown & Co., 1916

BOWKER, LEE. "Women and Crime: An International Perspective." Paper read at the Ninth World Congress of Sociology, August 1978, in Uppsala, Sweden. Mimeographed.

BRILLON, J. "Développement économique et criminalité en Afrique Occidentale". *Revue Internationale de Criminologie et de Police Technique* 26 (January–March 1973):65–70.

BRUSTON, MANFRED. "Crime Trends in West Germany." Paper read at ISA Research Symposium on Crime, August 1978, in Stockholm, Sweden. Mimeographed.

BRUUN, KETTIL; PAN, LYNN; AND REXED, INGEMAR. *The Gentlemen's Club: International Control of Drugs and Alcohol.* Chicago: University of Chicago Press, 1975.

BUCHOLZ, ERICH; HARTMANN, RICHARD; LEKSCHAS, JOHN; AND STILLER, G. *Socialist Criminology—Theoretical and Methodological Foundations.* Farnborough, Hants., England: Saxon House, 1974.

CANESTRI, F. "Venezuela—une criminologie Latino-Americaine." *Annales Internationales de Criminologie* 12 (1973):229–41.

CARSON, W. G. *Crime and Delinquency in Britain—Sociological Readings.* London: Martin Robertson, 1971.

CARTER, R. L. "Criminal's Image of the City and Urban Crime Patterns." *Social Science Quarterly* 57 (1976):597–607.

CASTLES, STEPHEN, and KOSACK, GODULA. *Immigrant Workers and Class Structures in Western Europe.* London: Oxford University Press, 1973.

CAVAN, R. S., AND CAVAN, J. *Delinquency and Crime: Cross-Cultural Perspectives.* Philadelphia: J. B. Lippincott, 1968.

CHANG, DAE H. "Environmental Influences on Criminal Activity in Korea." *Criminology* 10 (1972):338–52.

Selected Bibliography

————, ed *Criminology: A Cross-Cultural Perspective.* Vols. 1 and 2. New Delhi: Vikas, 1976.

CHAPPELL, DUNCAN, and WILSON, PAUL. *The Australian Criminal Justice System.* Sydney: Butterworth & Co., 1972.

CHEVALIER, LOUIS. *Laboring Classes and Dangerous Classes.* New York: Howard Fertig, 1973.

CHRISTIANSEN, KARL O. "Industrialization, Urbanization and Crime." In *Crime and Industrialization,* edited by Scandinavia Research Council of Criminology, pp. 46–57. Stockholm: University of Stockholm, 1974.

————. "Industrialization and Urbanization in Relation to Crime and Juvenile Delinquency." *International Review of Criminal Policy* 16 (1960):3–8.

CHRISTIANSEN, KARL O., and JENSEN, S. J. "Crime in Denmark." *Journal of Criminal Law, Criminology and Police Science* 60 (1972):82–92.

CLIFFORD, WILLIAM. *Crime Control in Japan.* Lexington, Mass.: D. C. Heath, 1976.

————. *Introduction to African Criminology.* Nairobi: Oxford University Press, 1974.

————. "New Dimensions in Criminality—National and Transnational." *Australian and New Zealand Journal of Criminology* 8 (1975):67–85.

CLINARD, MARSHALL B. *Cities with Little Crime.* Cambridge: At the University Press, 1978.

————. "A Cross-Cultural Replication of the Relations of Urbanism to Criminal Behavior." *American Sociological Review.* 25 (1960):253–57.

————. "The Organization of Urban Community Development Services in the Prevention of Crime and Juvenile Delinquency, with Particular Reference to Less Developed Countries." *International Review of Criminal Policy* 19 (1962):3–12.

————. "The Process of Urbanization and Criminal Behavior: A Study of Culture Conflicts." *American Journal of Sociology* 48 (1942):302–13.

————. "The Relation of Urbanization and Urbanism to Criminal Behavior." In *Contributions to Urban Sociology,* edited by E. W. Burgess and Donald J. Bogue. Chicago: University of Chicago Press, 1964.

————. "Urbanization and Criminal Behavior." Ph.D. diss., University of Chicago, 1941.

————, ed. *Anomie and Deviant Behavior.* New York: Free Press, 1964.

CLINARD, MARSHALL B., and ABBOTT, DANIEL J. "Community Organization and Property Crime: A Comparative Study of Social Control in the Slums of an African City." In *Delinquency, Crime and Society,* edited by James F. Short, Jr., pp. 186–206. Chicago: University of Chicago Press, 1976.

————. *Crime in Developing Countries: A Comparative Perspective.* New York: John Wiley & Sons, 1973.

CLOWARD, R. A., and OHLIN, L. E. *Delinquency and Opportunity.* Glencoe, Ill.: Free Press, 1960.

COHEN. ALBERT K. *Delinquent Boys.* Glencoe, Ill.: Free Press, 1955.

CONNOR, WALTER D. "Criminal Homicide, U.S.S.R./U.S.A. Reflections on Soviet Data in a Comparative Framework." *Journal of Criminal Law and Criminology* 64 (1973):111–17.

————. *Deviance in Soviet Society: Crime, Delinquency and Alcoholism.* New York: Columbia University Press, 1972.

————. "Deviance, Stress and Modernization in Eastern Europe." In *Social Consequences of Modernization in Communist Societies,* edited by Mark G. Field, pp. 181–203. Baltimore: Johns Hopkins University Press, 1976.

————. "Juvenile Delinquency in the U.S.S.R.: Some Quantitative and Qualitative Indicators." *American Sociological Review* 35 (1970):283–97.

Selected Bibliography

CONRAD, JOHN P. *Crime and Its Correction.* Berkeley and Los Angeles: University of California Press, 1970.

COOPER, H. H. A. "Ideology and Latin American Criminology." In *Politics, Crime and the International Scene,* edited by Freda Adler and G. O. W. Mueller. South Hackensack, N. J.: Fred B. Rothman, 1972.

COUNCIL OF EUROPE. *Activities in the Field of Crime Problems 1956–1976.* Strasbourg: Council of Europe, 1977.

——. *Criminological Aspects of Economic Crime.* Collected Studies in Criminological Research, vol. 15. Strasbourg: Council of Europe, 1977.

——. *Current Trends in Criminological Research.* Strasbourg: Librarie Bergen Levrault, 1970.

COURT, T. H. "Pornography and Sex-Crimes; A Re-evaluation in the Light of Recent Trends around the World." *International Journal of Criminology and Penology* 5 (1977):113–28.

CZUBINSKI, LUCJAN. "Crime Problems in Present-Day Poland." In *Problems of Crime Prevention in Poland,* edited by Brunon Hoyst, pp. 15–19. Warsaw: Polish Scientific Publishers, 1976.

DAVID, PEDRO R., and SCOTT, JOSEPH W. "A Cross-Cultural Comparison of Juvenile Offenders, Offenses, Due Processes, and Societies: The Cases of Toledo, Ohio, and Rosario, Argentina." *Criminology* 11 (August 1973):183–205.

DEFLEUR, LOIS B. "A Cross-Cultural Comparison of Juvenile Offenders and Offenses: Cordoba, Argentina, and the United States." *Social Problems* 14 (1967):483–92.

——. "Delinquent Gangs in Cross-Cultural Perspective: The Case of Cordoba." *Journal of Research in Crime and Delinquency* 4 (1967):132–41.

——. "Ecological Variables in the Cross-Cultural Study of Delinquency." *Social Forces* 45 (1967):556–70.

DEKKERS, R. "La Chine." In *Les frontières de la repression,* pp. 457–62. Brussels: Éditions de l'Université de Bruxelles, 1974.

La délinquance juvénile en Europe. Brussels: L'Instituté de Sociologie de L'université Libre de Bruxelles, 1968.

DOLESCHAL, EUGENE, ed. *Crime and Delinquency Research in Selected European Countries.* Washington, D. C.: U. S. Government Printing Office, 1972.

DOUGLAS, T. D., ed. *Deviance and Respectability.* New York: Basic Books, 1970.

DRESSLER, D. *Readings in Criminology and Penology.* New York: Columbia University Press, 1964.

DUNN, C. S. "Analysis of Environmental Attributes—Crime Incident Characteristics Relationships." In *Project Search—International Symposium. Criminal Justice Information and Statistical Systems April 30 to May 21, 1974:*569–86.

DURKHEIM, ÉMILE. *The Division of Labor in Society.* Translated by G. Simpson. New York: Free Press, 1933.

——. *The Rules of Sociological Method.* Glencoe, Ill. Free Press, 1964.

——. *Suicide: A Study in Sociology.* Glencoe, Ill.: Free Press, 1951.

EISENSTADT, S. N. *Tradition, Change and Modernity.* New York: John Wiley & Sons, 1973.

EL BACHA, ABDELLATIF. "Quelques aspects particuliers de la délinquance juvénile dans certaines villes du royaume du Maroc." *International Review of Criminal Policy* 20 (1962):11–21.

EMOVON, A. C., and LAMBO, T. A. "Survey of Criminal Homicide in Nigeria." *Scandinavian Journal of Social Medicine* 6 (1978):55–58.

ENGELS, FRIEDRICH. *The Position of the Working Class in England.* Moscow: Progress Publishers, 1973.

EVANS, R., JR. "Changing Labor Markets and Criminal Behavior in Japan." *Journal of Asian Studies* 36 (1977):477–89.

Selected Bibliography

FARLEY, JOHN E., and HANSEL, MARK. "The Ecological Context of Urban Crime: A Further Exploration." Paper read at Midwest Sociological Society, 1979, in Minneapolis. Mimeographed.

FERDINAND, THEODORE H. "Criminal Justice: From Colonial Intimacy to Bureaucratic Formality." In *Handbook of Contemporary Urban Life,* edited by David Streetem. San Francisco: Jossey-Bass, 1978.

FERRACUTI, FRANCO. "European Migration and Crime." In *Crime and Culture,* edited by Marvin E. Wolfgang, pp. 189–219. New York: John Wiley & Sons, 1968.

FERRACUTI, FRANCO; DINITZ, S.; and ACOSTADE BRENES, E. *Delinquents and Nondelinquents in the Puerto Rican Slum Culture.* Columbus, Ohio: Ohio State University Press, 1975.

FERRACUTI, FRANCO; LAZARI, R.; and WOLFGANG, MARVIN E. *Violence in Sardinia.* Rome: Bulzoni, 1973.

FIELD, MARK G. "Drink and Delinquency in the U.S.S.R." *Problems of Communism* 4 (1955):29–38.

"First International Symposium on Research in Comparative Criminology." *International Review of Criminal Policy* 28 (1970):113–18.

FLANGO, V. E., and SHERBENOU, E. L. "Poverty, Urbanization and Crime." *Criminology* 14 (November 1976):331–46.

FOUCAULT, MICHEL. *Discipline and Punish: The Birth of the Prison.* Translated by Alan Sheridan. New York: Pantheon Books, 1977.

FRANCIS, R.D. "Migration and Crime in Australia." In *The Australian Criminal Justice System,* pp. 201–22. Sydney: Butterworth & Co., 1972.

FRASER, GRAEME S. "Parent-Adolescent Relationships and Delinquent Behavior: A Cross-National Comparison." *Sociological Quarterly* 8 (1967):505–13.

FRIDAY, PAUL C. "Problems in Comparative Criminology: Comments on the Feasibility and Implications of Research." *International Journal of Criminology and Penology* 1 (1973):151–60.

FRIDAY, PAUL, and HAGE, JERALD. "Youth Crime in Postindustrial Societies." *Criminology* 14 (1976):347–67.

FRIDAY, PAUL C., and STEWART, V. LORNE, eds. *Youth Crime and Juvenile Justice—International Perspectives.* New York: Praeger, 1977.

FROLIC, MICHAEL B. "Noncomparative Communism: Chinese and Soviet Urbanization." In *Social Consequences of Modernization in Communist Societies,* edited by Mark G. Field, pp. 149–61. Baltimore: Johns Hopkins University Press, 1976.

GAIER, E. L. "Shifts in Delinquent Behavior, 1951–1973." *Juvenile Justice* 27 (August 1976):15–23.

GASTIL, R. D. "Homicide and a Regional Culture of Violence." *American Sociological Review* 36 (1971):412–27.

GATTRELL, V. A. C. and HADDEN, T. B. "Criminal Statistics and Their Interpretation." In *Nineteenth Century Society,* edited by E. A. Wrigley. Cambridge: At the University Press, 1972.

GERNET, M. N. *Izbrannye proizvedeniia.* Moscow: Juridicial Literature, 1974.

GIANNINI, M. C. "Economica y Delicuencia." *Criminologico* 1 (1973):125–38.

GIDDENS, ANTHONY. *Capitalism and Modern Social Theory.* Cambridge: At the University Press, 1971.

GODONY, JOSEF. "Criminality in Industrialized Countries." In *Crime and Industrialization,* edited by Scandinavian Research Council on Criminology pp. 91–109. Stockholm: University of Stockholm, 1974.

GOODMAN, NANCY. *Yugoslavia–A New Look at Crime.* London: Institute for the Study and Treatment of Delinquency, 1967.

GRAHAM, FRED P. "A Contemporary History of American Crime." In *Violence in America: Historical and Comparative Perspectives,* edited by Hugh Davis

Graham and Ted Robert Gurr, pp. 371–85. Washington, D. C.: U. S. Government Printing Office, 1969.

GRAHAM, HUGH DAVIS, and GURR, TED ROBERT *Violence in America: Historical and Comparative Perspectives.* Washington, D.C.: U.S. Government Printing Office, 1969.

GURR, TED ROBERT. "Crime Trends in Modern Democracies since 1945." *International Annals of Criminology* 16 (1977):84–86.

———. "The Criminal Ethos." *Center Magazine,* January/February 1978, pp. 74–79.

———. "On the History of Violent Crime in Europe and America." In *Violence in America: Historical and Comparative Perspectives,* edited by Hugh Davis Graham and Ted Robert Gurr. Beverly Hills: Sage, 1979.

———. *Rogues, Rebels and Reformers: A Political History of Urban Crime and Conflict.* Beverly Hills, Calif.: Sage, 1976.

GURR, TED ROBERT; GRABOSKY, PETER N.; and HULA, ROBERT C. *The Politics of Crime and Conflict: A Comparative History of Four Cities.* Beverly Hills, Calif.: Sage, 1977.

HAMPE, THEODOR. *Crime and Punishment in Germany.* London: Routledge and Sons, 1929.

HARRIES, KEITH D. "The Geography of American Crime, 1968." *Journal of Geography,* April 1971 pp. 204–13.

HAUGE, RAGNER, and WOLF, PREBEN. "Criminal Violence in Three Scandinavian Countries." In *Scandinavian Studies in Criminology,* vol. 5, pp. 25–33. London: Martin Robertson, 1974.

HAUSER, PHILIP M., and SCHNORE, LEO F., eds. *The Study of Urbanization.* New York: John Wiley & Sons, 1965.

HAZARD, JOHN N.; SHAPIRO, ISAAC; and MAGGS, PETER B. *The Soviet Legal System.* New York: Oceana Publications, 1969.

HELLMER, J. *Criminal Atlas of the Federal Republic of Germany and West Berlin—A Contribution to Criminal Geography.* Wiesbaden: Bundeskriminalamt, 1972.

HELLMER, J. *Criminality in Berlin.* Translated by the National Criminal Justice Reference Service. Berlin: Walter de Droyten, 1972.

HENRY, ANDREW F., and SHORT, JAMES F., JR. *Suicide and Homicide: Some Economic, Sociological and Psychological Aspects of Aggression.* New York: Free Press, 1954.

HIRSCHI, TRAVIS. *Causes of Delinquency.* Berkeley and Los Angeles: University of California Press, 1969.

HOBSBAWM, E. J. *Primitive Rebels.* New York: Praeger, 1959.

HOOD, ROGER, and SPARKS, RICHARD. *Key Issues in Criminology.* London: Weidenfeld and Nicholson, 1970.

HOUCHON, G. "Causation Research in Criminology." *Collected Studies in Criminological Review* 1 (1967):35–39.

INGRAHAM, B. L., and TOKORO, K. "Political Crime in the United States and Japan: A Comparative Study." *Issues in Criminology* 14 (1968):145–69.

INKELES, ALEX. "The Modernization of Man in Socialist and Nonsocialist Countries." In *Social Consequences of Modernization in Communist Societies,* edited by Mark G. Field, pp. 50–59. Baltimore: Johns Hopkins University Press, 1976.

INKELES, ALEX, and SMITH, DAVID H. *Becoming Modern.* Cambridge, Mass.: Harvard University Press, 1974.

International Center for Comparative Criminology. Annual Report 1972–3. Montreal: University of Montreal, 1973.

"Inventaire Bibliographique. Criminologie Comparée." *Annales Internationales de Criminologie* 12 (1973):245–66.

JASINSKI, JERZY. "Delinquent Generations in Poland." *British Journal of Criminology* 6 (April 1966):170–82.

Selected Bibliography

JASINSKI, JERZY. "Juvenile Delinquency in Poland 1961–67." *Archiwum Kryminologii* 4 (1966):229–40.

JASPERSE, C. W. G.; Leeuwen-Burow, A. V.; and Toornvliet, L. G. *Criminology Between the Rule of Law and the Outlaws.* Deventer, Holland: Kluwer, 1976.

JUD, G. D. "Tourism and Crime in Mexico." *Social Science Quarterly* 56 (September 1975):324–30.

JUNGER-TAS, J. "Crime and Dutch Society." Paper read at ISA Research Symposium on Crime, August 1978, in Stockholm, Sweden. Mimeographed.

———. "Some Issues and Problems in Cross-Cultural Research in Criminology." Paper read at American Society of Criminology, 1978, Dallas, Texas. Mimeographed.

JUVILER, PETER. *Revolutionary Law and Order.* New York: Free Press, 1976.

KALANJ, MALE, and LUKEZIC, ANTON. *Organizacija suzijanja kriminaliteta u turistickoj sezoni i turistickim mjestima.* Beograd: Savezni Sekretaryatza Unutrasnje Poslove, 1971.

KARAKASHEV, VESELIN. *Problemi na prest'pnostta i neinata struktura.* Sofia: Bulgarskata Akademiia na naukite, 1977.

KAYIIRA, L. A. "Violence in Kondoism—The Rise and Nature of Violent Crime in Uganda." Ph.D. dissertation, State University of New York at Albany, 1978.

KOLEV, STOIAN, "Povisheni iziskvaniia i efektiven kontrol." *Rabotnicheso Delo* 4 (June 1979):2.

KONRAD, GYORGY and SZELENYI, IVAN. "Social Conflicts of Underurbanization: The Hungarian Case." In *Social Consequences of Modernization in Communist Societies,* edited by Mark G. Field, pp. 162–78. Baltimore: Johns Hopkins University Press, 1976.

Kriminologiia, 2nd ed. Moscow: Juridicial Literature, 1968.

KUDRIAVTSEV, V. N. "The Structure of Criminality and Social Change," *Recent Contributions to Soviet Criminology,* pp. 23–37. Rome: United Nations Social Defense Research Institute, 1974.

KUZNETSOVA, N. *Prestuplenie i prestupnost'.* Moscow: Moscow University Press, 1969.

LANE, ROGER. *Policing the City: Boston, 1822–1885.* Cambridge, Mass.: Harvard University Press, 1967.

LEKSCHAS, JOHN "On Some Aspects of Criminality in Socialist Society." *Law and Legislation in the German Democratic Republic* 1 (1971):16–24.

LENSKI, GERHARD. *Power and Privilege.* New York: McGraw-Hill, 1966.

LENTZ, WILLIAM P. "Rural Urban Differentials and Juvenile Delinquency." *Journal of Criminal Law, Criminology and Police Science* 47 (September-October 1956):331–39.

LEWIS, OSCAR. *La Vida: A Puerto Rican Family in the Culture of Poverty.* New York: Random House, 1966.

LIN, TSUNG-YI. "Two Types of Delinquent Youth in Chinese Society." In *Comparative Social Problems,* edited by S. N. Eisenstadt, pp. 169–76. New York: Free Press, 1964.

LODHI, A. Q., and TILLY, CHARLES. "Urbanization, Crime and Collective Violence in Nineteenth Century France." *American Journal of Sociology* 79 (1973):297–318.

LOPEZ-RAY, MANUEL. *Crime: An Analytical Appraisal.* New York: Praeger, 1970.

———. "Economic Conditions and Crime with Special Reference to Less Developed Countries." *Annales Internationales de Criminologie* 1 (1964):33–40.

LUCAS, S. A. "Social Deviance and Crime in Selected Rural Communities of Tanzania." *Cahiers d'études Africaines* 16 (1976):499–518.

MANGIN, G. "La délinquance juvénile en Afrique noire Francophone." *Archives de Politique Criminelle* 1 (1975):225–40.

MANNHEIM, HERMANN. *Comparative Criminology.* Boston: Houghton Mifflin, 1965.

Selected Bibliography

————. *Group Problems in Crime and Punishment.* London: Routledge & Kegan Paul, 1955.

————. "Juvenile Delinquency." *British Journal of Delinquency* 7 (1956):148–52.

MANZANERA, LUIS R. *La Delincuencia de Menores en Mexico.* Mexico City: Messis, 1976.

MARCUS, STEVEN. *Engels, Manchester and the Working Class.* New York: Random House, 1974.

MARSH, ROBERT. *Comparative Sociology.* New York: Harcourt Brace and World, 1967.

MARX, KARL, and ENGELS, FRIEDRICH. *Sobranie Sochineniia,* vol. 5. Moscow, 1955.

MATZA, DAVID. *Delinquency and Drift.* New York: John Wiley & Sons, 1968.

MAYS, JOHN BARRON. *Crime and the Social Structure.* London, Faber & Faber, 1963.

MAZLOUMAN, R. "Polygamie et Criminalité." *Revue Internationale de Criminologie et de Police Technique* 26 (October–December 1973):400–404.

MCCARTHY, J. D., GALLE, O. R.; and ZIMMERN, W. "Population Density, Social Structure and Interpersonal Violence—An Inter Metropolitan Test of Competing Models." *American Behavioral Scientist* 8 (July–August 1975):771–91.

MCCLINTOCK, F. H., and AVISON, N. HOWARD. *Crime in England and Wales.* London: William Heinemann 1968.

MCGRATH, W. J. *Crime and Its Treatment in Canada.* Toronto: Macmillan Co., 1971.

MCLENNAN, BARBARA N., ed. *Crime in Urban Society.* New York: Dunellen, 1970.

MERGEN, ARMAND. "Les incidences du devéloppement économique sur la criminalité." *Annales Internationales de Criminologie* 1 (1964):41–55.

MERTON, ROBERT K. *Social Theory and Social Structure,* rev. ed. New York: Free Press, 1967.

MEYER, JOHN C., JR. "Methodological Issues in Comparative Criminal Justice Research." *Criminology* 10 (November 1972):295–313.

MICHALSKI, WOJCIECH. "The Effect of Social Changes on Crime in Poland in Light of Research by Criminologists," and "Phenomena in the Field of the Dynamics and Structure of Crime in Poland." In *Crime and Industrialization,* edited by Scandinavian Research Council on Criminology. Stockholm: University of Stockholm, 1974, 120–35.

MIDDENDORF, WOLF. "The Case of August Sangret." *Annales Internationales de Criminologie* 12 (1973):61–73.

————. "New Forms of Juvenile Delinquency: Their Origin, Prevention and Treatment." Second United Nations Conference on the Prevention of Crime and Treatment of Offenders New York: United Nations, 1960, pp. 33–36.

MILLER, WALTER B. "Lower Class Culture as a Generating Milieu of Gang Delinquency." *Journal of Social Issues* 14 (1958):5–19.

MOSCISKIER, ANDRZEJ. "Delinquency in Regions under Intensified Industrialization and the Relationship between the Dynamics of Delinquency and the Dynamics of Socio-Economic Processes (1958–60 and 1964–66)." *Archiwum Kriminologii* 4 (1969):223–28.

————. "Delinquency in Poland and the Processes of Industrialization and Urbanization." *Polish Sociological Bulletin* 1 (1976):53–63.

MUSHANGA, TIBAMANYA. *Criminal Homicide in Uganda.* Nairobi, Kenya: East Africa Literary Bureau, 1974.

MYRDAL, GUNNAR. "Corruption: Its Causes and Effects." In *Political Corruption,* edited by Arnold J. Heidenheimer. New York: Holt, Rinehart & Winston, 1970.

National Criminal Justice Reference Service. *International Summaries,* vols. 1 and 2. Washington, D. C.: National Institute of Law Enforcement and Criminal Justice, 1978.

Selected Bibliography

NAYAR, BALDEV RAY. *Violence and Crime in India.* New Delhi: Macmillan & Co., 1975.

NEPOTE, J. "Interpol and Organized Crime." *International Criminal Police Review* 282 (November 1974):230–36.

NEWMAN, GRAEME R. *Comparative Deviance.* New York: Elsevier, 1976.

———. "Problems of Method of Comparative Criminology." *International Journal of Comparative and Applied Criminal Justice* 1 (Spring 1977):17–31.

———. "Toward a Transnational Classification of Crime and Deviance." *Journal of Cross-Cultural Psychology* 16 (September 1975):297–315.

ODEKUNLE, F. "Capitalist Economy and the Crime Problem in Nigeria." *Contemporary Crises* 2 (January 1978):83–96.

OLMO, R. DEL. "Les limitations dans la prévention de la violence." *Revue de Droit Pénal et de Criminologie* 55 (March 1975):511–27.

OLURUNTIMEHIN, OLUFUNMILAYO. "A Study of Juvenile Delinquency in a Nigerian City." *British Journal of Criminology* 13 (1973):157–69.

PARSONS, TALCOTT. *The Social System.* Glencoe, Ill.: Free Press, 1951.

———. *The Structure of Social Action.* 2 vols. New York: Free Press, 1968.

PECAR, JANEZ "Vloga privlacujoah objektov v prostorski poraz delitvi odklonskosti." *Revija za kriminalistiko in kriminologijo* 26 (1975):183–200.

PEILLAD, A. *Criminologia del minor delincuente.* Santiago: Editorial Andres Bello, 1972.

Penal Code of the Polish People's Republic. Translated by William S. Kenney and Tadeusz Sadowski. South Hackensack, N. J.: Fred B. Rothman, 1973.

PHILLIPSON, COLEMAN. *Three Criminal Law Reformers.* Montclair, N. J.: Patterson Smith, 1970.

PIERRE, EVELYNE: FLAMAND, J. P. and COLLOMB, H. "La délinquance juvénile à Dakar." *International Review of Criminal Policy* 20 (1962):27–33.

PINATEL, JEAN. *La Société Criminogene.* Paris: Calmann, Levy, 1971.

POKORNY, ALEX D. "A Comparison of Homicide in Two Cities." *Journal of Criminal Law, Criminology and Police Science,* (December 1965):479–87.

"Quelques considerations sur la prévention de la délinquance juvénile dans les pays africains subissant des changements sociaux rapides." *International Review of Criminal Policy* 16 (1960):33–42.

QUINNEY, RICHARD. *The Social Reality of Crime.* Boston: Little, Brown & Co., 1970.

———. "Structural Characteristics, Population Areas and Crime Rates in the United States." *Journal of Criminal Law, Criminology and Police Science* 57 (1966):46–52.

RADVANYI, MIKLOS. "Die Kriminalitat in Ungarn." *Jahrbuch für Ostrecht* 18 (1977):87–120.

RADZINOWICZ, SIR LEON. *In Search of Criminology.* Cambridge Mass.: Harvard University Press, 1962.

RADZINOWICZ, SIR LEON, and KING, JOAN. *The Growth of Crime.* New York: Basic Books, 1977.

RAYMAEKERS, PAUL. "Prédelinquance et délinquance juvénile à Leopoldville." *International Review of Criminal Policy* 20 (1962):49–53.

Recent Contributions to Soviet Criminology. Rome: United Nations Social Defense Research Institute, 1974.

Research Bulletin of the Ministry of Justice of the Netherlands. The Hague: Research and Documentation Centre of the Ministry of Justice, 7 (1977):82–83.

RIZKALLA, S. "Crime and Criminal Justice in the Developing Countries." *Acta Criminologica* 7 (January 1974):169–89.

ROBERT, P.; BISMUTH, P.; and LAMBERT, T. *La criminalité des migrants en France.* Paris: Service D'Etudes Pénales et Criminologiques, 1970.

Selected Bibliography

ROSENQUIST, CARL M., and MEGARGEE, EDWIN I. *Delinquency in Three Cultures.* Austin: University of Texas Press, 1969.

ROSHCHIN, V. N., and LASHIN, M. P. "Characteristics of Criminals." *Soviet Review* 1 (1960):3–27

RUSSELL, W. "Criminal Ecology—Rising Crime Rate and the Criminal Population." *Police Research Bulletin* 5 (1968):13–16.

SALGADO, GAMINI. *The Elizabethan Underworld.* London: J. M. Dent & Sons, 1977.

SANCHEZ GALINDO, A. "El perfit del delincuente en el estado de Mexico." *Revista Mexicana de Prevencion y Readaptacion Social* 17 (April–June 1975):107–21.

Scandinavian Research Council on Criminology. *Crime and Industrialization.* Stockholm: University of Stockholm, 1974.

Scandinavian Studies in Criminology. Vols. 1,3, and 5. London: Martin Robertson, 1965, 1971, 1974.

SCHMID, CALVIN F. "Urban Crime Areas: Part II." *American Sociological Review* 25 (August 1960): 655–78.

SCHUR, EDWIN. *Crimes Without Victims.* Englewood-Cliffs, N. J. Prentice-Hall, 1965.

SCOTT, PETER. "Gangs and Delinquent Groups in London." *British Journal of Criminology* 7 (1956):4–26.

SELLIN, THORSTEN. *Culture Conflict and Crime.* New York: Social Science Research Council, 1938.

SELLIN, THORSTEN, and WOLFGANG, MARVIN E. *The Measurement of Delinquency.* New York: John Wiley & Sons, 1967.

SERRANO, GOMEZ, A. "La criminalidad en Espana y Francia." *Policia Espanola* 14 (September 1975):33–42.

———. "Robos con violencia o intimidacion en las personas." *Rivista Espanola de la opinion publica* 46 (October–December 1976):103–40.

SHARGORODSKII, M. D. "The Causes and Prevention of Crime." *Soviet Sociology* 3 (Summer 1964):24–39.

SHAW, CLIFFORD R. and McKAY, HENRY D. *Juvenile Delinquency and Urban Areas.* Chicago: University of Chicago Press, 1942.

SHICHOR, DAVID. "Some Correlations of Juvenile Delinquency in Israel Development Towns." In *Israel Studies in Criminology,* edited by Shlomo Shoham, vol. 2. Jerusalem: Jerusalem Academic Press, 1973.

SHOHAM, SHLOMO, ed. *Israel Studies in Criminology,* vol. 1, Jerusalem: Jerusalem Academic Press, 1970.

SHOHAM, SHLOMO, and SHAKOLSKY, LEON. "An Analysis of Delinquents and Nondelinquents in Israel: A Cross-Culture Perspective." *Sociology, and Social Research* 3 (1969):333–43.

SHOHAM, SHLOMO; SHOHAM, N.; and ABD-EL-RAZEK, A. "Immigration, Ethnicity and Ecology as Related to Juvenile Delinquency in Israel." *British Journal of Criminology* 6 (1966):391–409.

SHORT, JAMES F., JR., *Delinquency, Crime and Society.* Chicago: University of Chicago Press, 1976.

SILVER, ALLAN. "The Demand for Order in Civil Society, A Review of Some Themes in the History of Urban Crime, Police and Riot." In *The Police: Six Sociological Essays,* edited by David Bordua. New York: John Wiley & Sons, 1967.

SILVERMAN, ROBERT A. and TEEVAN, JAMES J., JR. *Crime in Canadian Society.* Toronto: Butterworth & Co., 1976.

SIMMEL, GEORG. *The Sociology of Georg Simmel.* Translated by K. Wolff. 4th Printing. New York: Free Press, 1959.

SIMON, RITA J. "American Women and Crime." *Annals of the American Academy of Political and Social Science* 423 (January 1976):31–46.

Selected Bibliography

SMITH, D. M. "Crime Rates as Territorial Social Indicators—The Case of the United States." Occasional Paper No. 1 University of London, London: Department of Geography, 1974.

STANCIU, V. V. *La criminalité à Paris.* Paris: Centre National de la Recherche Scientifique, 1968.

STANDISH, MYLES, and VILLALON, L. J. A., eds. *Tokyo: One City Where Crime Doesn't Pay.* Philadelphia: The Citizens Crime Commission, 1975.

STEPHENSON, LARRY K. "Spatial Dispersion of Intra-Urban Juvenile Delinquency." *Journal of Geography* 73 (March 1974):20–26.

STOFFLET, E. H. "The European Immigrant and his Children." In *Annals of the American Association of Political and Social Science* 217 (September 1941):84–92.

STRAUS, JACQUELINE H., and STRAUS, MURRAY A. "Suicide, Homicide and Social Structure in Ceylon." *American Journal of Sociology* 58 (1953):461–69.

STROMAS, A. "Crime, Law and Penal Practice in the U.S.S.R." *Review of Socialist Law* 3 (1977):297–324.

Summary of the White Paper on Crime, 1977. Tokyo: Research and Training Institute Ministry of Justice, 1978.

SUTHERLAND, EDWIN H. *The Professional Thief.* Chicago: University of Chicago Press, 1937.

———. *White Collar Crime.* New York: Dryden Press, 1949.

SUTHERLAND, EDWIN H., and CRESSEY, DONALD R. *Principles of Criminology.* 5th ed. New York: J. B. Lippincott Co., 1955.

SVERI, KNUT. "Criminality in Industrialized Countries." In *Crime and Industrialization,* edited by Scandinavian Research Council on Criminology. Stockholm: University of Stockholm, 1974.

SZABO, DENIS. "Comparative Criminology—Significance and Tasks." *Annales Internationales de Criminologie* 12 (1973):89–126.

———. *Crimes et villes: études statistiques de la criminalité urbaine et rurale en France et en Belgique.* Editions Ayas, 1960.

———. *International Center for Comparative Criminology Activities Report, 1969–1972.* Montreal: University of Montreal, 1972.

TACHOVSKY, JOHN CHARLES. "Crime in New Castle County, Delaware: A Multivariate Analysis of the Geographic Distribution of Crime Occurrence Rates." Ph.D. dissertation, University of Cincinnati, 1977.

TANNER, R. E. S. *Homicide in Uganda 1964.* Uppsala, Sweden: Scandinavian Institute of African Studies, 1970.

———. *Three Studies in East African Criminology.* Uppsala, Sweden: Scandinavian Institute of African Studies, 1970.

TARDE, GABRIEL. *La criminalité comparée.* Paris: Felix Alcan, 1902.

TARNIQUET, HENRI. "Note sur la criminalité en milieu urbaine à industrialization rapide." *Revue Internationale de Criminologie et de Police Technique* 22 (1968):49–58.

United Nations, General Assembly. "Crime Prevention and Control," Report of the Secretary General, 22 September 1977.

TAYLOR, I; WALTON, P.; and YOUNG J. *The New Criminology.* New York: Harper & Row, 1974.

"The Future Belongs to Parasites?" *Problems of Communism* 12 (1963):1–10.

THOMIS, MALCOLM I. *The Town Labourer and the Industrial Revolution.* New York: Barnes & Noble, 1974.

THOMPSON, E. P. *The Making of the English Working Class.* New York: Pantheon Books, 1963.

TILLY, CHARLES. "Collective Violence in European Perspective." In *Violence in America,* edited by Hugh Davis Graham and Ted Robert Gurr., vol. I, pp. 5–34. Washington, D. C.: U.S. Government Printing Office, 1969.

TILLY, CHARLES; TILLY, LOUISE; and TILLY, RICHARD. *The Rebellious Century: 1830–1930.* Cambridge, Mass.: Harvard University Press, 1975.

TOBIAS, J. J. *Crime and Industrial Society in the 19th Century.* New York: Schocken Books, 1967.

TOBY, JACKSON. "Affluence and Adolescent Crime." In *Task Force Report: Juvenile Delinquency and Youth Crime.* The President's Commission on Law Enforcement and Administration of Justice, app. H, pp. 132–94. Washington, D. C.: U.S. Government Printing Office, 1967.

TORNUDD, PATRIK. "Crime Trends in Finland 1950–1977." Paper read at ISA Research Symposium on Crime, August 1978, in Stockholm, Sweden. Mimeographed.

TORO-CALDER, J. "Apuntes sobre criminologia Caribena Puerto Rico 1975." In *Fundamentos para una sociologia penals en Puerto Rico,* pp. 147–70. Rio Piedras: Universidad de Puerto Rico, 1976.

TSCHOUNGUI, S. P., and ZUMBACH, P. "Diagnostic de la délinquance au Cameroun." *International Review of Criminal Policy* 20 (1962):35–44.

United Nations, "Social Change and Criminality." *International Journal of Comparative and Applied Criminal Justice* 3 (Spring 1979):79–94.

VAZ, EDMUND W., and CASPARIS, JOHN. "A Comparative Study of Youth Culture and Delinquency: Upper Middle-Class Canadian and Swiss Boys." *International Journal of Comparative Sociology* 12 (March 1971):1–23.

VENTER, HERMAN. "Urbanization and Industrialization as Criminogenic Factors in the Republic of South Africa. *International Review of Criminal Policy* 20 (1962):59–67.

VERMESH, M. "O nekotorykh kriminologicheskikh issledovaniiakh v Vengrii." *Voprosy bor'by s prestupnost'iu* 12 (1970):140–45.

VOLD, GEORGE B. "Crime in City and Country Areas." *Annals of the American Academy of Political and Social Science* 217 (September 1941):38–45.

VOLD, GEORGE B. *Theoretical Criminology.* New York: Oxford University Press, 1958.

VOLYGES, IVAN, ed. *Social Deviance in Eastern Europe.* Boulder, Colo.: Westview Press, 1978.

WEBER, MAX. *On Law in Economy and Society.* New York: Simon & Schuster, 1967.

———. *The Protestant Ethic and the Spirit of Capitalism.* New York: Charles Scribner's Sons, 1958.

———. *The Theory of Social and Economic Organization.* Edited by Talcott Parsons. New York: Free Press, 1966.

WEINBERG, S. KIRSON. "Shaw-McKay Theories of Delinquency in Cross-Cultural Context." In *Delinquency, Crime and Society,* edited by James F. Short Jr., pp. 167–85. Chicago: University of Chicago Press, 1976.

———. "Juvenile Delinquency in Ghana: A Comparative Analysis of Delinquents and Non-Delinquents." *Journal of Criminal Law, Criminology and Police Science* 155 (1964):471–81.

WIDOM, CATHY S., and STEWART, ABIGAIL J. "Female Criminality and the Changing Status of Women." Paper read at the American Society of Criminology, November 1977, in Atlanta, Georgia, Mimeographed.

WILSON, P. R., and BROWN, J. W. *Crime and the Community.* St. Lucia: University of Queensland Press, 1973.

WIRTH, LOUIS. "Urbanism as a Way of Life." *American Journal of Sociology* 44 (1938):3–24.

Selected Bibliography

WOLF, PREBEN. "Crime and Development: An International Comparison of Crime Rates." *Scandinavian Studies in Criminology* 3 (1971):107–20.

WOLFGANG, MARVIN E. "Crime and Punishment in Florence." *Journal of Criminal Law, Criminology and Police Science* 47 (1956):317–19.

———. "International Criminal Statistics: A Proposal." *Journal of Criminal Law, Criminology and Police Science* 58 (1967):65–69.

———. *Patterns in Criminal Homicide*. Philadelphia, Pennsylvania: University of Pennsylvania Press, 1958.

———, ed. *Studies in Homicide*. New York: Harper & Row, 1967.

———. "Urban Crime." In *The Metropolitan Enigma*, edited by James Q. Wilson, pp. 246–81. Cambridge, Mass.: Harvard University Press, 1968.

WOLFGANG, MARVIN E. and FERRACUTI, FRANCO. *The Subculture of Violence*. London: Methuen, 1967.

ZEHR, HOWARD. *Crime and the Development of Modern Society Patterns of Criminality in 19th Century Germany and France*. Totowa, New Jersey: Rowman & Littlefield, 1976.

———. "The Modernization of Crime in Germany and France, 1830–1913." *Journal of Social History* 8 (1974):117–41.

ZVIRBUL, V. K. "The Social and Historical Dimension in the Study of the Causes of Criminality." In *Recent Contributions to Soviet Criminology*, pp. 41–61 Rome: United Nations Social Defense Research Institute, 1974.

INDEX

Index

Highwaymen, 19
Historical tradition, impact of, 94
Homicide: definition for, xvii; high rates of in Latin America, 52; international rates for, 70; in Japan, 74; increased rates during and after wars, 69; in rural areas, 96; in Russia, 35; women offenders in, 56; study of in France and Germany, 29–30
Human conduct, regulations of, 6
Human degradation, 24
Hungary, crime in, 104, 111, 114, 116, 133

Illegal behavior. See Behavior, illegal
Illegal entry, 117
Imitation, criminological, theory of, 11–12
Immigrants, 51, 71–72
Immigration, 12, 64
India, female offenders in. See Female offender(s)
Individual crime commission, xv, 13
Individual disorientation, 25
Individualism, pervasive, 7
Industrialization: advent of, 11, 13, 35; and consequent depraved urban milieu, 24–26; development as related to, 24–25; crime in rural areas prior to the nineteenth century, 19–20; degree in developing countries, 63, 68; in England, 32–33; impact of, 27, 97; and intensification of violence, 30–31; and juvenile delinquency, 52, 56; level of, 94; in mid-twentieth century, 27–28; phenomenon of, 16–17; process of, 73; and rise in crime rates, 5–6; in socialist countries, 105; societal, 143; in Sweden, 33; and urbanization, 58–59; and youth, 12
Infanticide, 22, 89
Infant mortality, 94
Institutions, religious, 50
International crime patterns. See Crime patterns, international
International crime statistics. See Crime, statistics in
International drug traffic. See Drugs, traffic in
International Police Organization (Interpol), 68, 70, 86
Israel, religious and familial foundations of, 50–51

Japan: crime patterns and rates in, 67, 73–75; female crime data for, 86; juvenile offenders in, 80–81
Justice system. See Criminal justice system
Juvenile delinquency and crime: arrests in, 82; causes of, 14–15, 52–53, 55–56, 80–81, 84; increase in, xxi; international, 69; male, 141; in socialist countries, 104, 106, 108–10, 112, 123, 130; and subcultures, 6, 9, 11–12; urban character of, 128; and youth gangs, 9

Kampala, Uganda, crime in slum areas of, 61
Kickbacks, 45, 62
Kidnapping, high rate internationally, 70
Kondoism (Ugandan term for armed robbery), 44

Labor camps, women in, 132
Labor laws, child, 25, 53
Labor market trends, 69
Larceny, 79
Latin America, crime in, 45, 51–52, 103
Law enforcement, 93, 108, 117
Lenski, Gerhard, 22
Liu-mang (Chinese term for law-breaker), 54
Loan sharking, 118
Lombroso, Cesare, criminological theory of, 4, 6
Lombrosian thought, 6
London, crime patterns in, 31, 32, 34

"Machismo," cultural concept of in Latin America 44
Mafiosa (vendetta system), in organized crime, 71
Male offender(s), 52, 57, 79, 127. See also Female offender(s); Offender(s)
Male population. See Population, male
Male workers, youthful. See Work force
Marriage. See Prostitution, marriage and in traditional societies
Marx, Karl, 5, 14, 23, 24
Matza, David, 9
McKay, Henry D., xiii, 8, 60, 92
Merton, Robert K., 6–7, 9
Metropolitan areas. See Urban environment

Index

Mexico, gang subcultures and migration within, 59

Migrants, 11, 53, 59–60, 87–90

Migrant workers, employment of, 11

Migration: and crime in Poland, 125–26; in developing countries, 59; impact of on crime, 51, 87–88, 121; internal, xv; rural to urban, xx–xxi, 24, 58, 139

Mobility, of modern society, 11, 44, 49, 71, 77. *See also* Population, mobility of

Modern technology, 71, 137

Modernization: advent of, 12; and crime, xvii, xxi, 15, 26, 41–43, 53, 135–36, 139–40 and culture conflict, 11; effects of, xv, xix, 37, 79, 98; impact of on socialist countries, 105, 129; index of, 143; process of, 13–15, 54, 68; process of socialist, 112, 134; and prostitution, 46; of Russia, 35; theory of, 13, 14, 145; and urban population, 37

Morality, youth loss of, 69

Moral values, 8

Motorcycles. *See* Vehicular offenses

Murder, 20, 32, 70, 108

Need, motivation from, 28, 44, 53, 56

Netherlands, The, crime in, 93

New Zealand and transition to modernization, 67

Norway, homicide in, xvii

Offender(s), 3–4, 18–19, 100, 131–32

Offenses, criminal, xiv, 13, 32

Opium, illegal use of, 46

Opportunity theory: concept of, 9, 20–21

Organized crime. *See* Crime, organized

Parasite laws, 117

Parasitism, 113, 114

Parent-child relationships, 53–54

Passport laws and regulations, 117, 119

Patterns, crime. *See* Crime patterns

Payoffs, 45

Peace, breach of, 33

Peer culture in the United States. *See* Peers, adolescent influence of

Peers, adolescent influence of, xv, 55–56, 77, 83–84

Penal institutions, 64

Penalty, evasion of, 5

Person, crimes against the, xv, 36, 109

Petty theft. *See* Theft, petty

Picking pockets. *See* Theft, and picking pockets

Pilfering, 61

Piracy, 47

Poaching, 21

Poland: crimes in, 104, 116; crime rates compared to those in Hungary and Yugoslavia, 112; crime rates of urban and rural areas, 124–25; crimes against socialist property in, 114; Gdansk research in, 129; impact of modernization on, 129; juvenile delinquency in, 123, 127–28, 130; property crimes in, 106; rate of recidivism rising in, 132–33

Political crime. *See* Crime, political

Political criminality. *See* Criminality, political

Population: criminal, xv, xx–xxi, 4–5, 142; density of, 94, 96; health of, 25; male, 59; migration of, 105, 122, 134; mobility of, xvi, 87, 116–17

Pornography, 117

Position of the Working Class in England, The, (Engels), 5, 23

Poverty, 35, 51, 84–85, 122

Price-fixing, 72

Private entrepreneurial activity. *See* Economic crime(s)

Procuring, 114

Profession, effects of, 4

Professional thief, 7, 47

Property crime: absence of in rural areas, 20–21; increase in, xx–xxi, 42, 49, 63, 69; involving violence, 50; offenses related to, 19; in urban areas, 17, 44; women involvement in serious, 86; by youthful offenders, 82. *See also* Female offender(s); Male offender(s); Offender(s); Theft

Prostitution: in capitalist countries, 86; Chinese boys in, 54; growing rate of in developing countries, 45, 57, 59; marriage and in traditional societies, 46; as organized in Southeast Asia, 47; in socialist countries, 114, 118; in urban slums, 61–62

183

Index